Two Character
Chaos

By
Vin Morreale, Jr.

Cover Design by Amanda Michelle Morreale

ISBN: 978-0-9991473-7-5

All Rights Reserved.
Copyright © 2019 by Vin Morreale, Jr.

TABLE OF CONTENTS

ABOUT THIS BOOK	III
LIVING THE SCENE	V
THE INHERITANCE	1
AMBUSH	10
JOYS OF PARENTING	17
THE COURTSHIP *	20
HALFWAY HOME	28
TOO MANY MURDERS	33
MEATLOAF	37
MADE FOR EACH OTHER	40
MOVING IN	46
THE 'D' WORD	49
MARRIAGE *	55
SOUTHERN CROSS	63
SOUTHERN CROSS - 2	67
PLAIN SPEAKIN' - ACCOUNTING *	70
PHASE FIVE	73
SLIGHT INDULGENCES *	84
THE WILDLANDS	90
WILDLANDS - 2	93
WILDLANDS - 3	98
LITTLE LIES	101
A KNIGHTLY OCCURRENCE	104
VICTIM	109
JUST A SPRINKLE	116

ALL MY PASSIONS	121
ALL MY PASSIONS - 2	124
ALL MY PASSIONS - 3	128
ALL MY PASSIONS - 4	134
DAWN'S COMING *	141
PLAIN SPEAKIN' - LEGAL	147
CHALLENGE THE WIND	150
WHAT DO WE DO NOW?	153
CHASING PENELOPE	159
LITTLE IN COMMON	162
THE ENCOUNTER *	169
DENTAL CRUELTY	177
CRUSH	180
LAZLO'S MINE *	183
COLLABORATIONS	191
HER CHOICE	195
NIGHT AIR	198
NIGHT AIR - 2	201
BEWILDER BURGER	204
BIG PLANS	207
HOUSE OF THE SEVEN GABLES *	210
HOUSE OF THE SEVEN GABLES - 2 *	214
IT'S A MYSTERY	220
THE ASSIGNMENT	223
CRUEL WIT	227
PLAIN SPEAKIN' – POLITICAL TERMS	231
FISHING	234

WE NEED TO TALK	237
IN MYSTERIOUS WAYS	240
IN MYSTERIOUS WAYS - 2	244
IN MYSTERIOUS WAYS - 3	247
HERE TO HELP	249
NO GAS *	252
CAPTIVE CHRISTMAS	259
OTHERWISE ENGAGED	264
EXIT INTERVIEW	267
THE CARRIE VARIATIONS	269
EXPLOIT THE PRESS	279
KURT'S APOLOGY	282
BREAKING & ENTERING	285
BREAKING & ENTERING - 2	287
BREAKING & ENTERING - 3	292
BREAKING & ENTERING - 4 *	295
THANKS, MOM	304
A DAY AT THE WHITE HOUSE	307
BEING SOMEBODY	312
THE KISS ME CURSE	315
THE KISS ME CURSE - 2	320
BIG BUG	326
NASHVILLE *	329

EXCERPTED FROM SCRIPT PUBLISHED BY DRAMATIC PUBLISHING.
dramaticpublishing.com/authors/profile/view/url/vin-morreale-jr

About This Book

Within these pages you will find a diverse collection of original scenes designed for two actors. Each scene runs from one to fifteen minutes in length, and is designed specifically for you to play, to practice, to enjoy and to entertain others.

Like its companion books, **BURNING UP THE STAGE***, **300 MONOLOGUES** and **150 ACTING SCENES,** many of these pieces were written for my *Burning Up The Stage Acting Workshops*, which I have conducted in major cities across the United States over the past thirty years. Others were written for short play competitions, excerpted from various published and unpublished plays of mine, or taken from the more than twenty-five screenplays I have written to date. Together, they represent a variety of styles, emotions and acting challenges for actors from teens to seniors.

And therein lies the biggest advantage of a collection like this; the opportunity for actors to stretch their range and portray roles they might not otherwise have a chance to play. For actors who only settle for familiar pieces or roles they fit comfortably within, are in danger of seeing their talent grow safe and stale, sacrificing the emotional vibrancy needed to truly engage an audience.

As such, this collection is designed to be a valuable resource for the courageous actor, as well as an entertaining read for those who enjoy the spoken word brought to life.

So I invite you to use this book as part of your actor's toolkit. Practice these scenes in class, use them for auditions, add a hint of freshness to showcases, or incorporate them into your demo reel. All I ask is that you list the title of the piece and my name in any printed or screen credits.

If you would like to see the full version of any excerpted piece, or wish to use them in a paid performance, you can contact the publisher listed with each scene for royalty information, or to request a copy of the full play or movie script.

Two Character Chaos

Living The Scene

There is an elegant dance within every two-person scene. No matter how frivolous it may seem at first glance, each is a battle in miniature, an allegory of our grasping relationships with others, or possibly even ourselves. For what is theater but the gently teasing glimpse of all our chaotic emotions and self-delusions, allowing the actor to be both mirror and reflected subject, therapist and patient, prankster and joke, teacher and admonished pupil?

An often overlooked aspect of playing even a short piece is to realize that every word of dialogue is extremely important to your character at exactly that moment in the scene. Whether comedic or dramatic, silly or profound, it is crusial to realize that the scene is always completely real to your character. Nothing should be said simply because it is the next line in the script. Every word *needs to be said,* because it is your character's chosen way of engaging the other person in the scene, attempting to persuade him or her to gain a specific objective or reaction. And each cue line from your fellow actor is designed to accomplish the very same thing.

Identifying 'the want' or objective behind each line will inform how you choose to deliver that dialogue and portray the scene.

I intentionally crafted a number of scenes that are non-specific in nature. A subject may be unstated, a relationship undefined, the meaning of a line able to be taken any number of different ways. This forces the actor to make clear choices as to who these characters are, what is happening in the scene, what the relationship between the two characters may be, what each character hopes to gain or avoid, where the action is taking place, and why is it happening at that precise moment in time. If a scene fails to work, it is often because actors performing the scene have no clear idea, or hold wildly different views of what is really underpinning the dialogue.

For example, a line as simple as "What are you doing here?" takes on entirely different significance when it is uttered by someone discovering a thief in his living room in the middle of the night; an exhausted wife confronting the abusive husband she has thrown out weeks before; a frustrated boss bumping into an employee at a restaurant, after that employee had called in sick that morning; or a harried sibling, whose surprise party was ruined when the guest of honor arrives much too early. In each of these cases, the line of dialogue will be laced with different emotions, intensity, and familiarity.

For that reason, an insightful actor must be highly specific in order to discover and reinforce the reality of the scene. So even when the dilema, the relationship or even the subject being discussed has been left purposefully vague, you should view that as an opportunity to be bold, make strong choices, and bring your own unique interpretation to the piece. You can even take the same scene and play it a number of different ways, simply by changing the undefined specifics.

Most importantly, have fun with the scenes in this book. Don't lose the 'playing' part of your performance, which keeps your portrayal fresh, spontaneous, and helps you avoid over-thinking your choices.

All the best,

Vin Morreale, Jr.

The Inheritance

By
Vin Morreale, Jr.

CAST

Catherine — A 62 year-old widow

Wilma — Her estranged, slightly younger sister

SETTING

Catherine's kitchen.
The house they grew up in.

Vin's Notes: I am often told there is a lack of strong material for senior actors. I wrote this piece to give some of my older students an opportunity to really sink their teeth into nuanced, layered characters.

For royalty information and permission to use this scene in a paid performance, please contact Academy Arts Press - vin@academyarts.com

The Inheritance

AT RISE: *Lights come up on a simply dressed kitchen.* WILMA, 58, *sits at a worn table.* CATHERINE, *a few years older, stands by the counter, her back to the other woman. By their posture, we can sense the tension between them.*

CATHERINE. Would you like some coffee, Wilma?

WILMA. You know I don't drink coffee.

CATHERINE. Oh, that's right. I forgot. Tea? With lemon and honey?

WILMA. Just lemon. I'm watching my figure; in case you haven't noticed.

CATHERINE. I noticed.

(There is an awkward silence, as Catherine places two cups on the table. In Wilma's cup, she plops a tea bag. In her own, she spoons out some instant coffee.)

CATHERINE. It's good to see you again, Wilma.

WILMA. That's funny.

CATHERINE. Why is that funny?

WILMA. It is the same thing you said to me the last time I was invited over here. And that was twenty years ago.

CATHERINE. Has it been that long?

WILMA. The last time was when Daddy died.

CATHERINE. Really? There must have been some...

WILMA. There wasn't. But as to my comment, I was wondering why, if it so good to see me, you would let two decades pass before we get together?

CATHERINE.   Is that entirely my fault?

WILMA. Not entirely. Mostly, would be more accurate.

CATHERINE.   You never change, do you?

WILMA. Actually, I've changed a lot. It's you who never change, Catherine.

CATHERINE. You think so? That's funny. I could have sworn becoming a widow, teetering on the edge of bankruptcy, and fighting a four year bout with cancer might have changed me a little. *(A hard smile)* But I'm probably wrong. You always were so much more perceptive than me.

(Pause. Wilma sips her tea, not knowing what else to say.)

WILMA. This is good tea.

CATHERINE. Thank you. I dropped the bag in the water myself.

WILMA. Why do we do this, Catherine?

CATHERINE. I don't know. Because we are sisters, I suppose. Natural born antagonists linked by an accident of genetics.

WILMA. Cute.

CATHERINE. Thank you.

WILMA. I meant to call you when you were in the hospital.

CATHERINE. That's nice. I would have meant to answer, if you ever did. But I did get your card. What was the postmark? Denmark?

WILMA. Detroit.

CATHERINE. Ah, yes. That explains why you were unable to visit. Two tanks of gas can be so expensive these days.

WILMA. I was wrong about you not changing. You have developed quite a talent for sarcasm. Not to mention a slight edge of bitchiness.

CATHERINE. It keeps me sane. All alone in this big, empty house.

WILMA. I can imagine.

CATHERINE. I doubt it. But enough about me. How is your life? Roger and the kids?

WILMA. Roger left me for a twenty-three year-old intern. I thought you heard?

CATHERINE. I did. I just wanted to hear you admit it. *(Softly.)* I'm sorry. That was unkind.

WILMA. That's okay. It's always good to get my ego lacerated by my sister every couple of decades.

CATHERINE. I really am sorry, Wilma.

WILMA. Right.

CATHERINE. *(Too quickly.)* I guess…I guess knowing you've been through some tragedy too gives us something in common.

WILMA. As if the same parents, shared bedroom, and fifteen years of growing up together wasn't enough for you?

CATHERINE. Let's not do this.

WILMA. I was thinking the same thing. But I figured it would be more polite to finish my tea before I left for another twenty years.

CATHERINE. That's not what I meant. Please, let's not tear each other apart anymore. We aren't little girls fighting over Mommy's approval anymore.

WILMA. Or running from it.

CATHERINE. Or running from it. We can't change the past.

WILMA. I know. But I'm not sure I'm ready to let it go yet.

CATHERINE. Wilma, you are fifty-five years old.

WILMA. Fifty-eight.

CATHERINE. Whatever. The point is…when will you be able to let all that go?

WILMA. I don't know if I ever can.

CATHERINE. Of course you can. You just don't want to. Anger is a great motivator in life. But it is also poison. It makes even the great things you've accomplished seem inadequate.

WILMA. What do you know about what I've…?

CATHERINE. *(Cutting her off.)* I know everything you have accomplished. Graduated Magna cum laude from one of the top engineering schools in the country. You earned a Master's in engineering back when women in the profession were looked upon as oddities...

WILMA. Or freaks...

CATHERINE. Or freaks... But the point is, you did it. With no support from Mom and Dad...you did it. You made a name for yourself and a career. Then you eloped with Roger, because you didn't want any of the family to spoil your day. You gave birth to twin daughters... Darlene and Deborah... my only nieces, whom I have never seen...

WILMA. I sent you photos...

CATHERINE. Once. When they were five.

WILMA. You never wrote back.

CATHERINE. You never gave me your return address. I took that as a rather blatant hint.

WILMA. It wasn't.

CATHERINE. It was. Why deny it? As I said, the past is over.

WILMA. *(Softly.)* You would like them. Darlene especially. She is just like you. Practically perfect in every way.

CATHERINE. I was only perfect in your eyes, Wilma.

WILMA. And in our parents' eyes.

CATHERINE. Was that my fault?

WILMA. Wasn't it?

CATHERINE. No. No, it wasn't. Yet, you have wasted our entire lives torturing me, as if I had stolen them away from you. Well, here's a news flash, Wilma. Mommy and Daddy are dead. They have been for twenty years. Isn't it time to drop the sibling rivalry?

WILMA. That's easy for you to say.

CATHERINE. Is it? Is it easy to have that same door slammed in your face year after year? To know that your only living relative still hates you for something that you never did understand? *(Desperately.)* Listen, Wilma. I don't know why Mommy and Daddy lavished everything on me. I have no idea why I was their favorite, and you weren't. I don't know the reasons for any of that. And I don't even know why they left the house to me and not you. I never asked them for it!

WILMA. But you didn't refuse it.

CATHERINE. No, I didn't refuse it... Jonathan was just starting his business at the time. We, uh, didn't have a lot of money.

WILMA. I didn't have a lot of money either.

CATHERINE. I know that. I... I should have borrowed against the house and given you half. It would have been the fair thing to do.

WILMA. It would have. But you didn't do it.

CATHERINE. *(Takes a deep breath.)*. That is why I am doing it now.

WILMA. What?

CATHERINE. I am leaving you the house.

WILMA. *(Stunned.)* You're kidding.

CATHERINE. No, I'm not. I have had it longer than I deserved. It's your turn now.

WILMA. You're serious? You're giving me this house?

CATHERINE. It's just a house, Wilma.

WILMA. The only one you've ever lived in.

CATHERINE. While you have been able to travel all around the country. Maybe it's my turn to do that for a while.

WILMA. Two years after bankruptcy and suddenly you have enough to become a jet-setter? A world traveler?

CATHERINE. Look. I'm an old woman now. I've lost my husband. We never had any children. All I have left... All I have is my memories. They don't take much room.

WILMA. Catherine…

CATHERINE. I don't need this much space. I don't need much of anything anymore.

WILMA. *(Considers, then…)* I can't take your house.

CATHERINE. It's not my house. It's Mom and Dad's. Always was. Now it's yours.

WILMA. I don't want it.

CATHERINE. You don't have a choice. The paperwork is all drawn up.

> *(She grabs a large manila envelope from the counter and tosses it on the table. Wilma opens it slowly. Examines the papers inside.)*

CATHERINE. It's all perfectly legal. I had a lawyer draw it up last week.

WILMA. This isn't what I wanted.

CATHERINE. It doesn't matter. It's yours now.

WILMA. Stop being so damned noble and listen to what I am saying! *(She hesitates, then…)* I don't want the house because I don't need it anymore either… Roger is living in Omaha with his new Barbie doll wife. Darlene and Deborah have their own families now, and I only hear from them on Mother's Day and Christmas. One ten-minute phone call each. That's all. *(Softly.)* I am fifty-eight years old and completely alone. What makes you think I need this much space any more than you do?

CATHERINE. But you deserve it. This house is your inheritance. Either now, or when I die.

WILMA. What do you mean? When you die?

CATHERINE. Come on, Wilma. Let's face facts. I beat the last battle with cancer. It took everything I had left inside, but I beat it. When it comes back…

WILMA. If it comes back…

CATHERINE. If it comes back… I don't think I'll have the strength to fight it anymore. Or a reason to.

WILMA. Catherine…

CATHERINE. But none of that has absolutely anything to do with my giving you the house. Everything is already set in motion. It's officially yours as of the first of next month. No liens. No mortgages at all. The house is yours, free and clear.

(The two sisters stare at their cups in a long, oppressive silence.)

WILMA. Okay, Catherine. You win. I will take the house.

CATHERINE. Good.

WILMA. But I do have one condition.

CATHERINE. Why must you always look a gift horse in the…?

WILMA. My condition is that you agree to live here too.

CATHERINE. What are you talking about?

WILMA. You can't expect me to clean up this big old house all by myself. Not even you could be that inconsiderate.

CATHERINE. So hire a housekeeper.

WILMA. And spend what little money I have left? No way.

CATHERINE. So you're saying…

WILMA. We'll handle it this way… I'll live on the bottom floor. You take the top floor. We share the kitchen, basement and whatever bathroom is closest at the moment. If I want to pee in your bathroom, you can't stop me.

CATHERINE. This doesn't make any sense.

WILMA. It makes perfect sense. I will own the house and you will be sort of a permanent guest. You know, one of those annoying relations who come by to visit and you can never get rid of? We can be like that.

CATHERINE. *(Trying to hold back the tears.)* Wilma… I don't understand… Why are you doing this?

WILMA. Because, Catherine… maybe I've finally realized what my real inheritance is. *(Wipes her eyes with a napkin.)* Now stop your blubbering and make me another cup of tea.

(Catherine wipes the tears from her eyes. She crosses to the counter, keeping her back to her sister.)

CATHERINE. Lemon and honey?

WILMA. No honey. I'm watching my figure; in case you haven't noticed.

CATHERINE. I noticed.

CURTAIN

Ambush

By
Vin Morreale, Jr.

CAST

Madison — An attractive lawyer, 30

Munroe — A slacker in love, 27

SETTING

The local Starbucks

Vin's Notes: The Ruskin Theatre in Santa Monica has a long-standing tradition they call the Café Plays. One Sunday morning each month, five playwrights gather and are given photos of two actors, plus a specific theme for the month. The playwrghts then have only a few hours to craft a short play to be set in a café and revolving around the specified theme. The scripts are then rehearsed and performed the very same evening by the selected actors. This was one of my first Café Plays.

*For royalty information and permission to use this scene in a paid performance, please contact **Academy Arts Press** - vin@academyarts.com*

Ambush

AT RISE: Lights come up on a Starbucks café. MADISON, upscale, attractive and deadly serious, sits at a small table surrounded by a laptop, iPad, iPhone, briefcase, legal pads and colored pens, notebook and portable hotspot. MONROE enters. He is t-shirt and jeans casual and nervously eager. He looks around, confused. Checks his watch. Looks around again. Sees only Madison at a table. Monroe pulls out his cellphone. Dials. After a beat, Madison's phone RINGS.)

MADISON. *(Into phone.)* Madison Polk.

MONROE. *(Into phone.)* Uh…sorry. Wrong number.

(He looks twice as confused. Checks the number and dials it again. Madison's phone RINGS again. She answers it.)

MADISON. . *(Into phone.)* Madison Polk.

MONROE. *(Into phone.)* Uh…I think I have the wrong number again.

MADISON. *(Into phone.)* No, you don't.

MONROE. *(Into phone.)* Excuse me?

MADISON. *(Into phone.)* You are Monroe McConnell, and you are standing six feet away from me. Correct?

(He turns to see her on the phone at the table.)

MONROE. *(Into phone.)* Uh huh.

MADISON. *(Into phone.)* And you are dialing the number of your girlfriend, Hillary Reid. Correct?

MONROE. *(Into phone.)* I guess. But I don't see her.

MADISON. *(Into phone.)* And you won't, until we get all details locked down in writing.

MONROE. *(Into phone.)* What details? We were supposed to have a date.

MADISON. *(Into phone.)* That is negotiable.

MONROE. *(Into phone.)* Negotiable?

MADISON. *(Into phone.)* Depending on the terms of the agreement.

MONROE. *(Into phone.)* This is weird.

MADISON. *(Into phone.)* It may be less so if you hang up and we work this out face-to-face.

(He shoves his phone into his pocket and saunters over to her table. She stands and extends an aggressive hand.)

MADISON. Madison Polk. Attorney, CPA, Arbiter and Financial Facilitator.

MONROE. Uh, Monroe McConnell. Um, random guy.

MADISON. Precisely. Have a seat.

MONROE. Y'know, I'm not exactly sure what..?

MADISON. I am. Have a seat.

MONROE. This is weird.

MADISON. So you've said. Repeatedly. Clearly Ms. Reid is attracted to your linguistic expertise.

MONROE. Huh?

MADISON. My point exactly.

MONROE. Look, I'm just here to...

MADISON. Propose to my client, Hillary Reid.

MONROE. How did you know?

MADISON. The usual manner. Standard surveillance. Wire taps. Credit card monitoring. *(References notebook.)* You recently made a purchase in the jewelry department of Costco for two hundred, thirteen dollars...and twenty cents.

MONROE. I bought her an engagement ring.

MADISON. At Costco? For two hundred and thirteen, twenty?

MONROE. Plus tax.

MADISON. May I see the ring in question?

MONROE. I don't know.

MADISON. Mr. McConnell. Please be assured that I am Ms. Reid's official representative in all things related to this potential merger.

MONROE. Potential merger? You mean, our engagement?

MADISON. That remains to be seen. The ring, please.

(He pulls a small jewelry box from his pocket. Lays it on the table. Opens it.)

MADISON. And this is the engagement ring in question?

MONROE. Yeah.

MADISON. You overpaid.

MONROE. What the hell is this?! I come here to propose to my girlfriend. The love of my life. And suddenly I'm in the middle of a police interrogation.

MADISON. This is hardly a police interrogation…though we will need your fingerprints and DNA cheek swab before you leave.

MONROE. You're out of your mind.

MADISON. No. You are out of your depth, Mr. McConnell. My client, Ms. Reid, is an up-and-coming actress with significant career momentum. She has a rent controlled apartment on Venice Beach, a modest 401k, and earns continuing royalties for the cult classics *SNAKES ON A PLATE 2* and *SPRING BONK 4*.

MONROE. I know all that.

MADISON. You, by contrast, make your living donating plasma every other week for use in dog food and Chinese mascara.

MONROE. Some of my blood gets used in people.

MADISON. You must be so proud. *(Checks her laptop.)* Despite all that, and for some inexplicable reason, my client seems willing to consider taking you on as an on-going liability.

MONROE. She's going to say yes?

MADISON. Pending a detailed family history, criminal background check, and complete disclosure of every woman you have ever had intimate relations with.

MONROE. Hold up a minute. She starred in *SPRING BONK 4* and I have to account for everyone I ever slept with?

MADISON. Male, female, and domesticated animal, if applicable. Now then...what pets have you been particularly fond of?

MONROE. You're insane.

MADISON. I am merely protecting my client. (Slides paper to him.) I have taken the opportunity to draw up a pre-nuptial contract. In addition, you agree not to compromise Hillary's career through any embarrassing or illegal behavior and stay far in the background during any and all press and promotional events.

MONROE. Gee... Do I get to sit at the big people table at Thanksgiving?

MADISON. That is up for negotiation. Perhaps after a probationary period of three to five years. However, you may list her as a friend on Facebook.

MONROE. Listen, lady. I don't care about Hillary's money, or her fame. I care about her. Her heart, her smile. The way she crinkles her nose and laughs at the most inappropriate times.

MADISON. Those non-quantifiables are not listed in the dispositions.

MONROE. Which shows how little you know about your client. Those 'non-quantifiables' are everything I fell in love with. The way she can't walk past a kid's lemonade stand without dropping a dollar or two, laughs at my lame jokes, and throws an arm around me at night, no matter what a complete and utter loser I've been during the day.

MADISON. Be that as it may...

MONROE. Be that as it may... She's kind, she's good, she's beautiful - inside and out. And yes, she is absolutely, totally way too good for me.

MADISON. All the more reason for you to sign this pre-nuptial agreement.

MONROE. Unh-unh. No pre-nup. I will not cheapen what we have with some 'plan-to-break-up' legalese.

MADISON. *(Throws down her pen.)* Then we find ourselves at an impasse here. An emotional gridlock, so to speak.

MONROE. Maybe that's a sign. I mean, if Hillary is that paranoid, or that embarrassed by me...then maybe she's not the woman I thought she was.

(He grabs the ring box.)

MONROE. Sorry I wasted your time, counselor. Give Hillary my love. We both know she deserves so much better than me.

(He starts to stomp off.)

MADISON. Mr. McConnell... In addition to being financially secure, might I remind you that Hillary Reid is also sweet, gentle, compassionate, loving, faithful and trusting to a fault.

MONROE. Trusting to a fault? That's why she hired some tight-assed attorney to ambush her almost-fiancée?

MADISON. *(Uncomfortably.)* Well, 'hired' might not be entirely accurate.

MONROE. Meaning...you're not an attorney?

MADISON. No. I am an attorney. But I'm also a...

MONROE. Also a what?

MADISON. Older sister. A pretty protective one.

MONROE. Crazy protective?

MADISON. Sometimes.

MONROE. Paranoid protective?

MADISON. Guilty as charged.

MONROE. And Hillary doesn't even know you're here, does she?

MADISON. I was going to call her, but... *(Holds up her cell.)* ...somehow I ended up with her cell phone in my pocket.

MONROE. Right. And if she knew you were here trying to get me to sign a prenup?

MADISON. Then I'd probably be banned from the big people table on Thanksgiving.

(He sits back down. Smiles.)

MONROE. So how many more overly protective relatives do I have to worry about?

MADISON. Just two other sisters...plus an older brother who's a linebacker for the NFL. Big guy. Bad temper.

MONROE. Awesome.

MADISON. Oh, and you might want to keep an eye out for Dad. He works for the NSA.

MONROE. *(Stands.)* I'm outta here.

MADISON. *(Smiles wickedly.)* Just kidding. Welcome to the family, Monroe.

(She extends her hand. Instead he gives her a big hug, as she stands stiffly and grimaces, before finally relaxing with a smile.)

CURTAIN

Joys of Parenting

By
Vin Morreale, Jr.

CAST

Mandy — A bedraggled Mom

Brittany — Her best friend

SETTING

A comfortable suburban home.

Vin's Notes: I have taught my **Burnng Up The Stage Acting Workshops** all over the country. To give my students an extra advantage in cold auditions, I committed to writing at least two new scenes and five new monologuse for every class. In 2019, I compiled some of this origional material, including this piece, into two acting resource books; 300 MONOLOGUES and 150 ACTING SCENES.

*For royalty information and permission to use this scene in a paid performance, please contact **Academy Arts Press** - vin@academyarts.com*

The Joys of Parenting

AT RISE: *A suburban home. A very frustrated MANDY sits at her kitchen table, gulping coffee, with her best friend BRITTANY.*

MANDY.   I'm going to kill them! That's what I'm going to do. I'm going to kill them!

BRITTANY.   You can't.

MANDY.   Who says I can't?

BRITTANY.   Well, the police, very law on the books, basic morality and I'm pretty sure the Bible has, "Thou Shalt Not Kill Your Kids" written in there somewhere.

MANDY.   Yeah. But the people who wrote the Bible never met my kids. They would have changed their minds.

BRITTANY.   Okay, what did the little darlings do this time?

MANDY.   Freddy wet the bed.

BRITTANY.   That's not unusual. He's four. Accidents happen.

MANDY.   This was no accident. He used the garden hose. Fished it through my bedroom window and flooded the floor. Now my expensive Memory Foam mattress is a room-sized sponge.

BRITTANY.   Pretty creative for a four year-old.

MANDY.   Yeah. We started calling him Dr. Destructo. Oh, and then Ashlyn stayed out all night with Teddy.

BRITTANY.   Isn't she in preschool?

MANDY.   Uh huh, and Teddy is an invisible bear, who evidently likes two A.M. tea parties in the camping section of Target. The store's employees have me on speed dial. On top of that, she charged sixty-three dollars in Uber fares to my credit card just to get there.

BRITTANY.   *(Trying not to laugh.)* You have to admit that's...

MANDY. *(Cutting her off.)*. And my nine year-old sold our TV and dining room furniture on Craig's List, just so he could buy more Legos. We have to eat at a table made of Legos now! Why are you laughing?!

BRITTANY. I'm sorry. Lego furniture is serious business. What does their father say?

MANDY. He hasn't been coherent since they put a spy-cam in the bathroom.

BRITTANY. *(Laughing.)* You're kidding?

MANDY. I swear to God. His last bout of constipation is a top-rated YouTube video. Two million hits so far. Wherever he goes, people point and giggle.

(She turns to yell at someone offstage.)

MANDY. Ashlyn, put down that Sharpie! Freddy, do not Krazy Glue your brother to the toilet seat!

(Mandy downs the rest of her coffee in one gulp. Turns back to Brittany with a heavy sigh.)

MANDY. I don't know...Maybe if I had a night off now and then... *(Brightens.)* Hey, would you like to babysit for me this week?

BRITTANY. Unh-unh. Nope. No way. Never gonna happen.

CURTAIN

The Courtship

By
Vin Morreale, Jr.

CAST

Elizabeth — A young Victorian ingenue

Harold — Her elegant, but befuddled suitor

SETTING

A courtyard set within an elegant garden

Vin's Notes: One of my first staged successes was a play called PHASES, which I wrote at the age of 21. It was a unique concept (even to this day) where I mimicked the styles of different playwrights to illustrate the gradual dissolution of a relationship. In this first scene, our characters speak in the lively and witty style of Oscar Wilde, because we are never as charming and clever as when we are first attracted to someone. This scene also appears in my book *BURNING UP THE STAGE: Monologues, Short Scenes & Audition pieces for Actors From Six to Seventy,* which is carried by Dramatic Publishing.

TO PURCHASE BURNING UP THE STAGE, PLEASE CONTACT **DRAMATIC PUBLISHING -** dramaticpublishing.com/authors/profile/view/url/vin-morreale-jr

The Courtship

AT RISE: ELIZABETH, 23 and lovely, stands pensively in the garden. She wears a white dress reminiscent of an earlier time. HAROLD, 26, enters quietly, wearing a white suit. He sneaks up behind her.

HAROLD. There you are, my darling. I knew I would find you blossoming among the flowers in the garden.

ELIZABETH. *(Smiling.)* Harold.

HAROLD. Elizabeth. Your hair shines more fair than any of Nature's creations.

ELIZABETH. How perceptive you are, my love...And how handsome you look with the sun glinting off your perfectly formed teeth.

HAROLD. You always did like my teeth.

ELIZABETH. Adore them.

HAROLD. *(Embracing her.)* My one and only!

ELIZABETH. *(Pulling away.)* And also mine. Have you brought me a surprise today? I did so expect one.

HAROLD. Alas. My time was too limited. All I could bring you was my captive heart.

ELIZABETH. Nothing else? That is a surprise. Ah well. If your captive heart is all that you have brought me, I suppose I must amuse myself with that.

HAROLD. *(Happily.)* I must confess, my vacuous deity. I have deceived you totally! I really did bring you a surprise.

ELIZABETH. How wonderful! How clever and full of mirth you are! *(Sternly.)* Please don't attempt to pull that stunt again.

(Harold pulls a small box from his pocket. She reaches for it, eagerly.)

HAROLD. For you.

ELIZABETH. Such exquisite anxiety..! I wonder what it is?

HAROLD. Why don't you open it?

ELIZABETH. *(Sighs.)* If I must...

> *(She opens the box and pulls out a diamond ring, tossing the box over her shoulder.)*

ELIZABETH. Oooh! How expensive! I truly am surprised.

HAROLD. I'm glad. I was debating between an engagement ring and a new riding crop. I had hoped I made the right decision.

ELIZABETH. I...I'm speechless.

HAROLD. That makes me even happier. Try it on. If it fits, we can be married.

> *(Elizabeth turns her back to him, places the ring on her finger. She sighs.)*

ELIZABETH. *(Heavily.)* It fits...

HAROLD. Perhaps this is a foolish question, dearest one. But isn't the correct size supposed to be considered a positive sign?

ELIZABETH. So they say...

HAROLD. Yet, something is wrong. I can tell by your back. Tell me. Don't you like the ring?

> *(She pivots swiftly to escape him. She stumbles over her excuses.)*

ELIZABETH. The ring is perfect. It's so...circular, as it should be. It is of the type of metal to turn my friends green the longer I wear it...And I'm sure it was costly enough, so you will value my hand in marriage even more.

HAROLD. Then what is the matter? *(Realization, then smugly.)* Are you nervous?

ELIZABETH. Nervous? Hardly. I spent all my post-adolescent life worrying about this moment, so that when it came, I would be as calm as a professional.

HAROLD. Then, what?

ELIZABETH. It is not even the fact that you speak in abbreviated sentences! It's only that... All my life, I wished to marry a man I could pursue in vain. The man to whom I promised myself would have to play frightfully hard to get...Only by his utter rejection of all that I am...could I be sure I had found the man worthy of me.

HAROLD. I fail to understand the problem. Haven't I always treated you with indifference up to now?

ELIZABETH. Indeed you have. Only now that we are engaged, how could you possibly fit the bill? I could hardly be expected to suffer from afar, when you have vowed to remain always by my side.

HAROLD. Perhaps it would help if I broke off the engagement... temporarily. Then I could give you the ring right back. All sincere relationships need some arbitrary dissolution. It's what purifies them and allows them to survive the continual steadfastness which inflicted so many marriages of my parents' generation.

ELIZABETH. Naturally that would help. It is hard to respect a man who has never proven himself to be a cad. One would always be suspiciously waiting for the day he must inevitably reveal his true nature. *(As a prayer.)* Besides, what bitter memories would it leave me to cherish in later life -- after you depart this plane of existence we call Earth?

HAROLD. Then it is settled. I will terminate our engagement! (quickly) However, I will do so only if you promise to accept my repentance and take me back immediately after. *(Kneels, takes her hand.)* Do you so vow?

ELIZABETH. I do.

HAROLD. *(Rising abruptly, throwing her hand aside.)* Fine. The engagement is off! Please be discreet enough to hand over my ring. We must, above all, be attentive to detail. Detail alone separates us from the less concise masses.

ELIZABETH. *(Flinging it at him.)* There! Have your overly gaudy ring back! I wouldn't marry you if you were the last man who asked me!

HAROLD. Wait...We've missed a crucial detail! We need an excuse for our emotional unbinding.

ELIZABETH. Oh. Do make it something roguish on your part. Something so brutally unforgivable that I cannot help but love you more for it!

HAROLD. Let me think.

(*He paces, as she looks at him expectantly. Suddenly, he turns to her.*)

HAROLD. Ah! Just the thing. I regret to inform you that I have fallen quite totally for your sister, Marie.

ELIZABETH. For my sister?! I requested something unforgivable...not an exhibition of deficiency in taste.

HAROLD. But, my love..?

ELIZABETH. Besides, you took much too short a time in concocting a roguish deed...which makes me suspect you either possess a facile wit...or that you really love Marie. Since the former would deny the latter, I detest your incestuous desires toward my sister!

HAROLD. Incestuous?!

ELIZABETH. A close relation. Your ex-potential sister-in-law.

HAROLD. She cannot be a relation until we are formally betrothed. And since we just ended the possibility of our nuptial inevitability, there can be no sister-in-law -- ex-potential or otherwise -- and therefore, no incestuous desires.

ELIZABETH. Then, worse than reprehensible, your incestuous desires are inaccurate. More than anything, I do so detest inaccuracy.

HAROLD. And I detest your cynicism!

ELIZABETH. Cynicism? Me? Haven't you noticed that I'm the embodiment of flirtatious naiveté?

HAROLD. I suppose I hadn't -- distracted as I was by your claws in my back... Your sister Marie on the other hand... Now there's a woman who...

ELIZABETH. (*Sharply.*) What do you know of women? When I met you, you were a virgin. And one with little experience at that!

HAROLD. I am still a virgin! And so are you!

ELIZABETH. That's entirely different. On me, it signifies virtue. On you...ineptitude.

HAROLD. Inepti..?! How dare you..!

ELIZABETH. Oooh! You are speaking in abbreviated sentences again, knowing full well how I abhor it! And Marie of all possible rivals..? I shall never forgive the grievous wound inflicted on this trusting heart. You are a true cad, sir!

(They glare at each other for a long moment. Suddenly, Harold breaks the tension and turns happily away.)

HAROLD. Excellent! Now that I have fulfilled that criteria, will you accept my ring back and once more vow to be mine forever?

ELIZABETH. Never! I was foolish to accept it once. You will not find me so engaged again.

HAROLD. What? You promised!

ELIZABETH. How loathsome you are! We have not even been married long enough to foster recriminations, and already you throw in my face the things that I told you in strictest confidence.

HAROLD. This is entirely unfair! I broke off the engagement only because you vowed to reinstate it. They were your rules. I was merely gracious enough to condescend to them. Propriety alone demands you should accept my ring back.

ELIZABETH. What care I of propriety? I, who on this happiest of days -- the day my true love requested my hand for all time -- must be plunged into such pitiable despair by his total disregard for my impressionable emotions. *(Aside.)* Such dramatic angst. I love it!

HAROLD. This is too much! Will you now take my ring back or not?!

ELIZABETH. Never! How will I know I am not merely an infinitely preferable substitute for my sister Marie, whom you are so hopelessly devoted to?

HAROLD. You do not even have a sister Marie! You have a brother Mycroft!

ELIZABETH. Already finding fault with your in-laws, are you? And for you to be so enamored of my brother Mycroft would raise eyebrows in even the most liberal of societies. *(Looking up.)* Oh, kindly Lord. What did I ever see in this man, the dregs in the wine of your creation?

HAROLD. Dregs, is it? Well, then. As long as we are comparing our erstwhile affair to fine wines...you might do well to ferment a few years to remove the acid taste from your disposition.

ELIZABETH. Ooh!

HAROLD. Not to mention that you spring from one of the least notable vintners in the area!

ELIZABETH. Oooh!

HAROLD. Moreover, only my years of refinement prevent me from mentioning that you are developing an overly large cask! *(Smacks her backside.)*

ELIZABETH. Ooooh! You are a ruthless cad! An insect of disproportionate effemininity! An embarrassing stain on the fabric of human decency! *(Pause, then sweetly.)* Of course, I'll marry you.

HAROLD. My dearest one!

ELIZABETH. Darling lover of mine. Quickly, give me back the ring before my finger grows accustomed to the free air blowing around it.

HAROLD. At once, my epitome of feminine ambiguity. Would that I could afford a ring big enough to do justice to your overly large neck...so that I might run a chain from it to my heart. Then, we could go for walks in the park and everyone would know you belonged to me, my pet.

(He places the ring on her finger. They embrace.)

ELIZABETH. Words cannot express the passionate ambivalence you stir in me. Kiss me before I explode in righteous ennui!

HAROLD. I adore your constantly fresh nature. I prostrate myself before your moment-to-moment emotional upheavals. I worship your schizophrenic inconsistencies. *(Kisses her forehead.)* Promise me you'll never change?

ELIZABETH. I will, my malleable one. It is a promise I will keep with all the ardor of a drowning man thrown a bottle of champagne.

HAROLD. *(Hesitantly.)* Then our marriage can never fail.

ELIZABETH. Yes, my sweetbread. We are sentenced to a life of eternal contentment. Affection without end, amen.

HAROLD. Eternal contentment, eh?

ELIZABETH. And everlasting nuptial bliss. I fear it is so.

They walk apart, lost in thought, then...

HAROLD. *(Stiff upper lip.)* Cheer up, darling. It could be worse.

ELIZABETH. How?!

HAROLD. Why...we could have been born without refinement, of course.

ELIZABETH. Perish the thought! How could you even imagine such a thing?

HAROLD. Uh, sorry. It just slipped out...Ignorance is bliss and all that. It was almost...philosophical!

ELIZABETH. Honestly...The trivialities young men allow to wander through their minds when they are not concentrating on the woman at hand.

HAROLD. Forgive me, darling. A passing whimsy. I will not allow my thoughts such free rein in the future.

ELIZABETH. And neither will I! *(Takes his arm.)* Now, let us inform my brother Mycroft of our intentions...And I warn you, buster, if you so much as throw him a wink, I'll...

   (She drags him off stage.)

                                                                              CURTAIN

Halfway Home

By
Vin Morreale, Jr.

CAST

Rita — Caretaker in a halfway house

Terry — A slightly neurotic resident

SETTING

Terry's room in a transitional house for those with psychiatric issues.

Vin's Notes: Years ago, I was approached by Debi Kalman Pearl, an actor I had previously worked with, to expand a story idea ishe had nto a feature length screenplay. It wasn't really working for me, until I decided to merge her film concept with an original stage play I had been working on. The resulting screenplay featured both humor and heart, and would go on to win and place in a number of film festivals and national screenwriting contests.

For royalty information and permission to use this scene in a paid performance, or if you are a Film Producer interested in reading this award-winning screenplay, please contact **Academy Arts Entertainment** *- vin@academyarts.com.*

Halfway Home

AT RISE: Halfway Home Common Room. Terry is alone in the large room. He starts to hum, then sing to himself.

TERRY. *(singing)* "Feelings... Nothing more than feelings..."

    (RITA ALVEREZ enters, unseen by Terry. Rita is an attractive, middle-aged Puerto Rican woman in a white coat. She watches Terry, as he begins to sing more dramatically, as if before a large audience.)

TERRY. *(singing).* "Trying to forget my..."

RITA. Forgetting is not always the best way to deal with your problems.

    (Terry jumps, shocked to find he's not alone.)

RITA. Sorry. Didn't mean to scare you. I'm Rita. I work nights here.

TERRY. *(Embarrassed, he extends his hand.)* Terry. Terry. Matthews.

RITA. I know. I read your file. Getting your voice ready for the next karaoke riot?

TERRY. What? Oh, the song. No. That's nothing. *(He waves it away.)* A sappy old thing someone used to sing around the house when I was young.

RITA. Sounds like a mama's song. A sad mama's song.

TERRY. She wasn't sad as much as she was...

RITA. Bi-polar? *(Reacting to his shocked expression.)* I read that in your file, too. Your wife had similar issues, if I remember.

TERRY. *(Snapping.)* Leave my wife outa this, okay?!

    (A beat. Rita stares at him with gentle curiosity. Terry turns away, embarrassed.)

TERRY. I...I'm sorry. That wound's still too fresh.

RITA. I can see that. *(Gently.)* So tell me about your mom.

TERRY. I'm sure it's all in the file.

RITA. Just the facts. Not your memories.

TERRY. Is this some kind of therapy time?

RITA. Whatever you want to call it. But hey, it's not every day in life you find someone willing to listen.

TERRY. There's not much to tell.

RITA. That's okay. Tell me anyway.

TERRY. Do I have to do this?

RITA. No. But it lets me write positive things in your file. 'Willing to open up to staff members. Able to confront problems.' *(Carefully.)* It may help, in case other staff members put some less than positive things in your file.

TERRY. You heard about my little...disagreement with Dennis?

RITA. *(She smiles, changes the subject.)* We were talking about your mother.

TERRY. My mother... Um, should I sit?

RITA. Depends on how heavy your butt gets. Look, we can do this another day if it bothers you?

TERRY. I doesn't bother me. I mean, why should it? It's my mom. She had a few problems. But it's not like I didn't love her or anything. Or like she didn't love me.

RITA. She loved you.

TERRY. Is that in my file?

RITA. No. It's in your eyes.

(This comment, and Rita's gentle smile, helps Terry loosen up. He plops down on the sofa.)

TERRY. I don't know why everybody makes such a big fuss about it. It's not so bad, once you get used to it...

MORE

TERRY. *(Continued.)* I remember I used to get really scared at first. All that screaming. The crying. The way she gritted her teeth when it hit her. That was the worst part...You could always dodge the fancy china when it splattered against the wall and flew apart like a dozen little white moths. But the part I can never forget...is her teeth.

RITA. Her teeth?

TERRY. I used to see them sometimes at night. The way they'd clamp together... like some kind of wall, holding the Mom I used to know trapped inside. Pressed so tight together, she couldn't get out, even if she tried to...

(This is painful for him. Rita gives him a moment, then...)

RITA. Did it happen a lot?

TERRY. Not too much. My Dad would try to rush me out of the room, whenever she had one of her spells. He'd try to pretend like I didn't see any of it. He'd always have that same funny look on his face. His eyebrows would go way up on his head and his top lip would pull down and twitch a little. I think if I ever said a word to him...with his face like that...he would've just fallen over and cried. I bet he would have. He'd pick me up and rush me into bed, no matter what time it was. Then he'd go back in and try to calm her down until it stopped. *(He stands, wipes the tears from his eyes.)* And I'd just lie there in bed...listening to the dishes breaking and dreaming of little white butterflies...

(A long pause. Terry shakes it off. Tries to pull himself together. He turns and smiles at Rita, but the smile has pain behind it.)

RITA. How did your step-father handle it after your Dad died?

TERRY. *(Bitterly.)* Not as well...Can we stop now?

RITA. Sure. *(Rises.)* You need anything?

TERRY. No. I'm...I'm good.

RITA. We're all good, Terry. That doesn't mean we don't need.

TERRY. I'm fine. A little tired, that's all.

RITA. Fair enough. Now give old Rita a hug.

TERRY. Part of your job?

RITA. Part of my nature.

> *(He stiffens as she gives him a motherly hug. Slowly, he relaxes in her embrace.)*

RITA. *(Softly.)* You don't belong here, Terry. You know that, don't you?

TERRY. That's what I used to think. But lately...

> *(He can't finish the sentence. He breaks away, turns to the window.)*

RITA. Well, holler for me whenever you want to talk some more. Or if there's ever anything you need.

TERRY. Actually, I did seem to misplace some cash recently. I thought I put it in the dresser in my room, but... Well, I was just wondering if you might've seen it?

> *(Rita crosses to UL. She nods.)*

RITA. I haven't. But a word to the wise. Be careful where you put your valuables here. Things have a tendency to...disappear, if you know what I mean.

> *(Rita exits through the doorway leading to the upstairs bedrooms. Terry turns, then starts singing to himself, more softly this time.)*

TERRY. *(Singing.)* "Feelings... Nothing more than feelings..."

> *(The song dies on his lips. He crosses to the sofa and collapses on it.)*

CURTAIN

Too Many Murders

By
Vin Morreale, Jr.

CAST

Harry — A tough-talking cop

Natalie — His now-retired partner

SETTING

Natalie's Apartment

Vin's Notes: This was simply a fun piece I wrote for a 48-Hour Film Festival, where teams are given a genre, a character name, a prop, and one line that must all be incorporated into the piece. Each team has only 48 hours to write, cast, direct, produce, edit and deliver a finished seven-minute film short. I always loved a challenge, and this is an excerpt from a Film Noir style script I wrote for the contest.

*For royalty information and permission to use this scene in a paid performance, please contact **Academy Arts Press** - vin@academyarts.com*

Too Many Murders

AT RISE: It's midnight on a dark, film noir set, everything in sterile blacks, greys and shadows. HARRY, a rumpled detective in an equally rumpled trench coat, steps forward, addressing the audience.

HARRY.   It was getting to be a habit. Two weeks and fourteen stiffs. A regular crime wave that no one was complaining about. Because in this case, all the victims were hard core bad guys. Coke Eddie. Sammy The Shiv. Psycho Susan. Short Eyes Finnergan. It's like the TV show, *Survivor* where all the contestants was evil…and one by one, they were getting voted off the planet. The killer wasn't making it easier on us cops. No weapon. No prints. Not even any DNA. It's like the killer was wrapped in Plastic wrap. Perfect placement. He never saw it coming. Which was too bad. Chainsaw Jack was never that nice to his victims. He used to love making them suffer. Either way, it's like Operation Brightside cleaning up the scum of the city. My only question is…what happens when they run out of bad guys? But I didn't have time to think about that. I got one more stop to make…

(He walks to a doorway and knocks. NATALIE comes to the door. A still attractive, middle-aged woman. She takes a long look at Harry before speaking.)

NATALIE.   Harry. This is a surprise.

HARRY.   Is it, Natalie?

NATALIE.   Come on in. I got some cold spaghetti for breakfast.

(Lights come up on Natalie's pristine kitchen. Everything glaringly white.)

HARRY.   House is spotless, as always.

NATALIE.   What can I say? I'm a neat freak.

HARRY.   I always wondered what kind of freak you were.

NATALIE.   Sweet talker. You know, a guy your age shouldn't be working in the late night air. You'll catch your death.

HARRY. Already caught it. Fourteen, in fact.

NATALIE. Yeah. I've been reading the papers.

HARRY. I'll slice the garlic bread. You got a knife?

NATALIE. First drawer on the right.

HARRY. All I see is a butter knife.

NATALIE. Hmmm. I must have misplaced my Ginsu.

(Harry pulls up a plate. They both eat during the following)

HARRY. It's probably in the Ohio River. I'm guessing that's where you tossed it after you stabbed Itchy Hadler.

(She eyes him carefully. When she speaks, her words are hard and carefully measured.)

NATALIE. No. That's where I tossed it after I stabbed Paul the Pervert. Itchy Hadler I used the StaySharp Turkey Slicer on.

HARRY. My mistake. You know, Natalie… taking justice into your own hands is what got you bounced from the force in the first place.

NATALIE. I didn't get bounced. I retired. Voluntarily. After all, they couldn't prove anything.

HARRY. Just because they can't prove it, doesn't mean you're innocent.

NATALIE. Actually that's exactly what it means. Legally speaking.

HARRY. Legally, maybe. But you and I know better.

NATALIE. Do we, Harry?

HARRY. We do. You can't keep killing all the bad guys, Natalie.

NATALIE. Why not? I still read them their rights as they bleed all over the pavement.

HARRY. And I thought I was the cynic.

NATALIE. What do you want me to say, Harry? You want me to promise I won't do it again?

HARRY. That'd be a start.

NATALIE. I can't do that. Not when I see these creeps still walking the street after some high priced defense pimp makes up some stupid lie to confuse the jury, or gets the crooks sprung on some technicality.

HARRY. I feel ya. But what you're doing is wrong. It's murder.

NATALIE. It's justice. *(Hands him a cloth napkin.)* Wipe your mouth. You got sauce on your lips.

(She walks away sadly.)

HARRY. Thanks. You know I have to arrest you, Natalie.

NATALIE. You can't.

HARRY. I have a 9mm says I can.

NATALIE. Yeah. But your arms won't work anymore.

(A momentary confusion. He starts to sway. He collapses to the floor.)

HARRY. Poison? *(Gasping.)* You poisoned the spaghetti sauce?

NATALIE. An inert chemical. Harmless until it mixes with a reactant.

HARRY. ...where...

NATALIE. The napkin, silly. I told you I was a neat freak.

HARRY. ...why...

NATALIE. You left me no choice, Harry. You shouldn't have been so by the book. Now I'll just have to move across the river to chase down bad guys in Indiana.

HARRY. You...you killed me...

NATALIE. Sorry about that Harry. *(Kisses his forehead.)* I promise it won't happen again.

(Natalie grabs her purse and his gun. She steps over his body and heads to the door. Turns sadly.)

NATALIE. See ya, Harry.

Meatloaf

By
Vin Morreale, Jr.

CAST

Edna — A middle-aged housewife

Earl — Her lazy husband

SETTING

A den in a modest blue-collar home.

Vin's Notes: This was another scene I developed for my **Burning Up The Stage Acting Workshops** that can also be found in my collection 150 ACTING SCENES. I always believed the 'closer than they admit' dynamic of long-term relationships to be a rich source of gentle humor, and a perfect format for actors to develop chemistry in their work.

For royalty information and permission to use this scene in a paid performance, please contact **Academy Arts Press** *- vin@academyarts.com*

Meatloaf

AT RISE: A middle-aged couple, EDNA and EARL, sit watching TV on an old sofa.

EDNA.   Anything on TV tonight?

EARL.   No.

   (They both stare at the set watch anyway.)

EDNA.   You left your underwear on the floor again.

EARL.   Did I?

EDNA.   You do it to annoy me. Don't think I don't know that's why you do it.

EARL.   Guess underwear and subtlety don't mix.

EDNA.   What happened to us, Earl?

EARL.   I don't know. Dirty clothes. Gravity. Seems inevitable.

EDNA.   I don't mean the underwear… I mean what the hell happened to us?

EARL.   I don't know. My beer belly. Your boobs. Gravity. Seems inevitable.

EDNA.   Tell me this… Is there anything about me you still love? Is there?

EARL.   Give me a minute.

EDNA.   It shouldn't take a minute! You should be able to rattle off half a dozen lovable things about me in a heartbeat!

EARL.   Well, if you had half a dozen lovable things, maybe I could. *(Sees her hurt expression.)* I'm sorry. I was trying to be funny. Or stupid. Or male, which is all the same thing. *(Pause.)* I…I love your meatloaf.

EDNA.   That's romantic. I think Shakespeare wrote a sonnet about that once.

EARL.   Come on, Edna…

EDNA. Or maybe it was it a poem by Emily Dickinson? "Ode To Her Meatloaf" It might even have been Percy Bysshe Shelly during his Casserole Period…

EARL. You're smarter than me. I ain't never even heard of Percy Bysshe Shelly before I met you. If he didn't write for Car & Driver magazine, I wouldn't of heard of him at all. And I guarantee you, nobody going by the name of 'Percy Bysshe' ever wrote for Car & Driver.

EDNA. That's two. Smart and meatloaf. It's practically my Match.com profile.

EARL. Okay, you're funny, even when you're not trying to be. You have this cute way of squenching your eyes and throwing your hair back when you yawn that makes you look like a five-year-old. You put food out for robins in the winter, then yell at 'em all summer for pooping on the gas grill. You can't say no to any kid selling Girl Scout cookies or overpriced candy, even though we got three whole shelves stocked full of 'em. You can't sing worth a damn, but still do in the car, or when you think nobody's around. Even after all these years, you still look damn sexy when I sneak a peek at you in the shower. And every night before you fall asleep, you throw an arm around me and cuddle up close, as if you're holding onto some handsome movie star, instead of this old fat guy who's been stealing the covers and farting in your bed for the last three decades. Oh, and that crooked little smile of yours still melts me. That half a dozen yet? Counting the meatloaf?

EDNA. *(Stunned.)* Why, Earl Henry Dobson! All these years, and I never knew you were a closet romantic!

EARL. I ain't a closet anything. And don't you go thinkin' this means I'm gonna start picking my underwear up off the floor!

EDNA. You're nothin' but a lazy, old slob, Earl Henry Dobson. *(Pause, they watch TV.)* You want meatloaf tonight?

EARL. Sure.

Made For Each Other

By
Vin Morreale, Jr.

CAST

Danage   A cut-throat corporate tycoon

Cecily   His equally ambitious wife

SETTING

The bedroom of their luxurious estate

Vin's Notes: This scene was written specifically for this book, though I may choose to incorporate it into a larger play one day. I enjoy teasing and dissecting the fluid momentum of familiarity and contempt that occasionally bind people together, in spite of themselves.

*For royalty information and permission to use this scene in a paid performance, please contact **Academy Arts Press** - vin@academyarts.com*

Made For Each Other

AT RISE: *Lights come up on a lushly decorated bedroom of a true power couple.*

DANAGE.   Get out of here! Just get out! Leave me alone!

CECILY.   No.

DANAGE.   Why do you insist on making my life miserable? Don't you have anything better to do than make me feel like a total and absolute fraud in front of everyone I've been trying so hard to impress?

CECILY.   Not really.

DANAGE.   You hate me, don't you?

CECILY.   Of course. That's what makes our marriage work so well. Now don't tone down the histrionics. You're embarrassing yourself. If everyone wasn't so aware that I am so completely contemptuous of our marriage…you might run the risk of embarrassing me as well.

DANAGE.   That would be a catastrophe.

CECILY.   That would be an impossibility. I made sure never to grant you that power again after Seattle.

DANAGE.   Seattle was a long time ago.

CECILY.   So what? Time doesn't heal all wounds. That's the lie and plea of the guilty. Time just covers the open, festering sore with scars of multiple distractions.

DANAGE.   I don't have time for your hip cynicism right now. I have a dozen board members in the ballroom down the hall, who are using this party as an excuse to dissect me and sabotage my chances of taking over the company.

CECILY.   There go the histrionics again.

DANAGE. It's not histrionic. Histrionics and hysteria are women's words. Like hysterectomy. Men don't get hysterical. We get mad and angry and frantic. Most of all, we get even. That's what I'll do. If they try to cheat me out of what I rightfully shattered careers and climbed over bodies for, then I'll get even with every last one of them!

CECILY. Don't make it so dramatic. The board is far more afraid of you then you are of them. You've bribed a third of them, then threatened the rest. That job is yours, and you know it.

DANAGE. Of course I do. But I want it said. Said in public.

CECILY. The mystery to me is why you want it so badly. You've already pilfered the pension plan. You've given yourself a golden parachute that'll collapse the company finances for years. Yet you want to sit at the top of that crumbling tower of decaying morality.

DANAGE. I want the recognition. It's the principle of the thing.

CECILY. Come on. We both know that if principles were involved, you wouldn't be the man for the job.

DANAGE. Thank you so much.

CECILY. You're welcome. Now let's get out of here. I have hearts to break. Younger and more virile hearts.

DANAGE. You know, I just realized something.

CECILY. It can wait. Let's go back to the party before someone actually grows a backbone or gets liquored up enough to tell you what a contemptible excuse for a human being you really are.

DANAGE. No. It can't wait. Or maybe it's waited too long already.

CECILY. Well, even if it's important to you, it means nothing to me. I'm going.

(She rises elegantly and crosses to the door. As she opens it, she hesitates. Turns back to him.)

CECILY. You don't intend to move, do you? *(Sighs, walks back and sits on the sofa.)* Fine. Go ahead. Spew forth your great and wondrous realization. I await your enlightenment.

DANAGE. You never say my name.

CECILY. What?

DANAGE. You never say my name. I just realized we can have whole conversations…as unpleasant as they may be….you can talk and badger me for hours, but you never, ever say my name.

CECILY. That's ridiculous.

DANAGE. It's true. You seem physically incapable of allowing my first name to slip through your lips.

CECILY. I don't have time for this. *(Rises but goes nowhere.)*

DANAGE. Not once. In fact, I can't remember the last time you ever said my name to me. Not kindly. Not spitefully. Not at all.

CECILY. You're crazy.

DANAGE. That may be, but you still never say my name. It's ugly. It makes me think you don't love you.

CECILY. I don't love you. Haven't I made that painfully clear ever since Seattle?

DANAGE. Yes, you have. But even your hatred is nameless. I want you to say my name. Not to others, but to me. Say it now. Say it to my face.

CECILY. If this is some sort of bizarre power trip, I have no intention of falling for it.

(He crosses to her. Takes her gently in his arms. She tries to pull back, but only slightly.)

DANAGE. Say my name. Look me in the eye and say my name.

CECILY. Why should I? What's so special about you?

DANAGE. Nothing. Absolutely nothing. I'm just a belligerent, empty man in a loveless marriage, who feels the need to break others before they can rip him apart. That makes me just like everybody else these days. But I do have a name and I want you to use it.

(She hesitates, then breaks free. Turns to look at him now, with a more comfortable distance between them.)

CECILY. Well…Aren't we Mister Sensitive?

DANAGE. No. Not in the least. That died a long time ago. In a cheap and dingy studio apartment in Seattle. Where we watched everything that was good and decent in both of us bleed out and writhe on the floor. And then we buried it, far away, so no one could ever see. No one would ever know. Because we knew, even way back then, that people never really want to know you. They only want to know the worst about you. The malicious gossip. The dark and dirty details. Something they can salivate over in the privacy of their own abused consciences… something to distract them from their own cruel and twisted secrets.

CECILY. Don't…

DANAGE. It's okay. It doesn't hurt anymore. It's just sad. That's all. Just sad.

CECILY. Please, don't…

DANAGE. Why not? We've unsheathed the blade a million times. Why not plunge it deep into the heart where it belongs?

CECILY. This isn't healthy.

DANAGE. It never was. We lost all that was good about us in Seattle and left it behind without saying a word. That was the last time I ever remember you saying my name. The very last time.

CECILY. I say…

DANAGE. No. Not 'my husband,' not 'that slovenly scum I share an annuity with,' …but my name. You never say my name. *(Crosses to her again. Wants to touch her, but he stops. Falters.)* Just this once. I need you to say it… Say my name…

CECILY. *(Turns away.)* You've lost it. You've finally lost it! The accumulated crimes and ethical atrocities have finally pushed you over the edge. You're insane!

DANAGE. Say it. Say my name.

CECILY. Okay! Fine! You've lost it, Steven! You're completely insane, Stevie.

DANAGE. Say it again.

CECILY. *(Gently.)* You're completely insane.., Steve...

> *(A pause. A truce. A silent acknowledgment of things that can't be touched.)*

DANAGE. Let's go back to the party.

CECILY. Good... I'm glad that's over. Here.. Let me fix your tie.

DANAGE. No need. I've got people to badger, not impress.

CECILY. I'm glad to hear it. *(Turns away. Speaks softly, without looking at him.)* You know... you never say my name either.

> *(He takes her arm, leads her toward the door.)*

DANAGE. I know.

CECILY. *(Smiles.)* Bastard.

> *(They exit. Stage Left.)*

Moving In

By
Vin Morreale, Jr.

CAST

Phillip — A somewhat awkward, single guy

Felicity — His new neighbor

SETTING

The hallway of an apartment building

Vin's Notes: A familiar trope in romantic comedies is the clever woman and clueless guy. After all, don't many of us become both stunningly oblivious and desperately hopeful when an opportunity for true love suddenly presents itself? At least there's hope for this guy in this piece from 150 ACTING SCENES.

*For royalty information and permission to use this scene in a paid performance, please contact **Academy Arts Press** - vin@academyarts.com*

Moving In

AT RISE: A narrow hallway in an older apartment building. PHILLIP. Tall and gangly, wrestles with his piles of boxes and bags, as FELICITY enters behind him.

FELICITY.   Can you move your stuff out of the hallway? You're blocking my front door.

PHILLIP.   I'm sorry. Chaotic old me. I'll have this shoved in my apartment before you can say 'annoying neighbor.'

FELICITY.   You're new.

PHILLIP.   No, I'm old. Just new to this building. New to living alone after all these years. New to being the new guy. *(Pause.)* But um, evidently not new to awkward and uncomfortable conversations with um, new people I meet.

FELICITY.   Clearly.

PHILLIP.   Honestly, some people think I'm funny. I used to have a sense of humor.

FELICITY.   I guess you forgot to pack it.

PHILLIP.   Hey, you're funny too.

FELICITY.   Me? I'm just taking out the trash.

PHILLIP.   You are taking out your trash while I'm moving in mine. Kind of ironic, don't you think?

FELICITY.   Looks like we circled back to that awkward conversation again.

PHILLIP.   Sorry. Did I say sorry before? And here I am saying it again and acting like a sorry excuse for a neighbor. Don't worry. I'm not a serial killer or Grand Master Geek, or something…

FELICITY.   Chill. Stop trying so hard. It's cool.

PHILLIP.   I'm chill. I'm cool. I'm so cool I'm chilly. Although that may be the crappy heaters in this apartment building. That was me being funny again. Am I trying too hard?

FELICITY. Uh-huh.

PHILLIP. And you probably think I'm a total loser and waste of biomass at this point.

FELICITY. The jury is still out on that one. That was me being funny, by the way. Listen, we've all been there. Newly single after a relationship we thought was perfect shreds our soul. Suddenly, forced to get a new address and new friends, to hide the embarrassment of explaining to the old ones why it didn't work out with the former love of our life. So, you ratchet up the energy to hide the humiliation, and end up being twice as humiliated by discovering how hard it is to reconnect with people when you feel like a complete and utter loser.

PHILLIP. Wow. When you take out the trash, you really take out the trash.

FELICITY. Like I said, we've all been there.

PHILLIP. Tell me... Does it get any easier?

FELICITY. Not really. But wine helps. I have some in my apartment. That is, if I ever could get to my door.

PHILLIP. Oh, sorry, I...let me get this out of your way. Hey, was that an invitation? The wine thing, I mean?

FELICITY. Move your crap out of the hall, Grand Master Geek. I'll have a bottle uncorked in ten. We can get smashed and swap horrendous ex stories. I guarantee I'll win.

PHILLIP. Clean hallway in five. Uncorked wine in ten. Exes going down in flames shortly thereafter. I love this building! Wait a minute. Do you have a name?

FELICITY. Yes.

PHILLIP. Okay.... Uh, that was you being either funny or ironic again, wasn't it? Wasn't it?

FELICITY. Don't make me let the wine breathe too much. See you in ten.

(She exits.)

PHILLIP. I'm gonna love this building!

The 'D' Word

By
Vin Morreale, Jr.

CAST

Marky June   A hyper-energetic greeter

Gerald   A frustrated customer

SETTING

The guest entrance to the
Wet & Wacky Water Wonderland
amusement park.

Vin's Notes: This was one of my favorite scripts I wrote for the Ruskin Theatre's Café Plays. The theme was the California drought, and the two actors really crushed it with hilarious performances, despite the Marky June character having some real verbal gymnastics to learn in just a few short hours.

*For royalty information and permission to use this scene in a paid performance, please contact **Academy Arts Press** - vin@academyarts.com*

The 'D' Word

AT RISE: *The colorful entrance to a family amusement park. An overly bubbly woman stands behind a counter, all smiles and eagerness. She wears a brightly colored shirt and a nametag that reads* MARKY JUNE. *GERALD enters, looking around with confusion.*

GERALD. Uh, I'm not sure I'm in the right place.

MARKY JUNE. Of course you are! And you're about to have the time of your life!

GERALD. Is this the...

MARKY JUNE. Wet & Wacky Water Wonderland! That's us! Welcome to our Cafe and Guest Orientation Center. I'm Marky June, your Personal Ocean Commotion Specialist. Can I start you off with a complementary beverage?

GERALD. Sure. I'll take a large coffee.

MARKY JUNE. I'm sorry, sir. We don't serve large. We can offer you a Tall, Ginormous or Bladder Buster.

GERALD. Okay, I'll take a Ginormous. Black.

MARKY JUNE. No, I'm Caucasian. Okay, then! One Ginormous Coffee coming right up!

(She pulls out a tiny cup and pours a few dribbles of coffee in it.)

GERALD. That's Ginormous?

MARKY JUNE. Hasn't any woman told you that size doesn't matter?

GERALD. Well, at least it's free... *(Downs it in one tiny gulp.)* That was damn close to satisfying. So what time does the park open?

MARKY JUNE. Two hours ago, sir.

GERALD. Really? I just thought they'd be more...

MARKY JUNE. ...more Fun Fanatics besides you? There usually are. However, we have experienced a wee bit of a slowdown since the recent Multi-year Climactic Inconvenience.

GERALD. You mean the drought?

(Marky June hits a LOUD BUZZER and frowns.)

MARKY JUNE. Excuse me, sir. But management does not allow the use of 'the 'D' word' in this establishment.

GERALD. The 'D' word? What? You mean the drought?

(Marky June hits the LOUD BUZZER again.)

MARKY JUNE. I'm sorry, sir. But I'm going to have to ask you to refrain from using that kind of language here.

GERALD. You're telling me I can't say anything about the dr...

(She has her hand poised over the buzzer. He hesitates.)

GERALD. ...dr...rryyy weather conditions?

MARKY JUNE. Actually, the term 'dry' is also frowned upon. Fortunately, our head office has provided a list of acceptable euphemisms. *(Pulls out some paper.)*. They would rather our guests referred to the 'Long-Term Meteorological Abnormality' or 'Unintended Non-fluidity Interlude.'

GERALD. You're kidding, right?

MARKY JUNE. I don't believe so. Amusement is not part of my job description. In any event, the recent 'Minimized Liquidity Interphase' has somewhat reduced our guest bookings.

GERALD. How much?

MARKY JUNE. Only by ninety-seven percent. So are you ready to have the time of your life?!

GERALD. You mean it gets better than this?

MARKY JUNE. That would be sarcasm, I believe.

GERALD. More like dry humor. Well, at least I won't have to wait in line for the water rides.

MARKY JUNE. Actually, due to the recent 'Extended Non-Moisture Event,' a few of our regular water rides are temporarily out of service.

GERALD. How many?

MARKY JUNE. Only ninety-seven percent.

GERALD. So this is a water park without water rides? And you somehow forgot to mention it when I booked my reservation?!

MARKY JUNE. Sir... You are making it sound like this 'Multi-Month Precipitation-Free Period' is our fault. Trust me when I say, we here at Wet & Wacky Water Wonderland are every bit as vexed by this climactic inconvenience as you are.

GERALD. Vexed?! I paid $135 a day for a water park with no water!

MARKY JUNE. I see you are one of those 'glass half-empty' people.

GERALD. The glass isn't half-empty...It's completely empty because of the stupid drought!

(Marky June hits the LOUD BUZZER.)

MARKY JUNE. Uh-oh. There's that nasty old 'D' word again.

GERALD. Sorry. Okay. Just tell me what water activities you do have open?

MARKY JUNE. I'm so glad you asked! I suggest we start with the Wet & Wacky Water Wonderland Sensational Sea Spray Encounter!

GERALD. That sounds like fun. Let's do it.

MARKY JUNE. Okay, here goes!

(Marky June pulls out a spray bottle and squirts him two times.)

GERALD. That was the...

MARKY JUNE. Sensational Sea Spray Encounter. *(Squirts him again.)*. Yes, sir.

GERALD. Imagine my excitement. What else you got?

MARKY JUNE. How about our popular Wet & Wacky Water Wonderland Sudden Splash of Insanity?

GERALD. That's more like it. Bring it on!

(Marky June pulls out a small sponge from below the counter and places it in a dish. She carefully pours out one...two...then three droplets of water into it.)

GERALD. That's the Sudden Splash of Insanity?

MARKY JUNE. The ending is the best part.

GERALD. I can hardly wait.

(Marky June picks up the sponge, then slaps him twice in the face with it. Then adds a third slap.)

MARKY JUNE. That last splash is a bonus for preferred customers.

(Gerald starts to wipe his face off, when she stops him.)

MARKY JUNE. Uh-uh-uh! Please. We have to recycle!

(She pulls out a small Dollar Store squeegee and scrapes the water from his face back into the sponge.)

MARKY JUNE. In case you want to ride again.

GERALD. I'm good. So basically the only thing open in the whole Wet & Wacky Water Wonderland is this cafe?

MARKY JUNE. Well, there is our Giant Immersion Adventure Tank out back. But that's reserved.

GERALD. Giant Immersion Adventure Tank? You mean the Kiddie Pool I passed on the way in? What's it reserved for?

MARKY JUNE. They're shooting a remake of the old Kevin Costner movie, Water World. This one probably won't go over-budget. *(Holds up her hand.)* Ahh, missed a spot!

(She squeegees his face again.)

MARKY JUNE. There you go! Wasn't that all too much fun?!

GERALD. Yeah. A real splash. You got a restroom around here?

MARKY JUNE.   You mean our Personal Waste Water Reclamation Center? Third door on your left. Oh, but you'll need this...

(Hands him the spray bottle.)

GERALD.   What's this for?

(She unscrews the nozzle part. Hands him just the bottle.)

MARKY JUNE.   We all have to do our part!

GERALD.   You mean..? Wait a minute. Isn't this what you just sprayed me with...? No. Forget it. I don't want to know.

(Gerald starts to walk away. With the bottle.)

MARKY JUNE.   *(Calling after him.)* I hope you've enjoyed your visit to Wet & Wacky Water Wonderland! Tell your friends!

(He exits. Her smile fades and she slumps to the counter.)

MARKY JUNE.   Damn drought...

Catches herself and presses the LOUD BUZZER.

CURTAIN

Marriage

By
Vin Morreale, Jr.

CAST

Beth — A bored housewife

Harry — Her working-class husband

SETTING

The TV room in a modest home

Vin's Notes: In this second scene from PHASES, we revisit the characters of Harold & Elizabeth after they have been married a number of years. Although played by the same actors, their names are shortened to the casual familiarity of Harry and Beth, with dialogue reminiscent of a Sam Shepherd play, as they struggle to bridge that chasm of lost love and regret. This scene also appears in one of my favorite early plays *SOUTHERN DISCOMFORT,* available through Dramatic Publishing.

FOR ROYALTY INFORMATION, OR TO REQUEST A COPY OF
SOUTHERN DISCOMFORT, PLEASE CONTACT **DRAMATIC PUBLISHING** -
dramaticpublishing.com/authors/profile/view/url/vin-morreale-jr

Marriage

AT RISE: A modest room in a small apartment. All mismatched yard sale furniture and dingy curtains. HARRY, 40, slunk down on a worn loveseat, staring at a TV set. He lifts a remote every few minutes, bored with everything. Yet his eyes never leave the set. BETH, 38, is curled up beside him - an uncomfortable space between.

BETH. Hey. *(No reply.)* Hey. I said 'hey'.

HARRY. So what? Hey don't mean nothin'.

BETH. I was just trying to get your attention is all.

HARRY. Well, you got it.

(He continues to stare at the TV. She smacks his shoulder.)

BETH. Can't you do anything but watch TV when you get home?

HARRY. Can't you do anything but complain 'bout what I can and can't do?

BETH. I don't complain. You can't say I complain. I point out quirks, that's all.

HARRY. Quirks, she says. Quirks. That's a good one.

BETH. What's the matter? You don't think you got quirks?

HARRY. Listen, Lady. I got quirks. I got plenty of quirks!

BETH. You're tellin' me...

HARRY. I already said I got quirks, okay?! You don't have to keep pointing 'em out all the time. It don't make them go away. *(Softly.)* You got quirks, too, you know.

BETH. I know I got quirks. Everybody's got quirks.... *(A beat.)* What quirks?

HARRY. I dunno. Can't think of any right off.

BETH. 'Course not. I didn't think so.

HARRY. You snort when you laugh.

BETH. What?

HARRY. You snort when you laugh. It's embarrassing. Somebody tells a joke and you either squeak or snort. I don't know why in hell you can't enjoy yourself like a normal person.

BETH. Pardon me! They didn't cover laughing at finishing school.

HARRY. Finishing school... Ha!

BETH. I don't know what you're 'ha-ing' about. At least I finished finishing school.

HARRY. What's that supposed to mean?

BETH. Nothin'.

HARRY. You saying I'm dumb or something?

BETH. I'm not saying you're dumb.

HARRY. You saying I'm dumb 'cause I was dumb enough to get married instead of gettin' my diploma?

BETH. I'm not saying anything. I'm watching TV.

HARRY. Well, you're right. I was dumb.

BETH. Wasn't that dumb...

HARRY. Maybe not. But it would've been a hell of a lot smarter if I'd waited.

BETH. *(Musing.)* I guess you'd probably be a doctor or something by now.

HARRY. What's so fancy about a doctor, anyway? So you get blood all over your pants instead of grease. Is that so different?

BETH. It's easier to get out in the wash.

HARRY. Great. I'll become a doctor so you can have an easier time with the laundry!

BETH. At least it might make you more interesting.

HARRY. Whatta ya mean, interesting?

BETH. I dunno. More fun to talk to, I guess... More fun to show off.

HARRY. Hey. I'm sorry if I'm not entertaining enough for you! Sorry I embarrass you in front of your friends!

BETH. You don't embarrass me, Harry. I didn't mean it nasty.

HARRY. Sure.

BETH. It's just... It's just I can't get you to talk to me about anything new and stimulating anymore. You know, like you used to.

HARRY. If you want new and stimulating, why don't you buy a goddam home computer.

BETH. At least it wouldn't be rude! You can't say two words to me anymore without one of them being rude!

HARRY. I don't have to take this. I get enough frustration at the factory without having to take this when I get home. All day long I get the whine of the screw machine in my ear, then I have to come home and listen to you.

BETH. Are you calling me a screw machine?

HARRY. No. I didn't mean...

BETH. You called me a screw machine! That's the nastiest thing I ever heard anybody call anybody!

HARRY. Damn it all. I was just making a.., whaddaya call 'em.., an analogy.

BETH. You called me a screw machine. That's not a nice thing to call somebody...

HARRY. I didn't.

Pause. They both stare at the TV set.

BETH. So what's on tonight? *(No reply.)* I said, what's on tonight?

HARRY. I'm concentrating.

BETH. What the hell are you concentrating on? It's a damn deodorant commercial! There's only so much concentrating you can devote to deodorant.

HARRY. Have you noticed the poetry has gone out of our marriage?

BETH. Poetry? Ha! All I remember was a lot of heavy breathing.

HARRY. *(Softly.)* Well... maybe my memory's better than yours.

BETH. Okay... maybe there was a little poetry.

HARRY. A little. So what's on tonight?

BETH. I dunno. *(Pause.)* So where do you think it went?

HARRY. What went?

BETH. The poetry.

HARRY. Upstairs and first door on the left! Your mother locked it in her suitcase the day she unpacked the rest of her stuff!

BETH. Don't go blaming my mother! If anyone had poetry, it was her and Daddy.

HARRY. Sure! That's 'cause he kicked off before the second verse. Anyone can have poetry if they don't have to hang around and listen to it.

BETH. That's a cold thing to say, Harry. That was a cold thing to say...

HARRY. Hey... I didn't mean it to be all that cold... I'm sorry.

BETH. It's okay... *(Pause.)* So what's on tonight?

HARRY. I dunno. I didn't get a chance to pick up a TV Guide on the way home.

BETH. Oh. *(A beat, then....)* You know, Harry. This may sound crazy... *(Turns away.)* Naw... Forget it.

HARRY. Forget what?

BETH. Nothin. You'd probably think I was crazy.

HARRY. I already think everything you say is crazy. So tell me.

(She picks up a bag of pork rinds. Holds them tightly, as she talks, her back to Harry.)

BETH. I was just thinking.., maybe it'd be fun if, y'know, for a change.., we kinda shut off the TV and... you know...

HARRY. And what? Finish your sentences, will ya? You snort when you laugh, and you never finish your sentences.

BETH. Are you gonna pick on me or listen?!

HARRY. I'm listening. I'm listening and I'm not hearing. Maybe it's my ears, huh?

BETH. Maybe it is... *(Deep breath.)* What I meant was... it might be fun to go parkin' in the car.

HARRY. Parkin'? We already got us a driveway.

BETH. No. I mean 'parking'. Parking. You know.

HARRY. Oh, parking! Like we used to.

BETH. Yeah, like we used to, Harry. The windows steamin' up and you grabbing me real tight and all.

HARRY. And you always getting your foot caught in the steering wheel. I never could figure out how you did that...

BETH. *(Moving closer.)* But it was fun, wasn't it, Harry? We could lay right down on that front seat and see them stars right through the windshield. Way up there and twinklin' bright as ever. Twinklin' away like they was talking to us. Like they was tellin' us, it was okay what we was doing. Tellin' us they didn't mind... *(Melts into the memory.)* Them stars just winking and tellin' us that that's what they'd be doing if they were our age and feeling like we did about each other. Lord, how I loved them stars...

HARRY. *(Also entranced.)* Yeah. The stars...

BETH. Remember, Harry?

HARRY. Yeah.

BETH. What do you remember, Harry?

HARRY. I... I remember you... the way you were. Your blouse slippin' off your shoulders... How they looked so soft and creamy warm with you lying there on the front seat. Just that little bit of light hitting you...

(Smiling, she offers him her pork rinds.)

HARRY. That sure made me feel like something.

BETH. You always did like my shoulders.

HARRY. Your shoulders? Hell, all of you. You were so... beautiful. It used to make me so proud when you'd get all perfumed up and fancy looking just for me.

BETH. Thanks, Harry.

HARRY. It's true. You were so pretty; I'd get this tickly feeling in my ribs whenever I looked at you. The tickling was so bad sometimes, I almost had to giggle. No other girl ever did that to me with just her eyes.

BETH. Really?

HARRY. Yeah. *(Getting excited.)* And remember the smell of my new Chevy?! We'd get so close to the upholstery, you'd smell that new car smell wrapping all around you. It was like being right there up in Detroit watchin' some good old boy stitch that seat up right before your eyes. Man, that was something!

BETH. The stars... and the upholstery?

HARRY. *(Sighs.)*. Man, that was something...

BETH. The stars don't twinkle no more, do they, Harry?

HARRY. *(Sadly.)* Naw... The stars don't twinkle no more. And the upholstery ain't smelled for years.

BETH. Kinda sad, ain't it?

HARRY. Kinda. *(Trying to cheer her up.)* But, hell. We were kids then. Punk kids. We're all grown up now. You can't expect us to keep enjoying life like a couple of crazy kids.

BETH. Guess not.

HARRY. I mean, where would we be today if we spent our lives acting like crazy kids? We wouldn't have the house. We wouldn't have the pick-up truck. And we wouldn't have the kids.

BETH. *(Smiling.)* We'd have the kids.

HARRY. Yeah. I guess we'd have the kids. But we wouldn't have the microwave and we wouldn't have the color TV.

BETH. Guess not... *(Beat.)* New TVs don't smell... do they, Harry?

HARRY. No... And they don't twinkle either.

PAUSE.

BETH. What do you say, Harry? Let's take the car and let's go out and find the stars? Okay?

HARRY. *(Smiles.)* Maybe steam up a window or two?

(Gradually his smile fades.)

HARRY. Hell. Who are we kidding, Beth? We drive a Toyota now. Bucket seats. And besides, the weatherman said it's gonna be cloudy all night.

BETH. All night, Harry?

HARRY. That's what he said.

BETH. Well... Maybe the stars will be out tomorrow night.

HARRY. Maybe. He didn't give the long range forecast.

BETH. *(Sadly.)* They never do... *(Pause, then...)* So what's on TV tonight?

(She slides back to her end of the loveseat, as they both turn back to the TV.)

Southern Cross

By
Vin Morreale, Jr.

CAST

Detective Chaffee — A gruff police detective

Nevada Blue Piccoletti — A fast-talking private investigator

SETTING

A Police Interrogation Room

Vin's Notes: I often write late at night, when I believe our minds are more open to free-flowing dialogue. And so the first thing that came to me was the witty and brilliant voice of tough-as-nails private investigator Nevada Blue Piccoletti. Over the next few weeks, I created a TV pilot around her, which I later expanded to a full feature length script, and will soon spin her off into a series of crime novels.

For royalty information and permission to use this scene in a paid performance, or if you are a Film Producer interested in reading this award-winning screenplay, please contact **Academy Arts Entertainment** *- vin@academyarts.com.*

Southern Cross

AT RISE: Police Interrogation Room. Lovely and dangerous NEVADA BLUE 'NEV' PICCOLETTI, 33, is being interrogated by DETECTIVE CHAFFEE, 45, after she was arrested for beating up four gang members who attacked her.

CHAFFEE. Tea to your liking, princess?

NEV. Most things in life are. You should smile more. It might minimize those jowls.

CHAFFEE. I have jowls?

(She smiles. He scowls at her file.)

CHAFFEE. I see you're a regular around here. Pulled in nine times for aggravated assault.

NEV. Charges were dropped. Self-defense.

CHAFFEE. Nine times?

(Nev just smiles, which annoys him even more.)

CHAFFEE. Says here you used to be a cop… Poster child for the department's diversity push…'til you got booted for excessive force. Reckless discharging of a firearm. Conduct unbecoming an officer. And tonight you put three guys in the hospital.

NEV. C'mon, Detective. I know you're a newbie in this town, but don't tell me you didn't catch the gang tats on their necks?

CHAFFEE. Latin Kings. You got issues with them too?

(Nev sighs. As if explaining to a child.)

NEV. It's not like I was looking to start a turf war. I was meeting a client.

CHAFFEE. What client?

NEV. Dorothy Reedle. Sweet girl. Her Dad turned up missing yesterday.

CHAFFEE. So why'd she call you instead of us?

NEV. She did call. Got the standard forty-eight hour shove off. Typical cop-think. To you, she's just another hysterical female. Only her Dad is Mr. Punctuality. When he doesn't show up for Scrabble Tuesday, she knows something must be wrong.

CHAFFEE. So she calls Princess P.I.?

NEV. Nevada Blue Investigations, actually. She wanted results. I get them.

CHAFFEE. What makes you so special?

NEV. *(Smiles, then...)* You're recently divorced. A tough one, I bet. Tryin' hard to be an ex-smoker, but it's not taking. You feel a need to prove yourself by being the most cynical guy on the job. And you never had a problem firing your gun. Probably what got you transferred as one of Chief Hawthorne's charity cases. Don't quite fit in here and aren't sure you ever will. Oh, and you have a cat. *(Considers for a moment.)* Her cat.

CHAFFEE. *(Shaken.)* So...uh, you scoped my personnel files... or someone told you...

NEV. Oh, please... No woman would let you out the door with a brown belt and black pants. You know that and do it subconsciously to piss her off. You still have a white area and an indentation around your ring finger, but try to hide it around attractive women...

(She winks. He reddens.)

NEV. ...which I'll take as a compliment... You try to hide your Boston accent, but still can't say 'Louisville' like a native.

CHAFFEE. That don't mean...

NEV. You wear your badge prominently, but your jacket hasn't been cleaned in months and there's a bulge the size of a cigarette pack in the breast pocket. Only a trace of tobacco, meaning it's been a while since you lit up. Teeth are yellow at the top from smoking, but white below from cheap whitening strips. Should I go on?

(No reply. She rapidly clicks off more details.)

NEV. Okay...you're a Red Sox fan, because you shrug your right shoulder like someone who has loosened up his pitching arm, and well, you're a Boston boy, so that's a no-brainer. Cat hair on your pants, and scratches on your hand, meaning you hate the kitty, and the feeling is mutual. But you can't give it away because it's one last tie to your ex. Plus you are extremely conscious of the guys watching from behind the one way mirror... *(Waves to the mirror.)* Even though you try not to show it...

(He is stunned by her deductive abilities. She sees that and smiles.)

NEV. Or am I wrong?

Southern Cross - 2

By
Vin Morreale, Jr.

CAST

Lydia — A wealthy Southern lady

Nevada Blue Piccoletti — A fast-talking private investigator

SETTING

The lavish estate of a champion thoroughbred horse trainer

Vin's Notes: Here is another excerpt from my award-winning screenplay SOUTHERN CROSS. In this scene, Private investigator Nevada Blue Piccoletti (Nev to her friends) is subtly questioning the latest fiancee of a legendary thoroughbred trainer, after one of his employees is murdered on their famed Kentucky horse ranch.

*For royalty information and permission to use this scene in a paid performance, or if you are a Film Producer interested in reading this award-winning screenplay, please contact **Academy Arts Entertainment** - vin@academyarts.com.*

Southern Cross - 2

AT RISE: The luxurious estate of legendary horse trainer Bo Buckner. NEVADA BLUE 'NEV' PICCOLETTI, 33, is interviewing his most recent fiancée LYDIA, 29, after the mysterious death of one of his employees.

NEV. So, Lydia. How's it feel to be wife number five?

LYDIA. Actually, it's fiancée number six. Bo doesn't see the need to rush into marriage.

NEV. Yeah. Hate to mess up that track record of his.

(Lydia throws her an icy smile.)

NEV. So here you are... young, beautiful, stylish, and he's... well, none of the above. What's the attraction? Personality or bank account?

LYDIA. Have you met Bo?

NEV. 'Nuff said.

LYDIA. Am I supposed to not love someone just because he has a lot of money?

NEV. Hey, I hear you, sister! I've had the hots for Jeff Bezos ever since he made his fiftieth billion. But that old tease never returns my calls.

LYDIA. He returns Bo's.

NEV. I soooo want to be you right now.

LYDIA. Really?

NEV. No. That was sarcasm. So tell me... with all his winnings, why is this place so close to bankruptcy?

(Lydia hesitates. Offers Nev a seat in an outdoor rocking chair.)

LYDIA. Bo doesn't breed well.

NEV. I'm guessing it's the tight jeans.

LYDIA. Not him. The horses. That's where the real money is. In stud fees.

NEV. Stud fees?

LYDIA. Other owners pay hundreds of thousands for a Derby winner to impregnate their mares.

NEV. Everybody loves a winner.

LYDIA. You win a big race. Grab the glory. Then they put you out to stud for the rest of your days.

NEV. I'm guessing a man came up with that system.

(The women share a smile.)

NEV. So your fiancée with a rep as a ladies' man has horses that can't even do it for dollars?

LYDIA. Bo thinks someone is out to ruin him.

NEV. How?

LYDIA. He's not sure. Messing with their diet, maybe. Or dosing the horses.

NEV. That should be fairly easy to prove.

LYDIA. You would think so. But all the blood tests came back clean. Bo doesn't believe it though. That's what Greg was looking into before he... when he...

(She dabs her eye with a lace handkerchief. Nev reaches out a comforting hand.)

NEV. It's all right... You really don't have to pretend to care.

(Lydia stiffens. Fixes Nev with a stony gaze.)

LYDIA. I believe we are done here, Miss Picccoletti. You will find Little Bo in the South Building.

NEV. Thank you, Lydia. The sweet tea was delightful, by the way. Just the perfect touch of saccharin...

CURTAIN

Plain Speakin' Accounting Terms

By
Vin Morreale, Jr.

CAST

Joe Bob Dinkel — A redneck TV Host

Announcer — An Offstage Announcer

SETTING

A simple TV studio

Vin's Notes: In my early post-college days, I moved to Berkeley, California to give this crazy dream of writing, directing and acting a try. I founded the SENSELESS BICKERING COMEDY THEATRE, and was fortunate to work with so many talented comedians, who came and went as SENSELESS BICKERING moved with me to Los Angeles and then Kentucky. This was one of my favorite characters, who I imagined with a voice like old-time country actor Pat Butram of GREEN ACRES.

*For royalty information and permission to use this scene in a paid performance, please contact **Academy Arts Press** - vin@academyarts.com*

Plain Speakin' Financial Terms

AT RISE: An aging country gentlemen, JOE BOB DINKEL, sits in a rocking chair facing the audience. To his left, the ANNOUNCER stands before a podium (or may be played as an offstage voice only.)

JOE BOB. This is Joe Bob Dinkel with another lesson in *Plain Speakin'*. Today we're gonna look at some of them there financial *(pronounced finan-sea -al)* talk. You know the fancy pants, three dollar words that those dad-burned accountants throw at you so's they can charge you an arm and a leg to do your taxes. Let's look at a couple.

ANNOUNCER. Asset

JOE BOB. What I do when I'm tired. Asset on the front porch.

ANNOUNCER. Liability.

JOE BOB. A knack for twistin' the truth. My Uncle Goomer was always tellin' whoppers. He had a great lie-ability.

ANNOUNCER. Working Capital.

JOE BOB. Somethin' Washington, D.C. ain't been since the Democrats took over Congress.

ANNOUNCER. Balance Sheet.

JOE BOB. The favorite trick of someone who juggles horse manure.

ANNOUNCER. Penalty for Early Withdrawal.

JOE BOB. That's when the missus gets riled because you satisfied your own urges instead of hers.

ANNOUNCER. Ten-Forty *(1040)*

JOE BOB. It's either a tax form or a forty weight oil. Either way, it's slippery as hell.

ANNOUNCER. Wall Street

JOE BOB. A darn silly way to stop traffic.

ANNOUNCER. Depreciation.

JOE BOB. Joe Bob Dinkel's way of sayin' thankee. I depreciate your takin' the time to listen. I'll be talkin' at ya.

CURTAIN

Phase Five

By
Vin Morreale, Jr.

CAST

Harold — A male lecturer

Elizabeth — A female lecturer

SETTING

A bare stage with two podiums

Vin's Notes: There are two more scenes in PHASES, where a fragile Elizabeth breathes out a heartbreakingly lyrical monologue with a Tennesse Williams flair as she contemplates an affair, and Harold follows with an Edward Albee monologue of his own despair. The final scene offers a jarring Samuel Beckett detatched and self-deluding analysis, as the characters try to understand what went wrong, using poetic allusions interspersed with lines taken from the previous scenes. Sounds bizarre, but it actually proved quite effective.

*For royalty information and permission to use this scene in a paid performance, or to request a full copy of PHASES, please contact **Academy Arts Press** - vin@academyarts.com*

Phase Five

AT RISE: *Harold and Elizabeth enter from opposite sides of the stage and approach matching podiums, Downstage Left and Downstage Right. Upstage Center are two plain folding chairs, sitting empty in the semi-darkness. Spotlights illuminate the podiums, as the two characters begin in a clinical manner, as if they are giving a lecture to a science class. They speak directly to the audience.*

HAROLD. Phase.

ELIZABETH. Phases.

HAROLD. From the New Latin: "PHASIS", appearance.

ELIZABETH. From the Greek: "PHANEIN", to show.

HAROLD. Noun. One of a sequence of distinct apparent forms.

ELIZABETH. Verb. To introduce by one stage at a time.

HAROLD. A temporary manner, attitude or pattern of behavior; i.e., a passing phase.

ELIZABETH. To eliminate by one stage at a time.

HAROLD. A discreet homogeneous part of a material system that is mechanically separable from the rest, as is ice from water.

ELIZABETH. Phased...

HAROLD. Aspect, facet, angle...

ELIZABETH. Phasing...

HAROLD. ... Side, stage, as in going through a new phase...

ELIZABETH. Phased out.

HAROLD. Promise me you'll never change?

ELIZABETH. *(Trying to stay in character.).* Promises are the talons of memory.

HAROLD. I remember you...

ELIZABETH. The past always struggles...

HAROLD. You were so... beautiful...

ELIZABETH. Struggles to intrude at the most inopportune moments.

HAROLD. Have you noticed the poetry has gone out of our marriage?

ELIZABETH. The poetry?

HAROLD. The poetry.

ELIZABETH. ... poetry...

HAROLD. I remember...

ELIZABETH. The poetry...

HAROLD. *(Bitterly.).* Anyone can have poetry if they don't have to hang around to listen to it.

ELIZABETH. The poetry...

HAROLD. I remember.

ELIZABETH. *(Softly.)* And all the little Noovogoodlian children...

HAROLD. Like the night Robbie died...

ELIZABETH. Crane their long, wire-like necks...

HAROLD. The night he...

ELIZABETH. So as not to be seen seeing...

HAROLD. Children should be exempt.

ELIZABETH. That which they should not be seeing...

HAROLD. Repress your grief, so as not to impose too heavily on others.

ELIZABETH. Or, at least should not be able to recognize...

HAROLD. Sometimes, bad things happen to good people, too.

ELIZABETH. For many years hence...

HAROLD. They were your rules!

(She walks over to the folding chair, entranced. She sits.)

ELIZABETH. Rules give way to delusions, Delusions to dreams. Dreams to death...

HAROLD. I was merely gracious enough to condescend to them!

ELIZABETH. Rules to delusions to dreams to death.

HAROLD. I was merely gracious.

ELIZABETH. The stars don't twinkle no more... And the upholstery refuses to smell.

(Harold turns to her, though he cannot seem to move from the safety of the podium.)

HAROLD. You hurt me.

ELIZABETH. *(Softly.).* I didn't mean to...

HAROLD. But you hurt me.

ELIZABETH. I... I was young.

HAROLD. Wounded me.

ELIZABETH. I didn't know.

HAROLD. Slashed me. Scarred me.

ELIZABETH. I didn't see.

HAROLD. Crippled me.

ELIZABETH. I was afraid.

HAROLD. That's not enough.

ELIZABETH. *(Softly.)* Love is a spider.

HAROLD. Not nearly enough.

ELIZABETH. Besides, you hurt me!

HAROLD. I hurt you?

ELIZABETH. You hurt me.

(Harold hesitates, then abandons the podium for the chair. Lights fade

on podium, rise on the chairs.)

HAROLD.   I didn't intend to.

ELIZABETH.   But you hurt me.

HAROLD.   I... I was inexperienced.

ELIZABETH.   Injured me.

HAROLD.   I was unsure. I didn't know what to do.

ELIZABETH.   Tore me. Cut me off from myself.

HAROLD.   I was blind.

ELIZABETH.   Robbed me of my identity.

HAROLD.   I was afraid.

ELIZABETH.   That's not good enough.

HAROLD.   *(Softly.)*. Love is a spider...

ELIZABETH.   Not nearly enough.

HAROLD.   Besides, you hurt me.

ELIZABETH.   I did?

HAROLD.   You did.

ELIZABETH.   I am so terribly... sorry.

(The two stand, move half the distance to their respective podiums. Again they address the audience.)

HAROLD.   Impose...

ELIZABETH.   I have wasted all that I have been allowed to...

HAROLD.   Imposing...

ELIZABETH.   Treasured only things impossible to sustain.

HAROLD.   Imposition...

ELIZABETH.   Wasted the treasures.

HAROLD.   My whole life has been one, long imposition.

ELIZABETH. And treasured the wastes.

HAROLD. *(to Elizabeth).* Except for you.

ELIZABETH. I mourn for my irretrievable innocence.

HAROLD. Or so I thought.

ELIZABETH. Love is a spider.

(They turn to face each other, keeping a distance between.)

ELIZABETH. Love is a spider.

HAROLD. Beautiful and fearsome.

ELIZABETH. Waiting in its seemingly fragile snare.

HAROLD. Fiercely attractive.

ELIZABETH. Showing no mercy to its victims.

HAROLD. Such exquisite anxiety.

ELIZABETH. Feeding off their dreams and desperations. Leaving hollow husks where there was once feverish ambitions.

HAROLD. Love is a spider.

ELIZABETH. Or so I imagined.

(He crumples in the chair. She returns to the podium.)

HAROLD. What I need...

ELIZABETH. Need.

HAROLD. Need, is someone to cry for...

ELIZABETH. What are you asking from me?

HAROLD. Someone to distill me to my essence. Someone to wring out the truth in my emotions.

ELIZABETH. What are you asking from me?

HAROLD. Someone to pamper. Someone to bleed.

ELIZABETH. What are you asking?

HAROLD. Someone to make my life matter to me. To make my death fearsome, less inviting.

ELIZABETH. What are you asking..?

HAROLD. A gentle nightmare to extract and exorcise my fears.

ELIZABETH. What are you..?

HAROLD. A toy to bring tears to my eyes when it breaks. A thief to make me realize the value of what I have lost.

ELIZABETH. What?

HAROLD. A child I can cuddle and protect from all the pain within me. A pool of ice to reflect an inner beast I cannot alone create.

ELIZABETH. What are you?

HAROLD. A bleeding flame to purify. An all-consuming maelstrom to refresh memories never to be born.

ELIZABETH. What are you asking?

HAROLD. A simple touch.

ELIZABETH. What are you asking from me?

HAROLD. An unexpected embrace.

ELIZABETH. What are you asking from me?

HAROLD. *(Standing.)* Myself!! I'm asking you to give me a way to myself!

ELIZABETH. I... I can't...

(They face each other again.)

HAROLD. I see.

ELIZABETH. I'm sorry.

HAROLD. Ask and you shall deceive. Speak and you shall grind.

(They trade places. She sits in the chairs, as he walks to the podium.)

ELIZABETH. When I was a young girl...

HAROLD. A very young girl.

ELIZABETH. A very young girl. I prayed for a giant...

HAROLD. Not a prince.

ELIZABETH. A giant could protect me better.

HAROLD. Not a knight.

ELIZABETH. A giant is strong... without need of armor.

HAROLD. There was a giant.

ELIZABETH. Giants were always misunderstood. Clever children were always trying to slay them.

HAROLD. I remember a giant.

ELIZABETH. I prayed for a giant I could soothe.

HAROLD. I remember the giant.

ELIZABETH. I promised to understand his ugliness.

HAROLD. You were terrified and drawn to the giant.

ELIZABETH. No one else could appreciate his monstrous deformities.

HAROLD. I cannot be your giant.

ELIZABETH. Daddy was a giant.

HAROLD. I know.

ELIZABETH. You know?

HAROLD. I know.

ELIZABETH. How can you know?

HAROLD. I know your flights. I understand your need for wings.

ELIZABETH. You do?

HAROLD. You entice me with your flights. Entomb me with your wings.

(She moves away Downstage Center. All stage lights go down except one blue light shining down on her. Harold is left alone in shadows.)

ELIZABETH. My wings keep me falling forward.

HAROLD. *(Whispers.)*. Falling.

ELIZABETH. Straight ahead for miles.

HAROLD. I wait for you.

ELIZABETH. I am coming.

HAROLD. I wait.

ELIZABETH. I seek out the silver illusion you create for me. I plummet onward through the darkness.

HAROLD. It is no illusion.

ELIZABETH. I know that.

HAROLD. I wait.

ELIZABETH. Suddenly, you capture my freedom. I suffer the enticement of surrender.

HAROLD. I have you now.

ELIZABETH. But this fails to live up the crystalline beauty it promised..?

HAROLD. It always does.

ELIZABETH. I am entangled by your unrelenting needs. Truth tarnishes deception. I thrash in terror and confusion. Nothing is as it should be.

HAROLD. I cease to wait.

ELIZABETH. I scream into your eyes. I pull away deep into your soul.

HAROLD. I encroach upon you.

ELIZABETH. I am trusting you...

HAROLD. I move nearer.

ELIZABETH. I anticipate your embrace.

HAROLD. I seek only to crawl inside you.

ELIZABETH. I cannot let you.

HAROLD. It is too late to stop me.

ELIZABETH. I feel the jaws of your despair snap my wings. Your venom stills me with quiet need.

HAROLD. You are mine now.

ELIZABETH. Possess me.

HAROLD. You are mine.

ELIZABETH. I feel my very identity slipping away.

HAROLD. I drink your essence.

ELIZABETH. I am no more.

HAROLD. Then you become the spider.

ELIZABETH. Then I become the spider.

(A shift in lighting returns them to the podiums and their clinical postures.)

HAROLD. Cycles of interminable phases. Phases of infinite cycles. Cyclical phases...

ELIZABETH. The flesh stays willing, but the spirit grows weak.

HAROLD. Phasing cycles.

ELIZABETH. Phased...

HAROLD. Replace love with habit.

ELIZABETH. Phasing...

HAROLD. Devotion with tireless familiarity.

ELIZABETH. Phased out.

HAROLD. Is that what you left me? Or is that what you left?

(They escape the podium and stand facing each other, holding hands.)

ELIZABETH. Where are you now in my life?

HAROLD. I have always been here for you, my love.

ELIZABETH. I have always sought you out.

HAROLD. I have always been.

ELIZABETH. I have always sought.

HAROLD. I need to love. I love to need.

ELIZABETH. I know.

HAROLD. Be here for me now.

ELIZABETH. I am here.

HAROLD. Yes... But for how long?

(They exit from opposite sides of the stage, as the lights fade.)

CURTAIN

Slight Indulgences

By Vin Morreale, Jr.

CAST

Burton LeParge — A reclusive novelist

Bradley — A dashing super spy

SETTING

Bradley's office

Vin's Notes: This is an excerpt from one of my earliest published plays. Almost every writer tries to write a piece about being a writer. This was mine, as a shy and clumsy writer (me) creates a fictional alter ego who embodies everything his creator is not - dashing, brave and irresistably attractive to women. Of course, our fictional hero argues with the writer who created him. Well, it was highly original four decades ago, though others have used a similar device since. Still it is a charming one-act romantic comedy that was one of the very first productions of the THEATRE OF NOTE in Los Angeles. I am currently updating the play and may give it a new title.

For royalty information, or to request a copy of the full play, please contact **Dramatic Publishing** - dramaticpublishing.com/authors/profile/view/url/vin-morreale-jr

Slight Indulgences

AT RISE: The offices of BRADLEY AMES, 40, author of the wildly popular BURTON LEPARGE superspy series. Book and movie posters line the walls. But despite all this apparent success, the rumpled writer sits fretting over an old computer on a messy desk overflowing with papers and snack foods.

BRADLEY.   I don't know what got into her. She just doesn't understand. Real women never understand men at all. I mean really see the way we think.

> *(BURTON, the consummate James Bond elegant super spy enters from the shadows, wearing a red smoking jacket.)*

BURTON.   Fictional women aren't all that perceptive either. Sort of two-dimensional, you might say.

BRADLEY.   I don't know. I gave you some pretty wonderful women.

BURTON.   Grow up. None of them were half the woman Susan Morreale is.

BRADLEY.   I know that. But they are much easier to get along with.

BURTON.   You didn't spend the night with the Jungle Lady. I did.

BRADLEY.   She doesn't understand our relationship. I mean, I know I fashioned you and everything that happens to you out of my childish daydreams, right?

BURTON.   Right.

BRADLEY.   I know I could burn the three plays and eight novels, not to mention the Burton LeParge TV series, banishing you back to fantasyland forever. And you know that, too, don't you?

BURTON.   Of course I do.

BRADLEY.   Right. [Damn right.] So why does she care?

BURTON.   Because she does.

BRADLEY.   I never should have introduced you to that Zen master.

BURTON. Look, welterwit, she cares. She cares about you. Can't you see that?

BRADLEY. Huh? Don't confuse the issue. Of course she cares. Why shouldn't she? We've worked together for four years now. We're not strangers, you know.

BURTON. *(Sardonically.)* Sometimes I find it inconceivable that you are the one who puts words into my mouth. Must I spell it out for the world-famous writer? Anne Marie is in love with you.

BRADLEY. You're crazy. Why would she love me?

BURTON. I have no idea. Temporary lack of taste perhaps...But the point is...she does.

BRADLEY. I don't see how...

BURTON. If you trained your vision on the real world occasionally, you'd find it hard to miss an item like that.

BRADLEY. *(Pause, then...)* You really think so?

BURTON. Now there is a clever question.

BRADLEY. Don't worry. I know when I say "you," I mean "me" and I'm only outwardly manifesting my inner dialogue for the benefit of some unseen audience. Schizophrenia isn't even a consideration these days.

BURTON. Spare me the eulogies. I'm a super-hero, not a super-ego.

BRADLEY. Not a bad line. We'll have to use it in the next chapter.

BURTON. Forget the book, will you? It's more important to realize that Anne Marie loves you as much as you love her.

BRADLEY. Say what?

BURTON. Now don't try to deny that little fact.

BRADLEY. *(Defensively.)* I'm not necessarily denying it. *(A beat.)* But I haven't admitted it to myself either!

BURTON. Now there's a retort that deserves a place in history.

BRADLEY. Don't be sarcastic to me or I'll write a tapeworm into your character. Just you tell me how the great sleuth deduced the new recipient of my heart.

BURTON. You know, in all those stories you never once mentioned me going to school, any school. And yet, I'm not dumb enough to miss the similarity between Serena's hairstyle and Anne Marie's.

BRADLEY. A lot of women...

BURTON. Or the description of Lady Ethel's eyes and smile.

BRADLEY. Blue, big deal. And twinkles are common...

BURTON. Or even the Jungle Lady having, by sheer coincidence, the same unusual strawberry birthmark such as Anne Marie proudly possesses, and inch above her left knee.

BRADLEY. I'm sure many people have strawberry...

BURTON. Name twelve.

BRADLEY. Okay. So all you've proven is that I draw upon her for inspiration in the women I have you...uh...encounter.

BURTON. *(Smugly.)* I don't even have to mention the character of Antoinette...

BRADLEY. Okay. Enough! Guilty as charged, Mr. Mason. I'm in love with Anne Marie.

BURTON. Have you ever written me to be wrong?

BRADLEY. So now that I know, what do I do about it? Rescue her from a Bengal tiger? Make superior love to her in a U-2 spy plane hurtling over Mongolia? I'm no Burton LeParge, you know.

BURTON. Quite true. However, she is no Antoinette or Serena or Lady Ethel either. Have you ever considered merely asking her over for dinner? Prior to checking the rental fees for tigers and spy lanes, that is.

BRADLEY. I wouldn't know what to do over dinner. Or what to say. I feel infinitely more comfortable when I can script out what both people are thinking. An independent mind frightens me.

BURTON. So date a Democrat.

BRADLEY. Excuse me, I wrote you to not have any political opinions. Listen. When I write a love scene, I know what's going through the mind of the other person. I know in advance what she's going to say. Don't you see, there's no possibility of failure, no way I can embarrass myself by missing a cue or not being entertaining enough.

BURTON. In other words, you don't have the courage to live anywhere but in my safe little world.

BRADLEY. Remind me to have a gorilla rip out your tongue in the next chapter.

BURTON. He obviously got your guts years ago.

BRADLEY. I don't have to take this from you…uh…me. Self-abuse is immoral. Not to mention illegal in New England.

BURTON. Once again we whisk it all away with a minor witticism.

BRADLEY. I said that's enough! If you don't stop talking back, I'll write you into a Laverne and Shirley episode.

BURTON. Go split an infinitive.

BRADLEY. Go dangle your participle!

BURTON. Go take a …

(BRADLEY waves his hand angrily. Although BURTON continues to speak, no sound comes out. He turns in frustration.)

BRADLEY. Now. No more discussion about Anne Marie. Besides, I have work to do on chapter eleven.

BURTON. *(Yawning.)* Who do I seduce this time?

BRADLEY. Antoinette.

BURTON. Ha!

BRADLEY. Don't even think it! It has to be her. It's in the outline. I already wrote the notes on the scene and Antoin….Anne Marie typed them up for me.

BURTON. *(Laughing.)* How fast can a fictional character type?

(BRADLEY picks up a stack of paper and talks into the tape recorder.)

BRADLEY. *(Narrating vindictively.)* Burton LeParge walked into the room with great discomfort. Somehow during the night he had acquired a painfully stiff neck and now each step he took riddled him with agony.

(BURTON twists to conform to the description, wincing and muttering to himself as he walks into the upstage area.)

CURTAIN

The Wildlands

By
Vin Morreale, Jr.

CAST

Ellen   A 16 year-old pioneer girl

Simon   A 14 year-old pioneer boy

SETTING

A clearing in the Kentucky woods, circa 1769

Vin's Notes: The following three scenes are excerpted from a film trilogy I wrote with co-writer Devon Mitchell, based on the life of one of Kentucky's most colorful founders, frontiersman Simon Kenton. This larger than life woodsman was indeed larger than life, towering over most pioneers of his day. The series, which we hope to adapt to a TV series one day, traces his rise from a shy farmboy to a hero who served in the Revolutionary War and even saved Daiel Boone's life.

if you are a Film Producer interested in reading THE WILDLAND screenplays, please contact **Academy Arts Entertainment** *- vin@academyarts.com.*

The Wildlands

AT RISE: A clearing in the Kentucky forest, circa 1769. SIMON KENTON, a gangly young frontier boy sits beside ELLEN CUMMINS, 16. A flirtatious girl with long blond hair and big dreams.

ELLEN. You sure are good with that knife.

SIMON. *(Pleased she noticed.).* Been practicin'. I can split a squirrel from ten paces. Pa says I make a better hunter than a farmer.

ELLEN. A hunter ain't much these days. Huntin' don't get you anythin' but an old log cabin.

SIMON. A cabin would suit me fine.

ELLEN. But not a lady. She needs more.

SIMON. Uh, I reckon…

ELLEN. I foresee great things for you, Simon Kenton.

SIMON. What kinda things?

ELLEN. You're sure to be an important name around these parts. I can tell.

SIMON. Don't know nothin' 'bout that. I ain't much at learnin', and Ma says I'm less use in the fields than a parchment shovel.

ELLEN. You just ain't found your callin' yet. But you'll find it soon enough. *(Moves closer to him.)* You sure are growin' up tall, Simon. How old are you anyways?

SIMON. Fourteen.

ELLEN. And already a hand taller'n my pa.

(She plays with his long hair. Smiles as his face turns red.)

ELLEN. Someday I expect you and I are gonna up and run off together.

SIMON. Really?

ELLEN. Big strappin' boy like you. Handsome as the day is long. I could do worse.

SIMON. Is that a promise, Ellen? You and me, I mean?

ELLEN. You know better'n to ask a girl whether she's talkin' true or not...

SIMON. My sister almost died today. The green sickness almost got her.

ELLEN. That's why I'm never gonna be a farmwife. Or grow no tobacco.

(Sees that he is not really listening.)

ELLEN. Maybe I'll up and sail to Europe. Visit with kings and queens. Maybe live in a castle for a spell.

SIMON. You sure have a heap of strange ideas, Ellen Cummins.

ELLEN. It's not strange to know what you want. And what you don't. You won't see me with just one clean dress to my name. Trying to split two scrawny potatoes into a meal for six or seven squealin' babies... I seen what that kind of life can do to a woman. I seen my poor Ma old and broken before her time...

(She starts to sob softly. He doesn't know what to say.)

SIMON. I...I'm sorry, Ellen. I didn't mean to make you all sad and everything...

ELLEN. This life is hard enough on a man. But it kills its women young.

SIMON. I won't let that happen to you, Ellen. I swear I won't.

(She softens. Let's her shoulder lean into his chest.)

ELLEN. Neither will I...

CURTAIN

The Wildlands - 2

By
Vin Morreale, Jr.

CAST

Simon — An 18 year-old frontier boy

Jacob Butler — A widowed mill owner

SETTING

The workroom of an old Ohio mill, circa 1770

Vin's Notes: This second excerpt from THE WILDLANDS film series picks up after Young Simon runs away, believing he has killed a romatic rival. The frightened teenager changes his name and goes to work for a kindly miller in Ohio, who teaches him about being a man of kindness and integrity. Traits that will serve him well as he helps hundreds of stranded settlers in the expanding frontier.

if you are a Film Producer interested in reading THE WILDLAND screenplays, please contact **Academy Arts Entertainment** *- vin@academyarts.com.*

The Wildlands - 2

AT RISE: A small town along the Ohio frontier, circa 1770. SIMON KENTON, having run from his home, has been working for JACOB BUTLER, 44, a kindly miller.

SIMON. I'm sorry, Jacob. There's no more grain to be milled.

JACOB BUTLER. It's the end of the season. There's little more to do until the next winter wheat is ready to harvest.

SIMON. What do we do 'til then?

(A strange look comes over Jacob's face.)

JACOB BUTLER. How are you with a knife?

(Jacob leads Simon to the door of a locked room.)

JACOB BUTLER. You must promise you will tell no one what you see in here...

(A small workspace stacked with half-finished wooden objects.)

SIMON. What are they?

JACOB BUTLER. Cribs. I make them whenever the mill shuts down.

(Runs his hand along an unfinished crib rail.)

JACOB BUTLER. One for every new child born in town.

SIMON. *(Filled with wonder.)* My Ma had nine of us. On nothin' but an old straw mat. She would'a loved something like this. How much do folks pay you for 'em?

JACOB BUTLER. Not a penny. I place them on doorsteps in the dead of night. The parents never know who left them. The 'mystery cribmaker' has become a legend in these parts.

SIMON. Why do you do it? Jacob's eyes grow misty as he touches the crib.

JACOB BUTLER. Children are a blessing, Simon. A miracle. Someone to carry on your name after you're gone. Someone to teach... to encourage...and to care for. I hope you experience that joy for yourself one day. I've been blessed, Simon. A solid house. A steady business. Therefore, I must bless others any way I can. Not for praise or gratitude, but because it is the right thing to do. You understand all that?

SIMON. I reckon.

JACOB BUTLER. Good. Then off to work! That crib there needs smoothing. You'll find a planing tool on the shelf.

(Simon picks up an old planing tool.)

SIMON. This?

JACOB BUTLER. That's right. It has a small blade underneath. Run it gently along the grain until it's smooth enough for a child's hand. Not all blades are meant for harm, you know. *(Teaching him.)* Gently now. Smooth even movements...

(The two set down to work on their secret project. notices an older one hidden under a blanket. He pulls the blanket aside.)

SIMON. Who is this one for?

JACOB BUTLER. Don't touch that! It stays here!

(He snatches the blanket from Simon's hand. Throws it back over the old crib.)

JACOB BUTLER. Just get back to work... These two are for the orphanage. We lost so many to the fever last year.

(Simon gently smooths the upper rails.)

SIMON. Folks in town say...

JACOB BUTLER. Folks in town say what?

SIMON. They say Mrs. Butler was a good woman.

(Jacob's head snaps back, as if he's been slapped.)

SIMON. Just thought you'd like to know.

(A pause. Jacob's eyes droop. His voice, barely a whisper.)

JACOB BUTLER. She was. Too good for the likes of me. And beautiful. With a smile that could warm the coldest winter.

SIMON. Your Juliet.

JACOB BUTLER. That was my Bethany... She's out back. By the big elm tree. It was her favorite. She's lyin' out there with my boy, who never got the chance to open his eyes and see his father before... see me before... *(With pain.)* We don't get many days on this earth, Simon. My son didn't get more than a moment. You be sure to make the most of the days you're given, Simon.

SIMON. How do I do that, Jacob?

JACOB BUTLER. That's what each man has to answer for himself. I only wish you better luck than I had...

SIMON. You miss her, don't you? Mrs. Butler?

JACOB BUTLER. Only like I'd miss my arm if I suddenly woke and found it gone. Or my eyes, so that I was no longer able to see the sunrise. *(Smiles sadly.)* Let me tell you, Simon. It's painful when a man realizes the best part of him was inside someone else all along. And without her... well, he's not much of anything. Just a body grinding through his days like that old millstone grinds grain. *(Closes his book.)* Guess I've been reading poetry too long. What say you and I go into town? I'm dog-tired of hearing the sound of my own voice.

SIMON. I think you're wrong, Jacob.

JACOB BUTLER. About what?

SIMON. You said the best part of you was all in someone else. That's not what I see. You've been kind to the new mothers. You've been kind to me.

JACOB BUTLER. That's just plain selfishness on my part. It's hard to find good workhands these days. Especially one the size of you. I was hoping you'd stay and work another season or two. But that ain't going to happen, is it?

SIMON. I guess I'm just not meant for towns. Even one peaceful as this.

JACOB BUTLER. Still dead set on finding your way to the Kentucky cane lands?

SIMON. Strange how a place you never been to can pull at you so strong.

JACOB BUTLER. Is it what's pulling at you that has you itching to leave? Or what's chasing you?

SIMON. Both, I reckon.

JACOB BUTLER. Then I reckon you're like most your age.

(Simon stops. His face pales, even in the moonlight.)

SIMON. No, I'm not. I'm worse. A lot worse. I done things, Jacob. Things that shame me to my bones. And maybe I can't outrun 'em. But when I'm out there in the woods. With nothin' but the sound of birds and wind, and the soil itself settling all peaceful into place... Out there, maybe I'm not such a bad man. Maybe there's a chance for me to find somethin'.

JACOB BUTLER. Find what, Simon?

SIMON. I don't rightly know. Forgiveness, maybe...

JACOB BUTLER. You've seen hardships, son. That's plain enough. Hardships that left scars on you. But we all have scars. I find it's best not to let them carve too deep into your soul.

SIMON. And how do you do that?

JACOB BUTLER. You do what the Good Book says. Care for others. Lend a hand to those in need.

SIMON. Wish it were that easy...

JACOB BUTLER. No one says it'll be easy. Most of the time, it won't. You got debts to pay, I'm guessing. But every service you do for another helps those debts lessen a bit more. Before you know it, all that's left is the shadow of that harsh memory, soft and whispery as morning dew. And that too will fade before long.

SIMON. *(Tears in his eyes.)* Can't happen soon enough for me.

JACOB BUTLER. I know, son. I know.

The Wildlands -3

By
Vin Morreale, Jr.

CAST

Simon   A burly frontiersman

Girty   A trapper and woodsman

SETTING

A fort in the Ohio wilderness, circa 1773

Vin's Notes: This final excerpt from THE WILDLANDS film series finds a grownup Simon Kenton, now a famous scout and Indian fighter. Partnering with a far gruffer and brutal frontiersman named Girty. In the years that followed, Simon would change from Indian fighter to a major supporter of rights for Native American tribes, and go on to found the first school for Native American children in the US.

if you are a Film Producer interested in reading THE WILDLAND screenplays, please contact **Academy Arts Entertainment** *- vin@academyarts.com.*

The Wildlands - 3

AT RISE: A fort in the Ohio wilderness, circa 1773. SIMON KENTON, now a grown and experienced frontier man, watches a parade of new recruits with GIRTY, an even older frontier fighter. The soldiers, who we do not see, drill in the old European style of open field military marching.

SIMON. Look at all those new recruits in their shiny new uniforms.

GIRTY. Ain't that the dangdest thing?

SIMON. They sure march pretty.

GIRTY. That they do. And what d'ya think the tribes is gonna do when they see all them purty soldiers marchin' toward 'em lined up like that?

SIMON. Shoot at them from behind trees. Circle around to attack the sides and back. Anywhere but straight on.

GIRTY. Damned right. That style o' solderin' may work over there in England. But Chief Logan, Cornstalk and the rest o' that bunch ain't gonna have none of it.

SIMON. I tried to explain that to the Colonel. But he insists he knows how to fight an Indian War.

GIRTY. *(Spits.)* If he don't, he'll learn soon enough...

SIMON. Them boys in their new blue uniforms are gonna get themselves slaughtered. And for no reason.

GIRTY. No reason at all. The way I see it, more whites should get off their high horses and go live with the Indians a few years. There's lots they can teach ya. Not that they cain't be savages, you get on the wrong side of 'em. But we been stealing and killin' 'em for years. It's a wonder there ain't more dead whites than there be.

SIMON. They killed my partner. And a group of government surveyors. Hacked them to death.

GIRTY. And I seen whites do the same. Claimin' Indians are only good for killin'. Nothin' more. The last few years, I seen whole settlements wiped out on both sides. White and red. Both look the same when they's lyin' dead on the ground.

SIMON. Soldiers and braves are one thing. But when the Indians attacked the town not twenny miles from here, they even scalped the women.

GIRTY. Like I said. They can be savages, all right. And some tribes is worse than others. Don't never insult a Seneca chief, or trust a Cherokee with your horse or your woman. *(Grins.)* Then again, I wouldn't trust me with your woman neither.

SIMON. You speak their language?

GIRTY. A couple of 'em. Iroquois... Algonguin... I can stumble my way through a few others. I hire out as a translator for the army, so I'm usually the only one who knows who's lyin' to who.

SIMON. And who is lying?

GIRTY. Hell, we all are. It's how we get what we want. And there ain't no end to what we want neither. Them Indians want our guns, horses and liquor. All we want is their land and everything on it. But what all of 'em wants most is for the other to up and disappear and never trouble 'em again. Since that ain't gonna happen, I'd say we're all in a whole heap o' trouble.

SIMON. This ain't my fight. But I can't stand back and watch folks die. *(Desperately.)* I just need to know...who's right in all this?

GIRTY. Hell, ain't you learned yet, boy? There ain't no right... There's alive, and there's dead. You do what you can to keep breathin'... then hold your nose when the lies you tell yourself start to stink too bad...

CURTAIN

Little Lies

By
Vin Morreale, Jr.

CAST

Daphne — An attractive single woman

Josh — A charming single man

SETTING

A modern single's bar

Vin's Notes: This was another scene originally created for my **Burning Up The Stage Acting Workshops** that can also be found in my book 150 ACTING SCENES. People meeting for the first time, and the lies they tell or truths they withold from each other remains a great way to generate humor and explore the layers of a character.

*For royalty information and permission to use this scene in a paid performance, please contact **Academy Arts Press** - vin@academyarts.com*

Little Lies

AT RISE: A dim and sultry bar. All dark wood and secret intentions. At a small table sits DAPHNE, an attractive woman in her twenties. She yells at a man we do not see.)

DAPHNE. *(Yelling.)* Oh, and next time you try to pick up someone…be sure to hide your wedding ring! *(Muttering.)* Lying jerk.

(She gulps her drink, as JOSH, mid-twenties, slides in beside her.)

JOSH. I noticed your drink is almost empty.

DAPHNE. Thanks for the update.

JOSH. Can I get you another one?

(Daphne ignores him.)

JOSH. Anyway, my name is Josh. I just moved into the building. *(Still no reaction.)* Red's the perfect color on you. *(Still nothing.)* And just so you know, I'm not married like that other guy.

DAPHNE. What other guy?

JOSH. The one you scared off. I've been watching you.

DAPHNE. How comforting. Stalk much?

JOSH. In a good way. I noticed not one person has been able to talk to you for more than three minutes. A few have tried, but they left in a hurry. Ran for the hills.

DAPHNE. And that doesn't scare you off?

JOSH. Actually, I like the challenge.

DAPHNE. A sport dater, huh? It's not about me, or even the hope of a relationship. It's the challenge. The chase. The game. Alpha males on the prowl. I'm almost impressed.

JOSH. You got me all wrong. Others may be like that, but I…

DAPHNE. Look…Why don't we just tell all our lies up front and get them out of the way, okay? Then maybe we can attempt to have a real conversation afterwards. Okay?

JOSH. Fair enough. Here goes…

(He takes a deep breath.)

JOSH. *(With sincerity.)* I'm an amateur nuclear physicist and sole heir to the throne of Sweden. I'm four inches taller than I look, a decade younger than I appear, and far wiser than I ever imagined I'd be. I'm listed in the Guinness Book of World Records for stationary bungee jumping and won an Oscar last year for best nostrils in a dramatic feature. I play miniature golf every Saturday with Hillary Clinton, Justin Bieber, and the Pope, who has sometimes been known to cheat on his score card. I purchased a small Latin American country, but only get to visit occasionally. Many of my body parts are patent pending.
MORE

JOSH. *(Continued.)* I'm working on the Great American Novel, but it's not finished yet, because I'm writing it in five different languages at once, and those Chinese picture-letters can be a real bitch. In my free time, I darn socks, design US currency, and knit my own trash bags. *(Smiles.)* Now you lie to me.

DAPHNE. Okay. *(Just as sincerely.)* I think you have a great sense of humor.

(She gets up and leaves him with a wicked smile. He sits there, stunned.)

JOSH. I think she likes me.

CURTAIN

A Knightly Occurrence

By
Vin Morreale, Jr.

CAST

Rick — An awkward teen

Sir Lionel — The ghost of a Medieval knight

SETTING

The repair room of Psychic Cycles bicycle shop

Vin's Notes: Back when life seemed full of promise, this 23 year-old published playwright just had this third film script optioned by a low-budget film producer. Then I learned a sad truth of Hollywood. Options don't mean productions. So every three or four years since then, I rewrite every film script of mine that has yet to sell. I still have hope this family friendly comedy about a teen visited by a Medieval Knight, the ghost of his distant ancestor, someday makes it onto the big screen. Until then, enjoy this 'fish out of water' scene.

For royalty information and permission to use this scene in a paid performance, or if you are a Film Producer interested in reading this full screenplay, please contact **Academy Arts Entertainment** - *vin@academyarts.com.*

A Knightly Occurrence

AT RISE: The back repair room of Psychic Cycles bicycle repair shop. RICK, 17, is being haunted by the ghost of his long-dead ancestor, SIR LIONEL OF ANGSTAFF, a Medieval knight.)

LIONEL. So this is where you labor after school, eh?

RICK. Sir Lionel! You're going to give me a heart attack!

LIONEL. Easy, lad. I was merely curious about the manner of your apprenticeship. You must admit, the shop does have a rather unusual name.

RICK. Psychic Cycles? I think it's cute.

LIONEL. Cuteness appears to be an affliction of yours. What are these contraptions?

RICK. Bicycles. We sell and repair them.

LIONEL. Buy-sick-kills?

RICK. The modern day equivalent of a horse.

LIONEL. Ah. So you are a stable boy.

RICK. No. I am a salesman and repairman! I guess you didn't have many of either in your day.

LIONEL. We had gigolos and blacksmiths. And trust me, lad... you do not have the arms of a blacksmith.

RICK. And I don't have the morals of a gigolo either!

LIONEL. Nor the equipment, I might add.

RICK. Did you come back from the dead just to insult me?

LIONEL. Hardly. But as long as I am here, I may as well enjoy the sport. Now then, what does a salesman do? Barter?

RICK. The barter system went out five or six centuries ago, What I do is convince customers that this is the best bike they can get for their money.

LIONEL. Oh. They give you gold and silver for your wares?

RICK. Not exactly. Usually they pay with cash or credit. *(Pulls out a dollar.)* Look... This is a dollar.

LIONEL. Why, it is merely a painting of an old man on a piece of paper!

RICK. Well, yeah, But it's worth a certain amount of money...uh, gold.

LIONEL. Splendid! How much gold is it worth?

RICK. One dollar's worth.

LIONEL. Pray tell. How much is that?

RICK. Let me see... *(Searches on his phone.)* It says gold closed today at thirteen hundred dollars an ounce.

LIONEL. This is worth a thirteen hundredth of an ounce?! Hardly seems worth the time to paint the old man's portrait.

RICK. That's what it's worth today. It changes.

LIONEL. Who changes it?

RICK. Investors, I guess. It depends on how much they pay for dollars on the International Currency Exchange.

LIONEL. You mean to say people buy these dollars?

RICK. That's right.

LIONEL. With what? Bicycles?

RICK. No. With their own currency.

LIONEL. They buy these little paper portraits with other little paper portraits?

RICK. Sort of.

LIONEL. Why?

RICK. To make money.

LIONEL. This is all too muddled, Richard. Let us begin anew. Now, who declares this dollar is worth a certain amount of gold?

RICK. The market.

LIONEL. The one across the street?

RICK. Not that market. Wall Street.

LIONEL. *(Getting frustrated.)* Why would anyone put a wall in a street? Wouldn't that make it impassable?

RICK. *(Also frustrated.)* You don't understand. That's where all the financial big shots hang.

LIONEL. They hang them on Wall Street?

RICK. Not hang them. That's where they hang out....Gather. Work.

LIONEL. Can't they afford a building?

RICK. I give up.

LIONEL. Never give up, lad. There is little glory in doing so. Tell me, what if these fellows on Wall Street change their mind and decide they want a mountain of gold for each of these paper slips?

RICK. They can't.

LIONEL. Who would stop them?

RICK. The government, I guess.

LIONEL. Ah! But wouldn't the government be eager to gather more gold for themselves? Wouldn't they want to get as much as they can for each of their little paper portraits?

RICK. Yes. I mean, no...there are laws for that sort of thing.

LIONEL. But does not the government make the laws?

RICK. Yes, but...

LIONEL. Then why can't they make a law stating that the value of these little paper portraits is whatever they want it to be?

RICK. I guess they could. But they won't. At least I'm pretty sure they won't...

LIONEL. Suppose instead the government decides not to change their value. Why not keep painting more and more of these little paper portraits? If they are all worth a certain amount of gold, they could accumulate a fortune for the king's treasury.

RICK. *(Really frustrated.)* We don't have a king, and they can't just keep printing dollars!

LIONEL. Why not?

RICK. I don't know! I'm not an economist!!

LIONEL. You are not that talented of a barterer, either! I believe you have been made the fool with all this 'dollar' nonsense.

RICK. Look, Sir Lionel... Would you mind coming back later? I'm finding it hard to fix this bike while teaching you economics one-oh-one!

LIONEL. As you wish, my impatient heir. By the by, you will likely remove the malady, if you were to loosen this bolt here.

RICK. Look, Sir Lionel. I know you want to be helpful, but I've been working on these things since I was twelve. I really don't need your help!

LIONEL. Stubbornness seems to be a surer sign of youth than the inability to raise a credible beard! Very well. I will be waiting at your pitiable domicile. Good day!

(With a snarl, Lionel vanishes.)

RICK. Sir Lionel? *(Muttering.)* Why do I get all the touchy ancestors?

(Rick turns the screw that Lionel pointed out. The wheel spins.)

LIONEL. Aha! Did I not tell you!

(Rick jumps at the sound of the disembodied voice.)

CURTAIN

Victim

By Vin Morreale, Jr.

CAST

Mel   An inmate

Silvie   His new lawyer

SETTING

A conference room in a maximum security prison.

Vin's Notes: I wrote this script remembering a friend of mine who was attacked almost as described in the scene. The ending I wrote gave her a chance for justice that she would never receive in real life. Years later, I interviewed a real life serial killer in prison, seeing how little empathy he had for his victims. It made me realize there is genuine evil in this world, a kind that normal people can never really understand. This piece offers a unique challenge for strong actors. A short film of this script was produced by MWU Entertainment. This scene also appears in *BURNING UP THE STAGE: Monologues, Short Scenes & Audition pieces for Actors From Six to Seventy* under the title FACE TO FACE.

FOR ROYALTY INFORMATION, PLEASE CONTACT **DRAMATIC PUBLISHING** -
dramaticpublishing.com/authors/profile/view/url/vin-morreale-jr

Victim

AT RISE: The stark, concrete conference room of Gatlinger State Penitentiary. MEL 52, a frighteningly calm inmate, sits quietly as his lawyer, SYLVIE, 41, tries hard not to meet his eyes.

MEL. So… You're her.

SYLVIE. If you mean your new attorney. Yes. Sylvie Ellison.

MEL. Saint Sylvie.

SYLVIE. Excuse me?

MEL. Rich lawyer. Feeling guilty 'cause her life is way too perfect. So she plays crusader for a few hours to set a notorious scumbag free.

SYLVIE. *(Shaken.)* Why don't we concentrate on your case, Mr. Caldwell?

MEL. Gives you something to brag about at high-class dinner parties. Helps justify your million dollar salary. Man, you gotta love liberal guilt.

SYLVIE. Your case?

MEL. Hitting too close to home?

(Sylvie hesitates. Sits in the metal chair facing him. The metal table a cold hard barrier between their worlds. Her expression hardens.)

SYLVIE. You think you know me, Mel?

MEL. I know the type.

SYLVIE. Actually, you know me better than that.

MEL. Yeah? Not one of my ex-wives, are you?

SYLVIE. God, no. If I was one of your wives, I'd probably shoot myself.

MEL. *(Leaning forward.)* That's just what my first two exes said…Only they didn't have the balls to do it, so I had to help them pull the trigger.

SYLVIE. And you're proud of that?

MEL. *(Shrugs.)* Saved me a ton in alimony.

SYLVIE. You really are evil, aren't you?

MEL. Keep talking like that, lady, and it'll injure my self-esteem.

SYLVIE. That's a joke.

MEL. Yeah, it was. But you didn't come all the way out here just to hear my stand-up routine.

SYLVIE. No...I didn't.

MEL. Hell, I bet you ain't even been in one of these maximum security Disneylands before. Me? This is like home. I been kicking around concrete tombs like this since I graduated from Juvie hall. Some call it hard time. Don't mean shit to me.

SYLVIE. I can do without the profanity, if you please.

MEL. I imagine you could. So tell me...who are you? And why am I staring at your that ugly face of yours?

(His aggressiveness sparks something in her. A chord of defiance. She lifts her head and stares coolly back at him.)

SYLVIE. I wanted to see you...I wanted to remember your face.

MEL. *(Intrigued now.)* Now that's more like it. So we met before, huh? I like guessing games. It helps pass the time in a place like this. So where was it? Some bar you came on to me? Some quickie rendezvous in a cheap motel when your husband was outta town? Was I the best you ever had, and you couldn't get me off your mind? That's it, isn't it?

SYLVIE. You really don't remember, do you?

MEL. Don't have a clue, lady.

SYLVIE. Let me give you a hint...Interstate 95. Just outside Connecticut. Fourteen years ago.

MEL. Nope. Don't ring a bell.

SYLVIE. Let me refresh your memory... *(She stand and suddenly screams at the top of her lungs.)* AAARGHHH!

(Sylvie sits down again, trembling.)

MEL. I sure would enjoy another hint.

SYLVIE. Okay...How about ... *(Whimpering.)* Please don't kill me, Mister! Please...take anything you want...just please don't kill me!

MEL. *(Thinks for a moment.)* Nope...That doesn't narrow it down any. What kind of car were you driving?

SYLVIE. You really are a cold son of a bitch, aren't you?

MEL. I can do without the profanity, if you please.

SYLVIE. Fourteen years ago, I was driving home from work, when I saw what I thought was a human being stranded by the side of the road...That was the last peaceful moment of my entire life.

MEL. You're breaking my heart.

SYLVIE. You raped me!

MEL. Guess that depends on your perspective, doesn't it?

SYLVIE. There was no perspective about it! I gave you a ride and you raped me! And after you were done, you shot me. Twice... *(Points to her stomach.)* Here and here... Then you pushed me out and left me for dead by the side of the road.

MEL. Looks like I made an error in judgment. You're looking pretty healthy to me.

SYLVIE. Thanks to a trucker who happened to be driving by. A good man who saw a naked...bloody...half-dead woman claw her way back to the highway...With nothing but hatred keeping her alive.

MEL. I know a thing or two about hatred.

SYLVIE. I wasn't going to let you kill me and get away with it. That was all that was keeping me alive. Pure hatred.

MEL. My kinda woman.

SYLVIE. If I am...it's what you made me into.

MEL. So why not look me up earlier? I mean, fourteen years is a hell of a long time to let all that stuff boil up inside you.

SYLVIE. After that trucker scraped me off the road and ran me to the hospital...The doctors didn't hold out much hope. *(Reliving the pain.)* I...I was in a coma for two years...Two whole years wasting away, unconscious in some hospital bed. Two years you took from me.

MEL. Like I said...You're breaking my heart.

SYLVIE. When I came out of the coma, you were already locked up for two other murders.

MEL. *(Smiles cruelly.)* Two that they know about. There are a bunch more they ain't ever gonna find. But that's our little secret. *(Leaning back)* In case you ain't heard...The nice folks at the parole board are letting me out next week. Time off for good behavior, if you can believe that.

SYLVIE. That's why I'm here, Mr. Caldwell.

MEL. Yeah? Planning on looking me up after I get out?

SYLVIE. Exactly.

MEL. Some sort of roll in the hay for old time's sake?

SYLVIE. No... *(Coolly.)* A bullet in the gut for old time sake.

MEL. *(Amused.)* You're going to shoot me?

SYLVIE. Twice. *(Points to the two places she was shot.)* Once here...and once here. Then I'm going to strip off your clothes and leave you naked and bleeding by the side of the road. Just like you did to me.

MEL. And what makes you think I'll go along with your little plan?

SYLVIE. *(Matter-of-fact)* You won't have a choice. You'll never know when I'm going to be behind you with a nine millimeter pointed at your skull. Wherever you go, I'll be in the shadows...Watching you...

MEL. Sorry, Lady. But I've played tag with the big boys. When they let me outta here, I'll be invisible within the hour.

SYLVIE. *(Shrugs.)* You'll try.

MEL. Yeah? And how are you gonna find me?

(The roles have reversed now. Sylvie leans in with sadistic pleasure. Mel is increasingly unsure of this suddenly powerful woman.)

SYLVIE. Oh, I'll find you, Mel...I will make it my personal mission in life to find you. You see, I got married a few years after I came out of the coma...I could never have kids, you saw to that...But my husband, he's a good man. A supportive man...A man who's had to live with the hell you put me through all these years. Holding onto me all those nights I woke up screaming. Shaking. Begging for mercy...

MEL. And that concerns me...how?

SYLVIE. Did I mention he's with the FBI? And out of love for his wife, he's taken a special interest in your case, Mr. Caldwell. That's how I found out you were going to be released next Tuesday at exactly two-fifteen.

MEL. So you and your cuddly Fed hubby are going to track me down and kill me, huh?

SYLVIE. He'll track you down. I want the pleasure of killing you myself.

MEL. You don't have it in you, lady.

SYLVIE. Look into my eyes, Mel...then tell me I don't have it in me.

(He glares at her. She meets his stare with equal hatred. After a moment, he breaks.)

MEL. Okay, so maybe you got the stones... But that don't mean you'll be able to get me!

SYLVIE. I'll get you, Mel. However long it takes...I'll get you. I'm going to make you feel what it's like to see your life leaking out of your body on some cold deserted highway.

MEL. I ain't afraid of you.

SYLVIE. Then that's your mistake, Mr. Caldwell. You see, you gave me a reason to crawl back onto that highway. You gave me a reason to live. There's no way in hell I'm going to let you do to any other woman what you did to me. *(With pure hatred.)* I want you to feel what it's like to die for no other reason than some animal feels like killing you today... However long it takes, Mel. I'm going to hunt you down, and I'm going to take your life away.

(Mel stands, glaring at her. Suddenly, he kicks his chair, sending it clattering across the room. Sylvie doesn't flinch...which unnerves him even more.)

SYLVIE. *(With icy confidence.)* I'll be seeing you, Mel.

(She places the files in her briefcase. Snaps it shut. Then rises. Smooths her business suit and exits silently.)

SYLVIE. I'll be seeing you...

CURTAIN

Just A Sprinkle

By
Vin Morreale, Jr.

CAST

Jessie — A flirty stranger

George — A married man

SETTING

A small Italian restaurant

Vin's Notes: This was another piece written for The Ruskin Theatre's monthly Café Plays. Like the others, it was written in a little over two hours, according to a specific theme, and then performed before two different audiences that same night. Too much fun!

For royalty information and permission to use this scene in a paid performance, please contact **Academy Arts Press** *- vin@academyarts.com*

Just A Sprinkle

AT RISE: *Lights come up on a small Italian restaurant, GEORGE sits alone at a table, sipping coffee. Lost in thought. JESSIE enters, looks around. Spots him. Smiles, then squeezes into the seat beside him.*

JESSIE.   Is this seat taken?

(George shakes his head.)

JESSIE.   My name's Jessie, and may I say that you are absolutely...

GEORGE.   Married.

JESSIE.   Oh. *(Pause, then...)* Seriously married? Temporarily unavailable? Or just playing morally hard to get?

GEORGE.   You get shot down a lot, don't you?

JESSIE.   Is it that obvious?

GEORGE.   A bit.

JESSIE.   *(Face falls.)* I don't understand it. I used to be so smooth and comfortable around men! Especially guys like you. The kind that are so hot and studly and...

GEORGE.   Married.

JESSIE.   See? I can't even tempt you with flirty talk. *(Sighs & slumps back.)* My life is over.

GEORGE.   Maybe you just need to find someone a little more...available.

JESSIE.   That's the trouble. Guys are only available until they meet me. Then BAM, Door slams. Interest dries up.

GEORGE.   It could be that you're coming on too strong. Reeks of desperation.

JESSIE.   I reek?

GEORGE.   Not odor-wise...although I have to say, nobody has worn that particular brand of 'Laverne & Shirley' perfume since the 1970s.

JESSIE. I saw it on the Home Shopping Network. I bought four cases.

GEORGE. And you decided to wear them all today?

JESSIE. Okay. Dial down the perfume. Good suggestion. But it's more than that. I tried Match.com and even that was a disaster. I never knew people could email "Go to hell" in so many different languages. I probably shouldn't have used my high school graduation photo as my profile picture. Or listed my profession as brain surgeon cheerleader.

GEORGE. You're just going through a little slump, that's all. Everybody has them.

JESSIE. It's more than a slump. It's an absolute drought!

GEORGE. It can't be that bad.

JESSIE. It's worse. Four years ago, it was raining men. I was flooded with possibilities. Now every dating prospect has dried up. I'm reduced to hitting on married men in cheap restaurants on Tuesday afternoons.

GEORGE. At least you aren't one of those horny women who scour the produce departments at the supermarket.

JESSIE. Actually, I'm banned from Ralph's, Albertson's and Safeway. If it wasn't for Smart & Final, I'd starve to death. *(Softly.)* Sorry to dump this all on you.

GEORGE. It's okay. I wasn't doing much but sipping coffee and trying not to think. So what changed four years ago? When the drought started?

JESSIE. My husband, he...he...

GEORGE. Died?

JESSIE. I wish. No, he decided after ten years of marriage that he could do better. Or at least, he could do younger. Do it a few times a week, evidently. So he started working his way through every intern at his office. Then most of the college sororities, trying to prove that he was still Grade A middle-aged man meat.

GEORGE. Men are scum. I know. I'm one of them. But that's no reflection on you.

JESSIE.   It's funny. When I was unavailable, I couldn't stop all these guys from flirting with me. Now that I'm back on the market, I attract about as much attention as a Steven Segal movie marathon.

GEORGE.   I find that hard to believe.

JESSIE.   It's true. Some people go to astrologists to have their charts read. My love life is tied to the California meteorological chart. Severe drought, with no end in sight.

GEORGE.   That's crazy. You're attractive. Honest and funny.

JESSIE.   And withered. And drooping. And emotionally parched. The long range forecast is just as depressing. I'm waiting for Jerry Brown to declare my love life a National Disaster. Maybe he'll send in the National Guard. Some of them are cute.

GEORGE.   You just need to relax and let it happen for you.

JESSIE.   Bernie - my ex - used to say the same thing about female orgasms. I'm still waiting on that one. Hey, do you think those websites for Russian Mail Order Brides offer guys too? I have Amazon Prime, so I get second day shipping for free.

GEORGE.   Now cut that out. You are beautiful and charming, and sweet in a clumsy, endearingly awkward kind of way.

JESSIE.   Thanks... I think.

GEORGE.   All you have to do is find that one person who appreciates a real woman, instead of those 'make-up commercial - Victoria Secret' illusions they are always trying to sell us. Someone who appreciates a woman who knows how to communicate her feelings and is not afraid to share them.

JESSIE.   That kind of guy is extinct in California.

GEORGE.   Don't be so sure. You need a man who helps you find your laugh again, and makes your heart sing every time he loses himself in your soft, green eyes. Someone who values your opinions. And will challenge and cherish you every day of his life. *He said too much. Leans back, uncomfortably. She sighs, still carried away by his words.*

JESSIE.   Man, your wife must be the luckiest woman in the world.

GEORGE. She thinks so, too. *(Not harshly.).* At least while she's banging the 19 year-old kid who mows our lawn every other Tuesday.

JESSIE. While you're down here having coffee?

GEORGE. Trying to pretend I don't know. It's better that way. At least I tell myself it is. *(Softly.)* Droughts affect everyone, I guess.

JESSIE. *(A beat, then….)* Ready for another cup of coffee, Mr. Married Guy? My treat?

GEORGE. *(Sad smile.)* Maybe just a sprinkle.

JESSIE. Yeah. Maybe just a sprinkle.

(They lean closer, sharing a moment of silent commiseration.)

CURTAIN

All My Passions

By
Vin Morreale, Jr.

CAST

Melissa Mulcahey — A tough-talking soap opera producer

Hamilton — A conservative consultant from the Midwest

SETTING

The set of the soap opera ALL MY PASSIONS

Vin's Notes: What began as a silly sketch idea turned into a full-length comedy laced with social commentary and moments of surprising tenderness. That happens sometimes when you allow your characters the freedom to write themselves. ALL MY PASSIONS is a long-running soap opera trying to enhance its dwindling ratings by double dosing on sleaze. That is, until a conservative boycotter convinces the producers to let him try a less slimy version of the show.

For royalty information and permission to use this scene in a paid performance, or to request a full copy of ALL MY PASSIONS, please contact
Academy Arts Press - *vin@academyarts.com*

All My Passions

AT RISE: The TV studio where the long-running soap opera ALL MY PASSIONS is shot. Producer MELISSA MULCAHEY, 37, is frustrated that conservative outsider HAMILTON BENNETT, 34, has been elevated to a major creative position in the studio.)

MELISSA.   So, hick boy…are you ready to take on the entire studio establishment?

HAMILTON.   The question is… is the entire studio establishment ready for me? *(Softens.)* Listen, Melissa. I know I'm treading on your job as producer a bit, but I really believe we can make this work.

MELISSA.   I don't. You can fool Mr. Forrester, but I know what it takes to succeed in this business.

HAMILTON.   And what's that?

MELISSA.   A whole boatload of everything you don't got.

HAMILTON.   That may be true. But as Mister Forrester said, what have we got to lose?

MELISSA.   There is always something to lose. That's the first thing you learn in this town.

HAMILTON.   Okay. Maybe I do have a lot to learn. I would be happy to listen to whatever advice you'd be willing to share. *(Catches himself.)* To listen…not necessarily to follow.

MELISSA. Have you always been this pompous?

HAMILTON.   I majored in pomposity at Hick High School. *(Catching her smile.)* Please, Melissa. I would really love to work with you. No animosity. What do you say?

MELISSA.   *(Seeing the sincerity in his eyes.)* Okay…I'll go animosity-free for a day or two. That's the best I can do.

HAMILTON.   That's all I ask… *(Shyly.)* And maybe one more thing.

MELISSA.   Why is there always 'one more thing?'

HAMILTON. I was wondering… if you're not um… doing anything right now…Maybe you might go to lunch with me?

MELISSA. This is Hollywood, kid. We don't do lunch. We do meetings with food.

HAMILTON. So, uh…is that a yes?

MELISSA. You really are an Opie, aren't you?

HAMILTON. I'm sorry. Could you please hold up a cue card or something? Just so I know when I'm being insulted.

MELISSA. Assume it's continuous.

HAMILTON. Ah. Well, then. At least I know where I stand…So, back to my initial question… Can an Opie take his cynical, but talented, intelligent and ridiculously attractive producer to a meeting with food?

MELISSA. Are you really for real?

HAMILTON. Help me out here. How is one supposed to answer a question like that?

(She looks at him like a bug under a microscope, then softens.)
MELISSA. Okay, hick-boy. I'm willing to see what makes you tick. Lunch is on you, by the way.

(She exits, Stage Right. Hamilton is left alone on the set.)

HAMILTON. *(Sighs.)* Rampant insanity punctuated by meetings…

CURTAIN

All My Passions - 2

By
Vin Morreale, Jr.

CAST

Everett Montague   Aging soap opera star 40 years past his prime

Hamilton   A conservative consultant from the Midwest

SETTING

The set of the soap opera ALL MY PASSIONS

Vin's Notes: Everett Montague is the aging star of the long-running soap opera, ALL MY PASSIONS. He still believes he can pass for a young sex symbol, often with hilarious results. This behind the scenes look at daytime television offers a lot of potential for humor and social commentary.

For royalty information and permission to use this scene in a paid performance, or to request a full copy of ALL MY PASSIONS, please contact
Academy Arts Press - *vin@academyarts.com*

All My Passions - 2

AT RISE: The TV studio where ALL MY PASSIONS is shot. With the increasingly sleazy show spiraling down in ratings, outside consultant HAMILTON BENNETT, 34, is bringing a more family friendly feel to the long-running soap opera. EVERETT MONTAGUE, the show's aging and clueless star for the last 49 years, is trying to wrap his head around the changes.)

HAMILTON. Okay, let's take five, people!

EVERETT. Take five people where?

HAMILTON. We're on break, Everett.

EVERETT. Oh…Take five…

HAMILTON. Which presents me with an opportunity to explain this exciting new spin we have created for your character. I want you to picture a man…

EVERETT. Wait! *(Concentrates hard.)* Okay. Got him.

HAMILTON. Picture this man as the revered head of a powerful corporation. Wealthy. Wise. Loved by all.

EVERETT. Simultaneously?

HAMILTON. Yes. But…uh, not in the physical sense.

EVERETT. Really? How strange.

HAMILTON. He is loved because of his compassion and understanding for those around him.

EVERETT. I'm having trouble understanding this 'understanding' thing…

HAMILTON. He knows what they are feeling.

(Everett stares at him, as if he is speaking a different language.)

HAMILTON. He can sympathize with their needs and fears.

(Frustrated over Everett's continuing confusion.)

HAMILTON. He's, uh... read the script synopsis on their motivations.

EVERETT. Oh! Understanding. Why didn't you say so?

HAMILTON. People come to him with their problems. Their concerns.

EVERETT. And he sleeps with them?

HAMILTON. No. And that's the twist. He doesn't sleep with any of them!

EVERETT. For some reason I am losing the picture of this man...

HAMILTON. Everett, haven't you ever met anyone you looked up to?

EVERETT. Well, there was Ilsa. She was six-foot-five. When I looked up to her, I saw...

HAMILTON. I mean a role model. Someone who had a positive influence on your life? What about your father?

EVERETT. What about him?

HAMILTON. Was he a good man?

EVERETT. My father? Ha! He was a philandering bum who would sleep with anything on two legs. And even that was negotiable, depending on his mood.

HAMILTON. Okay. That was slightly more than I needed to know. But think back, Everett. How did you feel about him?

EVERETT. About my father? How could I feel? I was his seventh child from his sixth wife. I got to see him every other Arbor Day. And then again on Thanksgiving, when he'd gather all his ex-wives and mistresses, and all his kids together to thank the Lord for his bounty. *(Darkly.)* I wanted to beat him to death with the turkey leg.

HAMILTON. And how many illegitimate children and ex-lovers on *All My Passions* could say the same thing about your character?

EVERETT. Oh, we seldom have turkey here. I prefer ham.

HAMILTON. Why doesn't that surprise me? Okay, Everett. Here's the challenge. I want you to make your character on this show everything your father was not.

EVERETT. Everything my father was not?

HAMILTON. Instead of promiscuous, make him virtuous. Instead of irresponsible, make him strong and dependable. Instead of selfish, make him care about those in his family.

EVERETT. Everything my father never was.

HAMILTON. And everything your fans can look up to. I believe you can be that kind of man, Everett.

EVERETT. I can?

HAMILTON. Do it for your six brothers and sisters.

EVERETT. Fourteen. I was a middle child.

HAMILTON. That explains a lot. So what do you say? Is Everett Montague going to be remembered as a man to admire? Or someone who is one day found beaten to death with a turkey leg?

EVERETT. Ham. I like ham.

HAMILTON. *(Exasperated.)* Okay. Beaten to death with a ham shank.

(Everett considers this for a moment, then stands proudly.)

EVERETT. I believe I would rather be admired than killed by food!

HAMILTON. That is the first step on the path of nobility. I'm proud of you, Everett.

EVERETT. *(Genuinely surprised.)* You are?

HAMILTON. Definitely.

EVERETT. Do you look up to me?

HAMILTON. I'm starting to.

EVERETT. Well, I can understand how you would. *(Suddenly proud.)* Excuse me, Hamilton. I think I need to go to my dressing room and be profound for a while.

(Everett exits dramatically, Stage Left.)

CURTAIN

All My Passions - 3

By
Vin Morreale, Jr.

CAST

Everett Montague — Aging soap opera star 40 years past his prime

Melissa Mulcahey — A tough-talking soap opera producer

SETTING

The set of the soap opera ALL MY PASSIONS

Vin's Notes: This third excerpt from the full-length play allows me to once again showcase the charmingly clueless Everett Montague, who has been portraying the love interest on ALL MY PASSIONS for five decades. Over the years, he has become so identified with the role that he had his real name changed to the character's name, and actually believes the TV set is his home. Here he speaks with his strong-willed producer, Melissa Mulcahey.

For royalty information and permission to use this scene in a paid performance, or to request a full copy of ALL MY PASSIONS, please contact
Academy Arts Press - *vin@academyarts.com*

All My Passions - 3

AT RISE: The TV studio where ALL MY PASSIONS is shot. With the increasingly sleazy show spiraling down in ratings, Producer MELISSA MULCAHEY, 37, is fighting the more family friendly feel been brought to the long-running soap opera. EVERETT MONTAGUE, 79, the show's aging and clueless star for the last 49 years, is trying to wrap his head around the changes.)

MELISSA. What are you looking at?

EVERETT. I'm sorry, Miss Mulcahey. I was hoping you had a moment.

MELISSA. I'm extremely busy, Everett.

EVERETT. Ah.

>*(He nods and turns to leave. She hesitates, sees the disappointment in his face.)*

MELISSA. *(Sighs.)* Maybe I could spare a few minutes, Everett. What is it?

EVERETT. I was hoping to get your opinion on something.

MELISSA. My opinion?

EVERETT. A woman's perspective, if you don't mind.

MELISSA. *(Stunned.)* Everett Montague, in all the years I've known you, this is the first time I've ever heard you care about what a woman thinks.

EVERETT. Is that so? *(Considers this for a moment.)* That is rather sad, don't you think?

MELISSA. Sad, but typical. You're a man.

EVERETT. I have noticed that about me.

MELISSA. *(Wearily.)* So what do you need my opinion on, Everett? Are you unhappy with your wardrobe? You want another Juanita? Wanda is our fourteenth, you know.

EVERETT. Nothing like that. It's just... *(Looks stunned.)* She is not our original Juanita?

MELISSA. Not even close, Everett. Now, about your problem?

EVERETT. Not a problem really. More of a philosophical question.

MELISSA. A philosophical question?

EVERETT. Do women really like to know something about the men they sleep with?

MELISSA. *(Dryly.)* Not really. It complicates things. I prefer to not even know their names. I usually just ask them to take a number.

EVERETT. *(Softly.)* That would be sarcasm, if I am not mistaken.

MELISSA. Yes, it was. I'm sorry. But why would you even ask me such a question?

EVERETT. Oddly enough, it was something in the script that started me thinking. I suspect it is that Hamilton's influence.

MELISSA. Hamilton? He started you thinking about the right way to treat a woman?

EVERETT. Not the physical way, of course. I have been in the business long enough for that.

MELISSA. Yes. The first thing they teach you in this industry is how to screw people.

EVERETT. I believe that would be sarcasm again.

MELISSA. You're right. I'm sorry. A leftover defense mechanism from childhood.

EVERETT. Mine was delusions of grandeur. Can you imagine?

MELISSA. *(Trying to keep a straight face.)* Not at all, Everett. But to answer your question. Yes. Most women want to know a great deal about a man before we completely open ourselves up.

EVERETT. Really?

MELISSA. I prefer to know a man intimately, before I become intimate with him.

EVERETT. And that may take longer than one date?

MELISSA. Can you believe it?

EVERETT. *(Honestly surprised.)* I had no idea...

MELISSA. Everett, haven't you ever wanted to get to know a woman before you married her?

EVERETT. Not really. *(Struggles to remember.)* Although there was this one...but that was many years ago. *(Notices Melissa looking at her watch.)* But I am sure you are far too busy to care about the memories of anyone in your cast...

MELISSA. I'm sure I can spare a few more moments...

EVERETT. You are just being kind.

MELISSA. Spill it, Everett!

EVERETT. As you wish... *(Happily.)* It's funny. I can remember her voice to this day. She had the most amazing vocal tones. Clear, yet velvety. As if she caressed your name with every word she uttered.

MELISSA. What was her name?

EVERETT. Ah. Now you're asking me to really tax my memory. Hmmm... Melanie? Mindy? Monica? *(Shakes his head.)* No, those were three of my ex-wives... Melissa? No, that's you...

MELISSA. Thank you for remembering.

EVERETT. Eleanor...Eleanor Sweitzman!

MELISSA. And you loved this Eleanor Sweitzman?

EVERETT. Heavens no. *(Pauses, considers this.)* Well, maybe... *(Sadly.)* Perhaps I would have, if I had only had a little more time with her.

MELISSA. What happened, Everett? Did she die?

EVERETT. She chose a career outside the industry.

MELISSA. Virtually the same thing.

EVERETT. It was forty-nine years ago. I was so set on becoming a star. It was my destiny, and I would not let anything persuade me otherwise.

MELISSA. And she tried to?

EVERETT. Not at all. She was my biggest fan. It's just that an actor on the rise must devote himself entirely to his career. Eleanor demanded more of me than I had to give.

MELISSA. Time?

EVERETT. Compassion. *(Smiles sadly.)* How strange. I haven't thought of Eleanor Sweitzman in years...Yet, in some ways, she has never left my mind. Don't you find that strange?

MELISSA. No. I find it very sweet.

EVERETT. Really? I don't believe I was ever written to be sweet. Sophisticated. Sexy, and even statuesque. But never sweet. How odd...

MELISSA. Everett, can I ask you something?

EVERETT. Of course. You are the producer.

MELISSA. What do you really think of our Mister Bennett?

EVERETT. I believe he is a character far more complex than he is written to be.

MELISSA. That's an interesting way to put it.

EVERETT. And I believe he is quite smitten with you.

MELISSA. You're kidding?

EVERETT. Take it from someone whose had seven wives and thousands of affairs. I know a crush when I see one.

MELISSA. You think he likes me?

EVERETT. No. I think he loves you. It was in his eyes the very first moment he saw your face. His whole expression lit up with happiness. I almost envied him for it.

MELISSA. You mean, like love at first sight?

EVERETT. More like a flicker of recognition. Like he had fallen in love with you once before. Then suddenly, here you were again. It is not like you and I know love, of course. I believe this Hamilton fellow believes in that perverse, old-fashioned, forever-and-a-day brand of love. The kind that drives divorce lawyers crazy.

MELISSA. What do you think I should do?

EVERETT. I believe one should always be courageous enough to embrace the wind whenever it blows new hope in your direction.

MELISSA. Why, Everett Montague! I had no idea you were such a poet.

EVERETT. I'm not. That was dialogue from 1992. Episode nine thousand, four hundred and twelve, if I remember correctly. We had good writers back then.

MELISSA. So you think I should let Hamilton know I...I might be interested?

EVERETT. I also believe one should never turn true love into a missed opportunity.

MELISSA. Never turn true love into a missed opportunity. That's lovely. What episode was that from?

EVERETT. None. It was original. Miss Mulcahey, if you don't mind my offering a piece of advice... Eleanor Sweitzman was my missed opportunity. Don't let Hamilton Bennett be yours. Believe me... You won't like sitting here fifty years from now, wondering what might have been...if only you had gotten your priorities straight.

MELISSA. Thank you, Everett. It was really good talking to you.

EVERETT. Of course. Shall we sleep together now?

MELISSA. I don't think so.

EVERETT. Ah, well. Old habits are hard to break.

MELISSA. I'm starting to see that.

(She watches him wander off, Stage Left.)

CURTAIN

All My Passions - 4

By
Vin Morreale, Jr.

CAST

Everett Montague   Aging soap opera star 40 years past his prime

Eleanor Sweitzman   The woman he left behind 49 years ago

SETTING

The set of the soap opera ALL MY PASSIONS

Vin's Notes: ALL MY PASSIONS is a crowd-pleasing romantic comedy. In this fourth excerpt, I gave Everett Montague, the aging lothario who has been the show's focus for way too long, a chance to find his own true romance, and thus, regain his humanity. This timely play has continued to charm audiences in every outing, and I do believe it deserves many more productions in the years to come.

For royalty information and permission to use this scene in a paid performance, or to request a full copy of ALL MY PASSIONS, please contact **Academy Arts Press** - vin@academyarts.com

All My Passions - 4

AT RISE: The living room set of ALL MY PASSIONS. EVERETT MONTAGUE, 79, who has changed his name from Albert Mooney to match his character's name, enters the now empty set. He slowly crosses to a small mirror on the Stage Right wall. He checks again to make sure nobody else is around, drops his coat, then wistfully stares into the mirror. Gradually, as if the act is extremely painful for him, Everett removes his ridiculous toupee.)

ELEANOR. It's about time you acted your age, Albert Mooney.

EVERETT. *(Mystified.)* I know that voice...

   (ELEANOR enters, Stage Left. She is an elegant, silver-haired woman in her seventies.)

ELEANOR. I think you look quite distinguished without that lump of roadkill on the top of your head.

EVERETT. *(Turning, as if seeing a ghost.)* Eleanor? Eleanor Sweitzman?

ELEANOR. It's good to see you again, Albert. You are looking well.

EVERETT. Eleanor. It's been...

ELEANOR. Forty-nine years.

EVERETT. I left you on Santa Monica beach.

ELEANOR. I remember. I had to hitch a ride home in my swimsuit. I don't believe I ever properly thanked you for that.

EVERETT. *(Amazed.)* Forty-nine years.

ELEANOR. Ever since you first appeared on All My Passions.

EVERETT. Eleanor. Eleanor Sweitzman.

ELEANOR. It's Eleanor Abbott now. But thanks for remembering.

EVERETT. *(His face falls.)* You're married?

ELEANOR. You expected me to waste half a century pining over you? I got married two years later to the man who picked me up hitchhiking.

Herman Abbott. We were very happy. But Herman passed away three years ago.

EVERETT.   I am so sorry. *(Brightens.)* Wait. No, I'm not. That means you are single again!

ELEANOR.   What if I am? Are you planning to dump me on Santa Monica beach again? I'll have you know I'm much too old and wrinkled for a two-piece swimsuit. And my hitchhiking thumb ain't what it used to be.

EVERETT.   No. Never. I'd never leave you on that beach again. *(He sits down beside her. Takes her hand gently.)* I have regretted losing you for the past five decades.

ELEANOR.   *(Shrugs.)* You didn't lose me, Albert. You made a choice.

EVERETT.   And what has it brought me?

ELEANOR.   Money. Fame. All the women you can diddle.

EVERETT.   Well, there is that.

ELEANOR.   You were born to be a star, Albert Mooney. I always knew that. I just never understood why you believed I would ever want to hold you back.

EVERETT.   I...I was torn, Eleanor. An actor's life is hard. Unstable. You can be rich one moment and forgotten the next. I felt you deserved better than that.

ELEANOR.   I wish you had let me make that decision.

EVERETT.   What would you have chosen?

ELEANOR.   I was always your biggest fan, Albert Mooney.

EVERETT.   *(Hesitates.)* It is Everett Montague now.

ELEANOR.   Him, I can take or leave.

EVERETT.   I simply can't believe I have run into you again, Eleanor. And in my own studio! What are the odds?

ELEANOR.   *(Rises, sheepishly.)* Um...better than you might think. My husband, Herman...God rest his soul...was CEO of your biggest sponsor.

EVERETT.   You mean Abbott Laundry Detergent? That Herman Abbott?

ELEANOR. Okay, so I headed up the marketing department and insisted he sponsor your show for the last forty-nine years.

EVERETT. *(Comes up behind her. Touches her shoulder.)* Did he... did he know about us?

ELEANOR. He knew. He could see it in my face every time you appeared on our TV screen. *(Tenderly.)* But Herman was an understanding man. He was content to have most of my heart.

EVERETT. Most of it?

(They stare at each other for a long moment. Decades of separation fade away, and both seem to shed the years with each enhanced heartbeat.)

EVERETT. I have to ask you another question, if you don't mind.

ELEANOR. Yes.

EVERETT. Why now? I mean, after all this time? Why didn't you just...

ELEANOR. Look you up years ago?

EVERETT. Yes. Why did you have to wait so long?

ELEANOR. Three reasons. The first was that I was married, as I said. And unlike you show people, I took my wedding vows seriously.

EVERETT. I'll have you know I take all my wedding vows seriously.

ELEANOR. All seven of them?

EVERETT. Well, um...

ELEANOR. Which leads us to reason number two. Everett Montague.

EVERETT. Yes?

ELEANOR. No. I mean Everett Montague was the reason. The character you had become. The shallow, sex-obsessed. perpetual adolescent in the flabby, aging body.

EVERETT. This would be a well-chosen moment to soften that description with a compliment.

ELEANOR. Yes, it would.

EVERETT. But you are not going to, are you?

ELEANOR. Unlikely. Anyway, as I followed the show all these years, I found it harder and harder to separate the kind, considerate man I knew from the sleazy character he was playing.

EVERETT. I am an actor. I take on personas. That hardly means...

ELEANOR. You had your name changed, Albert! Every time you go out, it's always in your Everett Montague wardrobe. I even heard you had your mansion in Beverly Hills built to resemble this set in every detail!

EVERETT. *(Defensively.)* Not every detail. The drapes are different. They happen to be a lighter shade of teal!

ELEANOR. Albert...

EVERETT. Okay, so they're the same shade of teal! So why are my curtains suddenly an issue?!

ELEANOR. They are not.

EVERETT. *(Desperately.)* I walk differently than Everett Montague. Did you know that? He, I mean me...me, the character...or me, the actor playing the character. We walk like this. *(Walks jauntily across the stage.)* Now me, me not being the character...we...I mean, I walk like this. *(Walks jauntily back to her.)*

EVERETT. See! Ha!

ELEANOR. Looks the same to me.

EVERETT. You can't be serious. My real life walk has so much more 'intention' to it.

ELEANOR. As I was saying, I kept watching year after year, praying that one day the Albert I knew...the Albert I once looked up to...would somehow reappear. *(She moves closer, brightening.)* And from what I have seen of the last few episodes, it looks like he finally has.

EVERETT. *(Sighs.)* That was mostly Hamilton's doing.

ELEANOR. I know.

EVERETT. You do?

ELEANOR. Your producer called me. She said I should watch the new direction the show was taking.

EVERETT. Melissa called you? How did she..?

ELEANOR. As leading sponsor, she knew my name. Somehow, she even learned of our...history together. I think she was hoping we might still find something in common.

EVERETT. Melissa was plotting with you behind my back?

ELEANOR. Don't be mad at her. It's a producer's job to keep her talent happy. Melissa is very fond of you.

EVERETT. *(Dazed by it all.)* The world is changing too quickly, Eleanor.

ELEANOR. No, it's not. You just never noticed it before. Time betrays us all, Albert. It's not 1963 anymore. I hate to be the one to tell you this, but you are no longer a young, rising star.

EVERETT. Don't you dare tell me I'm old, Eleanor! I still have plenty of fire in me! I can still play a credible romantic lead!

ELEANOR. *(Softly.)* Only to me, Albert. Only to me. (Takes his hand.) And I'm just an old widow left with only a scrapbook of faded memories to keep me warm at night.

(She lowers her head, wonders if she made a mistake coming here, admitting so much. Tears trace her cheeks. Everett wipes away the tears and raises her chin with a gentle hand.)

EVERETT. You are not old.

ELEANOR. And you're obviously not seeing very clearly.

EVERETT. Perhaps. Or perhaps I am seeing more clearly than I have in a long, long time. *(Takes her hand.)* Eleanor. I mean, Mrs. Abbott...

ELEANOR. Yes, Mr. Mooney?

EVERETT. Would you do me the honor of having dinner with me tonight?

ELEANOR. I'd love to, Albert. *(Sternly.)* Provided you don't think I'm one of these soap opera strumpets who put out on the first date.

EVERETT. There is more to love than lust, Eleanor. If you watch the show in the coming weeks, you just might realize that.

ELEANOR. (*Tenderly.*) Get your coat, Everett Montague.

>   (*He smiles warmly. Everett grabs his coat, then reaches for his toupee.*)

ELEANOR. *That* you can leave.

>   (*Everett hesitates, then slowly drops the toupee on the loveseat. He takes her arm.*)

EVERETT. Your wish is my command, dear lady.

ELEANOR. It's about damn time.

>   (*They walk off, arm in arm, through the Upstage Center door. Stage Lights slowly dim.*)

CURTAIN

Dawn's Coming

By
Vin Morreale, Jr.

CAST

Wayne — A crusty old farmer

Earl — His nervous son

SETTING

The outskirts of a farm in Georgia

Vin's Notes: Having lived on both coasts in my early years, I foolishly believed there was only one true Southern accent. After I relocated to Kentucky, I quickly fell in love with the rich speech patterns that vary from state-to-state, and sometimes even from one side of the state to the other. I wrote a play called SOUTHERN DISCOMFORT to celebrate the rich flavor of the region's language and culture. This piece leads off the collection, and has won a few festival contests on its own.

FOR ROYALTY INFORMATION, OR TO REQUEST A COPY OF
SOUTHERN DISCOMFORT, PLEASE CONTACT **DRAMATIC PUBLISHING** -
dramaticpublishing.com/authors/profile/view/url/vin-morreale-jr

Dawn's Coming

AT RISE: *A farmland lost in the blue-gray haze before dawn. EARL, 17, overalls and a hunting rifle clutched in his sweaty hands. Beside him, WAYNE 53, rests on a hay bale, scanning the fields with a double-barreled shotgun. Wayne takes a swig from a jug of corn squeezing and passes it to his nervous son. Earl drinks, grimaces and looks up to the sky.*

EARL. Dawn's comin'.

WAYNE. Yup. Reckon it won't be long now.

EARL. You think?

WAYNE. Yup. Figure they'll move in at first light.

EARL. *(Muttering.)* Paw. Don't mind my asking this, but...

WAYNE. Speak your piece, boy.

EARL. Uh... Can't we get in real trouble for this?

WAYNE. Depends on what you mean by 'trouble.'

EARL. I mean, we might get ourselves killed and everything.

WAYNE. If you're killed, you ain't got no more troubles.

EARL. I suppose not... But what if we just get all shot up and wounded like?

WAYNE. *(Considers, then...)* That'd be trouble.

EARL. Or what if we kill a few of them and they lock us up for the rest of our lives?

WAYNE. That'd be trouble, too.

EARL. So what are we doin' this for?

WAYNE. It's the principle of the thing.

EARL. Oh.

(Earl accepts this. Looks off into the distance. Then...)

EARL. The principal of what thing, paw?

WAYNE. I'm not letting them take my land, boy. They'll have to drag me off it feet first!

EARL. But ain't there some other way?

WAYNE. You scared, Earl?

EARL. Hell, yeah! I ain't never killed anything bigger'n a pig before. And that was only so's we could have ham for Christmas dinner!

WAYNE. Well, these bank folk are a damn sight bigger'n any pig.

EARL. I imagine so. *(Suddenly.)* You don't think they'd send Charlie Waddell, do ya? His momma would sure be mad at me if I killed old Charlie.

WAYNE. Charlie would know better'n to come and take my land. If he don't, then he's no better than them Yankee bankers he works for. *(Confused.)* Besides. It don't seem right for a man to work all day playin' with other folks' money.

EARL. Whatta ya mean, paw?

WAYNE. Bankin'. It don't seem right somehow..? They take our money. Lock it up in that big old steel safe. Then they just sit there all day... watching that old safe, like somethin' magical's supposed to happen. Do it for weeks. Then, when I come to get my money back, they open up that big steel door again, take out my money... then take out a little more that got interested in it while it was just layin' there. And they give it all back to me, grinning like fools and sayin': "Have a nice day, Mister Packhammer!" *(Shakes his head.)* 'Course I'm gonna have a nice day! They gave me my money, didn't they?

EARL. Seems kinda silly when you put it that way, paw.

WAYNE. Don't seem natural. Like that three-legged calf that was born last winter. Bankin's a lot like that three-legged calf.

(Pause. Earl checks his sights by aiming his rifle across the field.)

EARL. Dawn's comin'.

WAYNE. Yep... Sorry I got you into this, boy.

EARL. That's okay, paw. We all gotta die sometimes.

WAYNE. That's sure enough true.

EARL. 'Though I was sorta hopin' I'd get a crack at Melinda May Tagget before my time was up. Y'know what I mean?

WAYNE. She's a purty one. No denying that. *(Suddenly harsh.)* You think I'm a fool for defendin' my land, boy?!

EARL. No, paw. I never, ever thought you was a fool! *(Under his breath.)* I was just sorta hopin' I'd have a chance at Melinda May is all.

WAYNE. I'm doing this for you, boy!

EARL. I know, paw.

WAYNE. My daddy farmed this land. And his daddy before him! And his daddy before him had to shoot a whole passel of Indians for this here land!

EARL. I know, paw.

WAYNE. What would they all say if we just let some silly bank folk take it away from us without a fight?

EARL. They probably wouldn't say nothin'... On account of them being dead and all. *(Softly.).* Like we's gonna be...

WAYNE. Maybe. *(Looking off.)* Dawn's coming up real strong now, ain't it?

EARL. Sure is.

WAYNE. Damn it all! This farm's been in my family for generations!

EARL. That's what I can't quite figure, paw. If this farm's been in our family for so many generations... how come we owe so much money on it?

WAYNE. Well, you remember when land values got real high and all? We borrowed mortgage money from the bank to buy that real fancy, brand new plow and harvester machine.

EARL. That was sure a pretty machine.

WAYNE. Expensive, too. But it was worth it. The salesman said it was gonna make us much better farmers.

EARL. So how come we didn't get to be much better farmers, paw?

WAYNE. The damn machine broke.

EARL. That's right. I forgot. *(Pause, then carefully.)* Can I tell you something, paw?

WAYNE. I suppose.

EARL. Something real personal like?

WAYNE. You got something to say, now's the time to spit it out.

EARL. I hate farmin'. paw.

WAYNE. What did you say?

EARL. I said, I really hate farmin'. Always have.

WAYNE. But you're a fifth generation farmer, boy!

EARL. I know. That's what's so darn funny about it all. I can't even stand the smell of pigs. I mean they really stink!

WAYNE. How come you never told me any of this before, Earl?

EARL. *(Shrugs.)* Didn't seem to matter none then.

(Wayne looks at his son, who can't meet his gaze. Then the older man shakes his head and spits. A pause, as the two stare out across the field.)

WAYNE. *(Softly.)* Pigs do kinda stink, don't they?

EARL. *(Smiling.)* That they do.

WAYNE. *(Starting to laugh.)* I mean, if people smelled that bad, we wouldn't have hardly anything to do with them, now would we?

EARL. *(Laughing.)* Not me. No way.

(Wayne suddenly grabs his binocular and stares off across the field.)

WAYNE. They're coming... Looks like Charlie Waddell, and three, maybe four sheriff's deputies with him.

EARL. *(Gulps.)* I guess this is it, then.

WAYNE. Looks like it...

(They both check their guns one last time. Pull out a few more boxes of ammunition. Together, they raise their rifles and aim at their targets.)

EARL. Paw?

WAYNE. Yes, son?

EARL. You gonna shoot Charlie, or you want me to?

(Wayne doesn't answer. Slowly, he lowers his rifle.)

WAYNE. How's about instead of shooting Charlie, you go out to the sty and shoot us a pig...

EARL. You serious?

WAYNE. That big, ornery one... and then we'll invite Charlie and those boys over for a big old ham breakfast.

EARL. But what about the farm, paw?

WAYNE. Earl?

EARL. Yes, paw?

WAYNE. I ever tell you how much I hate farmin'?

EARL. Go on! You?!

WAYNE. Never seemed quite natural for a man to play in dirt and pig shit for a livin'... *(Unloads his rifle.)* Sort of ironic, don't ya think?

EARL. Does this mean I get a chance with Melinda May Tagget?

WAYNE. Might as well. And maybe I'll try my hand at banking. *(Throws his arm around his son..)* Banking... yep, I could grow to like that...

EARL. Maybe you could ask Charlie for a job, paw?

WAYNE. Maybe...

CURTAIN

Plain Speakin' Legal Terms

By
Vin Morreale, Jr.

CAST

Joe Bob Dinkel — A redneck TV Host

Announcer — An Offstage Announcer

SETTING

A simple TV studio

Vin's Notes: Another somewhat silly sketch from my tenure with the SENSELESS BICKERING COMEDY THEATRE. By the time I reformed the group in Kentucky, we were entirely focused on radio comedy. The character of Joe Bob Dinkel was voiced by the amazingly talented Claude Wayne Fulkerson, who could do over two hundred impressions. Looking back I have to say that working with SENSELESS BICKERING was one of the most fun-filled times of my life.

*For royalty information and permission to use this scene in a paid performance, please contact **Academy Arts Press** - vin@academyarts.com*

Plain Speakin' - Legal

AT RISE: An aging country gentlemen, JOE BOB DINKEL, sits in a rocking chair facing the audience. To his left, the ANNOUNCER stands before a podium (or may be played as an offstage voice only.)

JOE BOB.   This is Joe Bob Dinkel with another lesson in Plain Speakin'. Today we're gonna look at some of them there legal blabber. You know them smarty pants, three dollar words that those dad-burned lawyers throw at you so's they can charge you an arm and a leg to not understand them. Let's take a listen to a few.

ANNOUNCER.   Lawsuit.

JOE BOB.   The fancy clothes a lawyer can buy because he's chargin' you so much for doin' nothin.

ANNOUNCER.   Litigate.

JOE BOB.   Another way to beautify your home. My brother Elwood litigate by puttin' a spotlight by his fence.

ANNOUNCER.   Hung Jury.

JOE BOB.   Twelve happy men.

ANNOUNCER.   Conviction.

JOE BOB.   Something lawyers try too hard to get for other people but never have any for themselves.

ANNOUNCER.   Mistrial

JOE BOB.   A first date with a virgin.

ANNOUNCER.   Misdemeanor.

JOE BOB.   That's a batter with a bad temper. The more he miss, de meaner he gets.

ANNOUNCER.   Felony.

JOE BOB.   It's what happens when I trip sometimes.

ANNOUNCER. Perjury.

JOE BOB. It's how normal folks go to jail and politicians go to Washington.

ANNOUNCER. Motion to adjourn.

JOE BOB. It's my fancy way of saying 'that's all, folks.' This is Joe Bob Dinkel for Plain Speakin'. I'll be talkin' at ya.

CURTAIN

Challenge The Wind

By
Vin Morreale, Jr.

CAST

Lydia — A 104 year-old woman in a wheelchair

Charlene — A neglectful mother

SETTING

Lydia's room at the Paradise Acres Nursing Home

Vin's Notes: Another piece where I first found a character's voice and started writing lines without knowing anything about her or where the story was going. I wrote eight pages of Lydia's fiesty dialogue, then wrapped a plot around them of an extremely old women who happened to live through many key events of the Twetieth Century. As the movie starts, we find her in a nursing home telling the story of her life to a precocious child. In this scene, the child's mother abandons her child in the care of the 104 year-old woman.

For royalty information and permission to use this scene in a paid performance, or if you are a Film Producer interested in reading the award-winning screenplay, please contact **Academy Arts Entertainment** *- vin@academyarts.com.*

Challenge The Wind

AT RISE: Lydia's room at the Paradise Acres Nursing Home. CHARLENE, 27, everything about her screaming 'trailer park.' is pawning her four year-old daughter off on LYDIA, 104, aged but feisty.)

CHARLENE. And I can't tell you how excited Tori's been these past few weeks. All she can talk about is... "Miss Lydia this" and "Miss Lydia that." She says your stories are better than TV.

LYDIA. That's the best compliment I've had all minute. After all, what's in my bedpan is better than most of what's on TV.

CHARLENE. Tori said you was funny.

LYDIA. Did she now?

CHARLENE. Uh-huh. She couldn't wait 'til Saturday came 'round so's I could bring her to see you. She 'bout drove me crazy!

LYDIA. Your daughter does seem to have a mind of her own.

CHARLENE. She's showed her butt more than once, I tell you what.

LYDIA. I beg your pardon?

CHARLENE. Sometimes that girl gets too big for her britches. Y'know what I mean?

LYDIA. Not in the least.

CHARLENE. She's a handful.

LYDIA. Oh, I see. My parents used to say that about me... only in English.

CHARLENE. Sometimes that girl runs me plum ragged.

LYDIA. Where is Tori's father?

CHARLENE. How the hell should I know? I ain't heard word one from him since she was two months old.

LYDIA. I am so sorry.

CHARLENE. I'm not. The man was a shit-kickin' bastard…uh, Pardon my French…

LYDIA. You speak the language beautifully.

CHARLENE. Yeah… Well, don't mean nothin' by it. Just heard so much about your stories and all.

LYDIA. Forgive me. Sarcasm is one of the few benefits of living forever. Would you like me to start my story at the beginning? I'm afraid it might be tiresome for Tori to hear it all again.

CHARLENE. Oh, that's real nice of you an' all, but I can't stay. What with work and all, I don't get much chance to run around much. I was kinda figurin' I'd take some time for myself while you sat with Tori. If that's okay with you.

(Lydia eyes the other woman with chilly politeness.)

LYDIA. Why of course, dearie. Who better to trust your baby to than a hundred and four year-old stranger in a wheelchair?

CHARLENE. Tori said you was funny. Don't worry. That girl won't be givin' you no trouble. If she does, just smack her butt a few times. That'll learn her. *(Heading to the door.)* I'll be by to pick her up later. You can just have her hang out in the waiting area if you're asleep. Bye.

CURTAIN

What Do We Do Now?

By
Vin Morreale, Jr.

CAST

Collette ... A woman of indistinct age

Ellis ... A man with ill-defined background

SETTING

An empty stage except for a single blanket

Vin's Notes: This experimental piece was written specifically for this book. It is always fun to surprise the audience, while leaving the characters equally mystified about what will happen next. Since confusion is part of the human condition, the key to bringing these kind of experimental pieces to life is to play the characters as real people caught in a situation they do not understand..

For royalty information and permission to use this scene in a paid performance, please contact **Academy Arts Press** *- vin@academyarts.com*

What Do We Do?

AT RISE: COLLETTE and ELLIS sit on the floor facing the audience. A blanket over their laps. She looks over at him.

COLLETTE. This is ridiculous. Don't you think this is ridiculous? I said, this is ridiculous. Hey, are you asleep? Because sleeping in a situation like this would be ridiculous.

ELLIS. I'm not asleep. I'm disengaged.

COLLETTE. Disengaged? What the hell does that mean?

ELLIS. It means I am choosing not to answer.

COLLETTE. Why not?

ELLIS. Because it doesn't help the situation.

COLLETTE. Of course it helps the situation! We are in this together. It's up to us to figure a way out. You and I are all we have!

ELLIS. Hmmm.

COLLETTE. I said we are all we have.

ELLIS. I heard you.

COLLETTE. Don't you dare disengage on me again.

ELLIS. Okay.

COLLETTE. Disengage is such a cruel word. It's like you don't want to be married to me anymore. I said it's like you don't want to be married to me anymore.

ELLIS. Hmmm.

COLLETTE. Is that it? That's all you can say? I say you don't want to be married anymore and all you have is a Hmmm?! You are worse than they are. I don't know what I ever saw in you.

ELLIS. I don't either.

COLLETTE. Well, it sure wasn't your conversational abilities, that's for sure.

ELLIS. Hmmm.

COLLETTE. You're a real sonofabitch. You know that?

ELLIS. That's unkind.

COLLETTE. Unkind? Unkind?! Dammit! When a woman says you don't want to marry me anymore and all you say is Hmm. That makes you a real sonovabitch.

ELLIS. What do you want me to say?

COLLETTE. I don't know. Say you still want to be married to me. Say you love me. Say you're scared. Say you're afraid we'll never get out of this ridiculous situation.

ELLIS. Okay, First: I don't want to be married to you anymore. Never did. Second: I don't love you. Never did that either. Third: I am scared. Petrified, actually, that we won't ever be able to get out.

COLLETTE. Wow. I liked you so much better when you were disengaged. So you don't love me? You don't want to be married to me anymore?

ELLIS. I've known you for what? Fourteen hours? Ever since I woke up and found myself lying here, in this strange room…

(He pulls his arm out from under the blanket to reveal a chain around his wrist. He raises it higher and it pulls up Collette's wrist, connected to the other end of the chain.)

ELLIS. …chained to a woman I never met before, who talks incessantly and is somehow is under the delusion that we are married.

COLLETTE. We are married. Chained together on what could be the last day of our lives constitutes a marriage. What's a marriage if not being chained to someone you really don't know and aren't sure you like for what is probable the rest of your life?

ELLIS. That's rather cynical.

COLLETTE. Hmmm.

ELLIS. Hmm is right.

COLLETTE. Well, at least you're scared. That's something.

ELLIS. I'm glad it brings you comfort.

COLLETTE. On a scale of one to ten; one being a general feeling of anxiety and ten being piss your pants terror, how scared are you? Answer me.

ELLIS. Seven.

COLLETTE. Seven? That's all?

ELLIS. Hmm.

COLLETTE. They're going to kill us, you know.

ELLIS. Hmmm.

COLLETTE. I said they're going to kill us. Chop us up into little pieces of dead meat, and then do who knows what obscene things to our body parts. Either that, or they'll never come back and just let us starve to death down here. Just two rotting corpses, scared, alone and forgotten to the world.

ELLIS. Hmmm.

COLLETTE. Why don't you talk to me?

ELLIS. I choose not to.

COLLETTE. Why?

ELLIS. Because you're a chatterist.

COLLETTE. A chatterist? That's not even a word.

ELLIS. Maybe not, but it fits you. For the past seven hours you have been spewing inanities at a rate of 143 useless words a minute. Not caring if I was listening. Not caring if I was caring. Not caring if you made any sense at all, considering our situation. That is a textbook chatterist.

COLLETTE. So I'm a chatterist and you're a sonovabitch.

ELLIS. Evidently.

COLLETTE. Maybe that's why they chose us?

ELLIS. Possibly.

COLLETTE. Do you think we're going to live through this?

ELLIS. No.

COLLETTE. You know, you could use a little chatteristness about you too.

ELLIS. I suppose.

COLLETTE. Maybe I wouldn't be as scared.

ELLIS. How scared are you? On a scale from one to ten? One being mild anxiety and ten being piss you pants terrified?

COLLETTE. Want to feel my pants?

ELLIS. I don't know you well enough.

COLLETTE. Was that a joke? Did you just make a joke?

ELLIS. It's not a big deal.

COLLETTE. You made a joke to a complete stranger you are chained to in some Godforsaken dark room, with no clue as to who she is or why we are here!

MAN
I thought it might help ease the tension.

COLLETTE. It did. Thank you. Maybe you are not a total sonovabitch. So are we going to talk about the elephant in the room?

ELLIS. What elephant?

COLLETTE. You know. The elephant in the room.

ELLIS. That's not an elephant. That's an audience. And they are watching us. Trying to figure out what happens next.

COLLETTE. As if we know.

ELLIS. Right. As if we know.

COLLETTE. So what should we do? It's creepy having them watching us. Analyzing our every move.

ELLIS.   I choose to ignore them. Eventually they'll go away. But only after something dramatic happens. But maybe that's like that *Waiting For Godot* play, where nothing happens, and for some reason people assume it's profound.

COLLETTE.   Don't worry. We are in no danger of anyone assuming we are profound.

ELLIS.   Possibly. Your spewed inanities could be seen as absurdist, a lack of meaning which some mistake for deep and meaningful. It's all very contemporary.

COLLETTE.   I hate people assuming I'm deep. It's so retro PC. Like the polar opposite of assuming blondes are dumb. Or my lazy ex-brother-in-law is morally superior because he's poor, instead of the fact that he drinks like a sewer pipe and screws everything within sniffing distance.

COLLETTE.   So what should we do with that audience? They kind of creep me out, staring at me like that.

ELLIS.   I don't know. We could stare back. See how comfortable it makes them.

COLLETTE.   Good idea.

(The two sit up and stare at the audience for a full 90 seconds, before the LIGHTS DIM. Over the BLACKOUT, we hear...)

COLLETTE.   Well, that was pretty anti-climactic.

ELLIS.   Hmmm.

CURTAIN

Chasing Penelope

By
Vin Morreale, Jr.

CAST

Chase Longshot — A rough-edged Private Investigator

Margot — A mysterious woman

SETTING

An airport lounge, late at night.

Vin's Notes: I always loved the cuttingly clever patter of Film Noir detectives. This piece appears in my collection, 150 ACTING SCENES, and lets me play with two deviously witty people flirting at cross purposes. Even if it's all just for fun.

For royalty information and permission to use this scene in a paid performance, please contact **Academy Arts Press** *- vin@academyarts.com*

Chasing Penelope

AT RISE: A dark and sleazy bar, mid-afternoon. CHASE LONGSHOT, a rough-edged Private Investigator is sucking down a neatly placed row of bourbon shots. He does not look surprised when MARGOT, a sexy redhead, saunters up to him.

MARGOT. Fancy meeting you here.

CHASE. Nothing fancy about this place. That's why I like it. I suppose you're gonna sit down?

MARGOT. I suppose I am. *(Sits.)* I didn't take it, by the way.

CHASE. Didn't take what?

MARGOT. The money.

CHASE. I didn't say you did.

MARGOT. No. But you think I did. I can see it in your eyes.

CHASE. Those are bourbon tracks, baby. And for your information, eyes don't talk. Mouths do.

MARGOT. Except yours. I'm sure nothing even remotely useful ever comes out of your mouth.

CHASE. It's an art form. I practiced for years to be this obtuse.

MARGOT. Obtuse? Well, aren't we the college graduate?

CHASE. Not me. Junior High was tough enough. So, let's just say you did take the money…

MARGOT. Which I didn't.

CHASE. Seems only my bloodshot eyes think you did. But assuming they're right…

MARGOT. Which they're not.

CHASE. Hey, they're eyes. Not IQs.

MARGOT. Funny. How long you been saving that one up?

CHASE. About six months. Which is close to the time you opened that secret bank account in the Cayman Islands. Under the name Penelope Streeter, I believe.

MARGOT. Oh, you're good.

CHASE. And you're not. Didn't anyone ever tell you it's not nice to take other people's stuff?

MARGOT. Just my dad. He was a big time Wall Street banker. But after they put him away for some big-time embezzling, all those cute little daddy lessons took on a somewhat ironic twist. So, what do we do now?

CHASE. I dunno. I'm rather enjoying this conversation.

MARGOT. Me, too.

CHASE. But that whole 'Penelope Streeter' thing might make things a little awkward.

MARGOT. Penelope can do that. What do you say we leave her in the Cayman Islands? Then you and me can go make some more little bourbon tracks on your eyeballs.

CHASE. You buying?

MARGOT. Sorry. All my funds are tied up at the moment.

CHASE. okay. I know where to find them. And this Penelope. I bet she can really rock a bikini down there in the Caribbean.

MARGOT. You have no idea.

CURTAIN

Little In Common

By
Vin Morreale, Jr.

CAST

Mitchell — A woman on a blind date

Augustus — An older, obnoxious man

SETTING

A table in an upscale bar

Vin's Notes: Another piece from my time working with the Ruskin Theatre's Café Play series. So much fun sitting with four other talented writers, each trying to devise a play around the same theme in just a few hours. Then experiencing the almost immediate gratification of seeing actors and directors bring your words to life a few hours later. If you ever find yourself in Santa Monica, California on the third Sunday of the month, be sure to check out the Café Plays.

For royalty information and permission to use this scene in a paid performance, please contact **Academy Arts Press** *- vin@academyarts.com*

Little In Common

AT RISE: Lights come up on an upscale bar. MITCHELL, 30, female, sits alone at a table, sipping coffee. She looks around nervously. She grimaces as she answers her phone on the third ring..

MITCHELL. *(Into phone.)* Yes, Mom. I'm here. And yes, I promise to keep an open mind. Love you, too.

(She throws her phone down. Hard. Sticks her tongue out at it. AUGUSTUS, 60 enters shyly. Head spinning in every direction. He has a charmingly oafish nervousness about him and holds a ridiculous bouquet of sticks, weeds & ugly flowers. After a few beats, their eyes finally find each other.)

MITCHELL. Don't even think it.

(He nods. Goes back to searching the room for his date. All the while, he squirms in discomfort. She does too. After a moment, he looks at the empty chair beside her.)

AUGUSTUS. Do you mind?

MITCHELL. I do.

AUGUSTUS. Right.

(He goes back to trying to lean against a wall. Clearly in pain standing for long periods, but his attempt to look cool, while doing so becomes increasingly comical.)

MITCHELL. What is wrong with you?

AUGUSTUS. Uh, I had an accident. It hurts to stand for any length of time.

MITCHELL. Not my problem.

(She continues to look around. He continues to do his feeble attempt to look casual, while in pain. Finally, she kicks the chair away from the table.)

MITCHELL. Just for a minute. I'm waiting for my fiancée.

(He scrambles into the chair, gratefully.)

AUGUSTUS. Thank you so much. I'm waiting for someone, too.

MITCHELL. I could tell by... *(Gestures to the flowers.)* ...whatever those are supposed to be.

AUGUSTUS. The salesman called it an urban bouquet. He said repurposed weeds are supposed to be very trendy.

MITCHELL. You paid someone for those?

AUGUSTUS. Too much?

MITCHELL. Too something. It looks like they raped an abandoned cemetery. Just keep them away from me. I don't want my date to think I have the same complete disregard for taste as you.

AUGUSTUS. Perhaps you're right.

(He looks around for a place to throw the ugly flowers. Can't find one. Finally hands them to a woman in the audience.)

AUGUSTUS. These are for you.

(Sits back down. Turns to Mitchell.)

AUGUSTUS. Can you believe how crowded this place is?

MITCHELL. Day after Valentine's Day. You can almost smell the single desperation in the air.

AUGUSTUS. That might be my cologne.

(Pulls out a bottle with the label SINGLE DESPERATION. Hands it to her.)

MITCHELL. I don't know what's worse. The fact that you have a cologne actually called 'Single Desperation'... or that you carry it with you on a date.

AUGUSTUS. Right again.

(He gets up and hands the bottle to a single man in the audience.)

AUGUSTUS. Looks like you could use it. *(Sits back down.)* So is your fiancée always this late?

MITCHELL. I don't know. Never met him.

AUGUSTUS. But he's your fiancée?

MITCHELL. *(Heavy sigh.)* My mom signed me up on a website called 'Arranged Marriages Dot Com.'

AUGUSTUS. That's so...traditional. While being both cutting edge and deeply disturbing.

MITCHELL. Yeah. My Mom's a force of nature. She insisted on picking out my husband this time.

AUGUSTUS. This time? How many times have you been married?

MITCHELL. Three or four.

AUGUSTUS. You don't remember?

MITCHELL. Okay, five. But Randy doesn't really count. It only lasted a week and involved a Harley, case of tequila, and a Sons of Anarchy binge marathon.

AUGUSTUS. Who hasn't been there before? So you think this Arranged Marriages Dot Com thing will work out better?

MITCHELL. Couldn't be any worse. I'm thirty years old, a four-time divorcee, with one annulment and three restraining orders.

AUGUSTUS. So you're attracted to dangerous men?

MITCHELL. The restraining orders are all against me.

AUGUSTUS. Oh, charming. On the bright side, they say arranged marriages used to be all the rage. In the...uh, Dark Ages.

MITCHELL. Yeah, back when people died of plague by age thirty-five. How's that for a ringing endorsement?

AUGUSTUS. What's your uh, fiancée look like?

MITCHELL. According to his online profile, Norman is forty-eight, unemployed, lives with his parents, is morbidly obese, and really into comb-overs, Nerds of Warcraft, and fantasy frisbee. *(Sighs.)* But according to my Mom, he comes from a good family.

AUGUSTUS. Sounds like a real catch.

MITCHELL. So was Moby Dick. Please, just shoot me now. So who are you waiting for?

AUGUSTUS. My ex-wife. She said she wants to give it another try.

MITCHELL. How long have you been divorced?

AUGUSTUS. Which time?

MITCHELL. What?

AUGUSTUS. We've been married and divorced three times so far. But she says she's ready to try again. Especially since she heard about the legal settlement from my accident.

MITCHELL. Big payoff?

AUGUSTUS. The jury awarded me eleven million for corporate negligence. Of course, that doesn't begin to cover the emotional scars.

MITCHELL. What happened?

AUGUSTUS. Well, you know those weedwhackers? The handheld machines you use to trim your lawn?

MITCHELL. With the spinning wire?

AUGUSTUS. Right. Well, with all those instructions and warning labels, they never once tell you not to use your weedwhacker in the nude. *(Shudders.)* Turns out it wasn't my brightest moment.

MITCHELL. You, uh…?

AUGUSTUS. Got trimmed. Yes.

MITCHELL. I can imagine how painful that was.

AUGUSTUS. No, you can't.

MITCHELL. That's right. I can't.

(They both shudder.)

AUGUSTUS. On the bright side, they now put an extra warning label on every weedwhacker sold in America. I carry one around with me.

(He pulls out a small laminated card. Hands it to her.)

MITCHELL. *(Reading.)* "Do not attempt to use this device while naked."

AUGUSTUS. I feel I've done my part to make the world a safer place.

MITCHELL. So your wife left you after the accident?

AUGUSTUS. She said I wasn't half the man I used to be. But that's an exaggeration. It only chopped off the top three inches.

MITCHELL. And now you can't...?

AUGUSTUS. No, the remaining eight inches work just fine. But she's willing to overlook my reduced size. Especially since the manufacturer settled for a million dollars per original inch.

MITCHELL. That's big of her. And, um, big of you, evidently.

AUGUSTUS. Love stinks, doesn't it?

MITCHELL. You got that right.

AUGUSTUS. *(Standing.)* Anyway. I've wasted too much of your time. Good luck with Norman, and the whole...uh, restraining order, Arranged Marriages Dot Com thing.

MITCHELL. Thanks. Good luck with your size-obsessed, gold-digger ex-wife.

(He starts to walk away. Turns back to the woman in the audience with the sickly flowers.)

AUGUSTUS. May I have those back? *(Turns to the guy with the Single Desperation cologne.).* You can keep the cologne.

(He grabs the flowers, and is almost out the door, when Mitchell calls to him.)

MITCHELL. Hey, mister?

AUGUSTUS. It's Augustus.

MITCHELL. Yet another point of embarrassment.

AUGUSTUS. Thanks for reminding me.

MITCHELL. Look, you're old, I'm young. You're a wimp to your wife, and I'm emotionally unstable, at least according to the police in three states. *(Stands.)* We have absolutely nothing in common, except a shared appreciation for eleven million dollars...and possibly your remaining eight inches.

AUGUSTUS. Your point being?

MITCHELL. We both agree Love Stinks. How about we take love off the table, and just wallow in a little shared misery over sushi? Whatta ya say?

(Pause. Looks at her.)

AUGUSTUS. Why the hell not? But no sushi. Anything sliced brings back traumatic memories.

(He twitches. She walks over to him.)

MITCHELL. I'm guessing Benihana's is out of the question?

AUGUSTUS. Right. And no obvious weedwhacker jokes. I've heard them all.

MITCHELL. I wasn't going to..!

AUGUSTUS. I can see in your eyes you're dying to make one.

MITCHELL. You're right, I was. It's just that the phrase 'whacking off' seems so rudely appropriate...

(They exit.)

CURTAIN

The Encounter

By
Vin Morreale, Jr.

CAST

Harlan — A burly Southerner, 59 years-old

Tricia — A 41 year-old African-American woman

SETTING

A rustic office in the Deep South

Vin's Notes: Another piece from my play *SOUTHERN DISCOMFORT* with the Dramatic Publishing Company. In this visually suspenseful fifteen-minute play, I tried to tackle the idea that the roots of racism and hatred are not always as clear-cut as they may seem. THE ENCOUNTER won the Bunbury Theatre's 15th Anniversary Play Festival,, which featured an especially powerful performance by Kentucky actor Charlie Hunter as Harlan.

FOR ROYALTY INFORMATION, OR TO REQUEST A COPY OF SOUTHERN DISCOMFORT, PLEASE CONTACT **DRAMATIC PUBLISHING** - dramaticpublishing.com/authors/profile/view/url/vin-morreale-jr

The Encounter

AT RISE: *A run-down office that reeks of old Southern masculinity. Beer keg. Motorcycle calendar. Antlers on the wall. An old sign reads:* IN GUNS WE TRUST. *Old black & white photos and two flags adorn the walls: the stars & stripes and the Confederate battle flag.*

HARLAN.   *(Offstage.)* Take it easy, Gil. I'll be done and out in two! So you boys just control your damn butt muscles!!

   (A door swings open and out steps HARLAN, a burly and balding 59. He adjust the corded sash on his white robe.)

HARLAN.   *(Muttering.)* Never seen grown men so all-fired anxious to dress up like the Pillsbury Doughboy...

   (He pulls a white cloth from his pocket. The pointed distinctive hood of the Klu Klux Klan.)

TRICIA.   Nice outfit.

   (Suddenly, the leather chair behind him swivels around to reveal TRICIA, 41. An attractive African-American woman.)

TRICIA.   Who's your tailor? Casper the friendly ghost?

HARLAN.   Christ! You done scared the heart right outa me!

TRICIA.   I could tell. You're as white as a sheet.

HARLAN.   How'd you get in here?! And what the hell you doing in my office?!

TRICIA.   I came to see you.

HARLAN.   What for?

TRICIA.   Sure wasn't for fashion advice.

HARLAN.   This here's private property, little girl. I could shoot you down for just bein' here.

TRICIA. And get nigger blood all over this pretty leather chair? That'd be a real shame.

HARLAN. You got a smart mouth. You know that?

TRICIA. Yes, sir. I get it from my momma.

HARLAN. A smart mouth can get you in real trouble 'round these parts.

TRICIA. Tell me something I don't know. My momma got in trouble once. Nine months later, there I was.

HARLAN. You think you're funny, don't ya?

TRICIA. My teachers always said I had a noticeable ability to amuse myself.

(Tricia rises. Casually examines the photos. Harlan, clad in his white sheet seems far more nervous.)

HARLAN. I don't know what your game is, little girl. But I don't think you know what you're dealing with here.

TRICIA. First of all, the name is Tricia. Tricia Hardwick. Not little girl. Got it? And second of all, I know exactly what I'm dealing with. Some low-rent cracker so afraid of us black folk, he gotta hide behind a white sheet and an army of brain-dead, whisky-sucking rednecks, who burp for a living, cheat on their wives, and try to convince themselves that they're really the superior race!

(Tense pause as they glare at each other. Slowly, Harlan's face softens.)

HARLAN. Okay... so you do know what you're dealing with. Now why don't you tell me what the hell you want?

TRICIA. Like I said. I came to see you.

HARLAN. Listen, if you need insurance, these ain't my normal business hours. Why don't you come on back when the office is open?

She crosses past him. Talks directly to the Confederate flag.

TRICIA. I come to tell you she's dead.

HARLAN. Who's dead?

TRICIA. Lydia.

(This registers, but Harlan tries not to let it show.)

HARLAN. Yeah? Lydia who?

TRICIA. Lydia Hardwick! Don't you dare tell me you don't know who I'm talking about! After what you and your kind did to her!

HARLAN. *(Pause, then...)* How'd she die?

TRICIA. Figure it out.

HARLAN. *(Nods slowly.)* She always did have a bad heart...

TRICIA. No, Mister Jenkins. She had a good heart. A wonderful heart. It just never beat like everybody else's.

HARLAN. So, you kin to her, or what?

TRICIA. Her daughter. She never had none but me.

HARLAN. What about her husband? He with her when she passed?

TRICIA. She didn't 'pass' Mr. Jenkins. She died... She died alone. While I was at college. And to answer the question you don't have the guts to ask, she never did choose to marry.

HARLAN. So that makes you some kind of bastard, huh?

TRICIA. *(Bitterly.)* That makes us both some kind of bastard, Mister Jenkins. I'm forty-one. Do the math.

HARLAN. Christ...

TRICIA. The Good Lord had nothing to do with this.

HARLAN. So... what exactly you want with me?

TRICIA. Nothing... I'm just here to tell you the news is all.

HARLAN. Bullshit. You may think I'm some dumb heap of white trash, but even I don't buy that.

TRICIA. Fair enough... I don't know. I had to see you, I guess. Had to see the man who raped my momma.

HARLAN. *(Turns away from her.)* He ain't in this room, little girl.

TRICIA. You raped my momma, Mr. Jenkins! You raped my momma and left me as some walking-talking trophy of your pitiful white aggression!

HARLAN. *(Calmly.)* That what she told you?

TRICIA. No. Momma never mentioned one word about you... But I could see the pain in her eyes. It never left her. Lord, that woman hurt more than one human being has a right to bear.

HARLAN. So who told you I raped her? Your uncles?

TRICIA. *(Near tears.)* At her funeral. I had to know. They told me how you raped her when she was only seventeen. Left her bleeding and begging for mercy in the tobacco field.

HARLAN. Well, they got half the story right, anyways.

TRICIA. You trying to deny it? You trying to tell me you're not my daddy?!

HARLAN. Look, little girl...

TRICIA. Tricia! At least you can learn my name, you bastard!

HARLAN. Look, Tricia... I... I knew your momma.

TRICIA. *(Sarcastically.)* Nice way to phrase it.

HARLAN. Okay, let me phrase it better... I didn't just know your momma. I loved her. That make you feel better?! Huh?!

(Harlan towers over her, menacingly. Tricia looks stunned.)

HARLAN. You wanna hear me say it again? I loved Lydia. Loved her more than anybody I ever met in my whole, damn useless life!

TRICIA. If you loved her so much, how could you...?!

HARLAN. Just sit down and shut up, okay?! If you're gonna make me tell you this, I'm gonna see you're at least respectful enough to listen!

TRICIA. You can't talk to me like that!

HARLAN. I can do whatever the hell I please! I'm your daddy, remember?!

(He pushes her back into the chair. She looks up at the big man with a combination of fear and defiance. The look is too similar to her mothers, and it startles him. When he meets her gaze again, he softens.)

HARLAN. Look... Just sit... please. I ain't talked this out in near on twenty years... Old wounds ain't pretty when they open up again. Best not to stand too close...

TRICIA. *(Crossing her arms.)* Speak your piece.

HARLAN. Lydia... your momma... She was everything to me. Beautiful... like you. Smart mouth, like you. Full of life, y'know? I was on the football team at Southland. You might not guess that to look at me now...

TRICIA. Let me guess. Tackling dummy?

HARLAN. Wide receiver.

TRICIA. I can understand the 'wide' part.

HARLAN. Your momma, she kept to herself mostly. But I loved her from the first moment I caught that strange look in her eyes... You say you saw pain in her eyes, and maybe that's so. But I saw only life. Pure, sweet life and laughter, oozing outa her like nobody else in the world had any claim to it. That woman made me feel... Hell, let's just say I loved her and leave it at that. I didn't care what nobody else thought. The hell with my friends. The hell with everybody. All I cared about was marrying Lydia Hardwick and losing myself in those soft sparkling eyes forever.

TRICIA. You trying to tell me you didn't rape her?

HARLAN. *(Softly.)* No. I didn't rape her... But we were stupid. Carryin' on in secret. Before you know it, your momma got pregnant. What could I do? I couldn't tell my family. Hell, my daddy woulda shot me for fraternizin' with a Negro. So I figured we'd best up and run off together. New Orleans or something. Didn't matter where. Not to me. And not to Lydia.

TRICIA. But you never made it to New Orleans.

HARLAN. No. We never made it... your momma, she was so pig-headed. But in a lovable way, y'know?

TRICIA. *(A sad smile.)* Yeah. I know.

HARLAN. She couldn't just sneak off. We were already halfway down the road, when she made me turn that old pickup around and drive on back. She just had to tell her Daddy goodbye. I tried to talk her out of it. Told her what would happen if anybody found out about us. But you know your momma.

(Tricia nods silently.)

HARLAN. When we got back, her brothers were waiting for me. Pulled me straight outa the driver's seat.

(As he speaks, he unconsciously twists the rope around his waist with increasing anger.)

HARLAN. They weren't gonna let their sister marry no big dumb white boy. They blamed me for what some handful of people I ain't never met up and did two hundred years before my kin even came to this country! Like it was my fault and always will be! I done told them I was gonna marry her. Protect her. Do it all right and proper. But they wouldn't have none of it. They took a pick-axe to my truck and told me I was next. So, I grabbed your momma right then and there and we took off 'cross the tobacco field. When she couldn't keep up, her being pregnant and all, I carried her. Running like crazy with her in my arms like a baby. Some lovesick wide receiver running for his life. For both our lives. *(Hesitates.)* Anyways, your uncles, they caught up to us. And tried hard to convince me that your momma and me wasn't right for each other.

TRICIA. Just like that? You get her pregnant and they just convince you to walk away?

HARLAN. Well... They did a bit more than convincing...

(He pulls the white robe off his shoulders to reveal an angry patchwork of scars across his back.)

TRICIA. Oh, my god..!

HARLAN. Didn't all happen that night. I got some from the second or third lesson. Finally, I guess I just got tired of seein' the doctor.

TRICIA. Why didn't you..?

HARLAN. Why didn't I, what? Put here through more pain havin' to choose between her family and me? You knew how fragile her heart was. I couldn't put her through that anymore. No matter what it cost me...

(He drags a meaty paw across his tear-filled eyes.)

HARLAN.   Anyway, now you know the story. Not that any of it matters all that much.

TRICIA. Mr. Jenkins... I... I...

HARLAN.   Don't say nothin'. That was all too many tears ago. I'm too old and squeezed empty to try and live through all that again.

(He grabs his hood and crosses to the door. With his hand on the knob, he pauses.)

HARLAN.   You best wait here about twenty minutes, then leave out the back door. You don't want Gil and the boys to catch you around here. No telling what those brain-dead, whisky-suckin' rednecks would do.

TRICIA. You mean, you're still gonna march?!

(He faces the door. It's less painful than meeting her eyes.)

HARLAN.   I... I'd rather you didn't stop by again, y'hear?

TRICIA. Yeah... Good-bye, Mr. Jenkins... *(Almost to herself.)* ...daddy...

HARLAN. *(Without turning around.)* Good-bye, little girl. *(Painfully.)* Look, if there's anything you need...

TRICIA. *(Too quickly.)* Nothing...

(Harlan nods. Then he slowly puts on his Klu Klux Klan hood, and slowly turns to look at his daughter. Tricia does not look away. Suddenly, the big man turns and escapes through the door. Slamming it behind him. As the angry rumble of their truck fades into the distance, Tricia sits back down, and slowly swivels the chair until her face is once more hidden from the audience.)

CURTAIN

Dental Cruelty

By
Vin Morreale, Jr.

CAST

Daniel   A zany 'Dentist to the Stars'

Lisa   His artist girlfriend

SETTING

An Upscale Beverly Hills Apartment

Vin's Notes: When I first arrived in Los Angeles with dreams of big screen success, I was quickly approached by an independent producer, who promised he would hire me to write a screenplay for him to produce. His only stipulation was that it was a comedy involving a dentist. In my eagerness and naivete, I finished a feature-length screenplay called *DENTAL CRUELTY* in two weeks, before I actually had anything in writing. The producer loved my script and said the money would come any day, as he was putting the final funding together. Sadly, that proved to be even more fictional than my script, which is still a fun read that has yet to be produced. Welcome to Hollywood, Vin!

*For royalty information and permission to use this scene in a paid performance, or if you are a Film Producer interested in reading the feature screenplay, please contact **Academy Arts Entertainment** - vin@academyarts.com.*

Dental Cruelty

AT RISE: *The apartment of Dr. Daniel Bingham, Beverly Hills dentist. The sparkling white walls are decorated with many large paintings of teeth. DANIEL, 50, angrily attacks everything in the room with furniture polish. His girlfriend, LISA, 38, eyes him from the sofa.*

LISA. Want to talk about it?

DANIEL. What? I'm just straightening up the place!

LISA. Exactly. Usually they have to put a shotgun to your head to make you pick up a dust rag. So why the Mister Clean act?

DANIEL. You had Margo send your files to Dr. Letson.

LISA. And?

DANIEL. And you don't need an orthodontist! You have the world's most obsessively perfect teeth.

LISA. Worried about losing a patient? Or your girlfriend?

DANIEL. Neither. Both. Should I be?

LISA. Don't be silly, toothman. If I'm obsessed with anything, it's you.

DANIEL. Obsessions fade, Lisa. Just ask Elvis and Princess Di. No, bad examples. Just tell me I'm not alone in this relationship, okay?

LISA. And would Captain Insecurity believe me if I did? Look, Daniel. I can't guarantee the future. Nobody can.

DANIEL. I bet some online company could make a fortune peddling broken-heart insurance. Like Geico. I bet that horny little gecko gets as much tail as he can handle.

LISA. Thank you for that disturbing image. But lizard love aside, you'll just have to take my word for it. I'm here for the long haul. Or at least until your paranoia drives me away.

DANIEL. I know. I'm sorry. I'm just so crazy in love with you, Lisa. You may be out of my league, but I'm all in here.

(She pulls him to the sofa. Spreads her long legs on his lap.)

LISA. Then stop pushing so hard and let's see how this plays out, okay? If it feels this good, isn't it worth the risk?

DANIEL. Ask me again when we're ninety and surrounded by great-grandchildren.

LISA. It's a deal. Just remind me in about forty or fifty years. My memory may not be that good by then.

(She moves closer. Lays her head on his chest.)

LISA. Trust me, Daniel. You're a keeper.

DANIEL. A keeper, she says.

CURTAIN

Crush

By
Vin Morreale, Jr.

CAST

Daniel — A zany 'Dentist to the Stars'

Laurie — A young dental assistant

SETTING

A Beverly Hills Dental Office

Vin's Notes: This is the second excerpt from my romantic comedy entitled *DENTAL CRUELTY*. It is actually a zany, fun screenplay. However, I chose to include two scenes in this book that are less comical, but show Daniel's bad luck with finding a real relationship. Later in the script, he has a drunken rant about him women hate dentists because they remind them of drills and pain. Oh, and there is a comical terrorist plot as well, that culminates in a laughing gas fueled food fight. Lots of fun.

For royalty information and permission to use this scene in a paid performance, or if you are a Film Producer interested in reading the full feature-length screenplay, please contact **Academy Arts Entertainment** *- vin@academyarts.com.*

Crush

AT RISE: *The dental offices of Dr. Daniel Bingham, Beverly Hills dentist. DANIEL, 50 is cleaning up. His wide-eyed dental assistant, LAURIE, 18, pops her head in.*

LAURIE.   Need some help, Dr. Bingham?

DANIEL.   More than you know. *(Shakes his head.)* Thanks anyway, Laurie. I think I just need to be alone for a while.

LAURIE.   No problem.

(She helps him anyway.)

LAURIE.   You seem to be in a little better mood than yesterday.

DANIEL.   One of my patients made me realize something. No matter how old we get, we all have to grow up sometimes.

LAURIE.   Growing up's not so hot. *(Softly.)* Especially when no one ever notices...

(Daniel studies her face. Seeing her for the first time. She fidgets under his gaze.)

LAURIE.   I...I better be going now.

DANIEL.   *(Gently.)* I'm sorry, Laurie. I guess I've been so caught up in my own troubles, I haven't been there for you. Come here.

(She approaches him hesitantly -- the frightened innocence of young love.)

DANIEL.   You've always been so sweet and helpful, Laurie. I guess I never took the time to notice you were also a very beautiful woman.

LAURIE.   That don't mean much in this town. Look at Margo. And Jeannie. And half your patients. You're surrounded by beautiful women all the time...

DANIEL.   And not one of them is half as kind and compassionate as you. Listen to me, Laurie. You're far too precious to waste on a neurotic old lunatic like me.

LAURIE. You're not old!

DANIEL. I'm old enough to be your father... which I guarantee depresses me way more than it depresses you. I've not only been around the block.., I've broken down by the curb. *(Gently.)* You deserve so much more than that.

LAURIE. And what if I don't want more?

DANIEL. You will. Someday you will. Love is like a surprise party. Just when we think no one really cares, someone comes from out of nowhere and knocks us flat. Then, suddenly, that face we see smiling down on us puts a strangle-hold on our hearts we can never escape from. That's love, Laurie. It's an ambush. A beautiful, crazy, terrifying ambush.

LAURIE. Is this a brush off, Dr. Bingham?

DANIEL. No, Laurie. You'll always have a special place in my heart. I just want you to find the right guy to fit in yours.

(She steps back slowly, then flings herself into his arms, smothering him in one brief kiss. Just as suddenly, she pulls away and dashes out the door.)

DANIEL. *(Softly.)* Oh, sweetheart... Where were you when I was nineteen..?

CURTAIN

Lazlo's Mine

By
Vin Morreale, Jr.

CAST

Corrigan — A young miner

Potter — A grizzled old miner

SETTING

A collapsed West Virginia coal mine

Vin's Notes: Yet another powerful short play from my collection *SOUTHERN DISCOMFORT* with the Dramatic Publishing Company. This one set in West Virginia. The opening scene in darkness, with sound effects and flashlights quickly capturtes the audience's attention, while the shift of fear and resignation from one character to the other offers a unique challenge for strong actors.

For royalty information, or to request a copy of SOUTHERN DISCOMFORT, please contact **Dramatic Publishing** - dramaticpublishing.com/authors/profile/view/url/vin-morreale-jr

Lazlo's Mine

AT RISE: *The stage is in darkness. Throughout the play, handheld flashlights and mine helmet lights will be the only illumination. Suddenly, we hear a tremendous RUMBLING CRASH, as part of the mine collapses.*

POTTER. *(Offstage)* Look out! She's givin' way! Look OUT!

> *A few moments of desperate silence, as the sound of the last few boulders FALL and SETTLE into place, followed by ROUGH COUGHING.*

CORRIGAN. *(Frantically.)* Beamis? Linville? Ruthorford?! *(No reply.)* Morgan?! Potter?!! Oh, please, God... Tell me you're not all dead!

POTTER. *(Weakly)* ... Corrigan..?

CORRIGAN. Yeah! It's me. Webster Corrigan! I'm still alive!

POTTER. Well... ain't that just dandy for you? *(Painfully.)* Now, can I inconvenience you in your bellowin' long enough to git this damn plank off'un my legs?!

CORRIGAN. Where you at, Potter?

> *(A FLASHLIGHT splits the darkness, Stage Right. It scans the audience, supplemented by the light on two helmet, which illuminate the miner's faces. WEBSTER CORRIGAN is in his mid-20's, thin and hunched over. His face and clothing blackened with coal and soot.)*

POTTER. Over here, ya durn fool..!

> *(The flashlight swings around to reveal SAMUEL POTTER, a crusty old miner in his 50s, sprawled Upstage Left. A wooden beam covers his legs. Corrigan sees him and gasps.)*

CORRIGAN. Jesus, Sam... your legs...

POTTER. Yeah... They's busted all to hell. Just my luck. I was supposed to take the old lady dancing come Saturday night.

CORRIGAN. Jesus, Sam...

POTTER. You said that. Only I'd rather you'd pick up that plank then say it again.

CORRIGAN. Uh... sorry. I got it.

POTTER. Real gentle-like. Any big moves may cause this whole section to collapse around our ears.

(Corrigan heaves the plank off the older miner's damaged legs.)

POTTER. Arrrrrgggh!

CORRIGAN. Does it hurt, Sam?

POTTER. No, you idiot. I'm auditionin' for the Grand Ol' Opry! Course it hurts! Hurts like hell!

CORRIGAN. I'm sorry, Sam.

POTTER. *(Trying to regain his composure.)* Okay. Apologizin' for stupid questions is a good thing. *(Sits up, painfully.)* Stayin' alive's a good thing, too.

(With a great amount of exertion, Potter pulls himself to a seated position, his back against a large rock. His useless legs stretched out in front of him. His grabs his helmet and places it on his head, switching on the helmet light. Then he grabs his own flashlight and lets the light sweeps over the stage and audience.)

CORRIGAN. Where are the others? Beamis and Rutherford and all?

POTTER. Beamis and Rutherford and Morgan were tryin' to scramble out of Section 247, last I heard.

CORRIGAN. Jesus, Sam. Section 247 was one of the worst hit! If they was in there when it let go, then they's sure to be...

POTTER. You don't think I know that, Corrigan?! You don't think I know what fifty tons of fallin' rock can do to a man's skull? You don't think I know there won't be enough left of those poor bastards to scrape outta there?! Huh?!

CORRIGAN. Sorry, Sam... Just weren't sure you knew...

POTTER. Well, I do know! I know at least three friends of mine are dead because the damn coal company pushed us to go too deep too fast. I know that everything from 311 to 247 behind us is under more'n a mile of dirt and rock. And I also figure everything from 241 to daylight is sealed off in front of us.

CORRIGAN. Ya think?

POTTER. And I know that all that means we're about as screwed as two livin' men can get!

CORRIGAN. You think we're trapped down here?

(Potter points his flashlight at the other man's face.)

CORRIGAN. I... I'm sorry, Sam...

POTTER. Apologizin' for stupidity is good, Corrigan. But I'm losin' my patience for it real quick-like. *(Trying to sound casual.)* Hell, these things happen every twenny years or so. We's just unlucky enough to be the ones down here when the whole kit 'n caboodle collapsed.

CORRIGAN. *(Terrified.)* I heard tales... lotsa tales about this kinda thing... But I never thought this would happen to me.

POTTER. Nobody does, Corrigan. If I'da knowed it was gonna happen, I'da prob'ly called in sick today.

CORRIGAN. I guess.

POTTER. Jus' you stay sharp, boy. I ain't got no patience for any hysterics. You hear me?

CORRIGAN. I hear you...

POTTER. Hell, we's still alive. That's a good thing. If they can open up a passage, we just might make it outta this mine alive.

CORRIGAN. Ya think?

POTTER. *(Pause, then...)* I was in one of these before, ya know. 'Bout twenny years back, over in Milton County. They put some durn fool kid with three months' experience blastin' a new section of the mine. It weren't hard to figure out what was gonna happen.

MORE

POTTER (CONT'D)   The kid used too much dynamite and placed it in the wrongest possible spot. He shouts, "Fire in the hole!" and there's this big deep rumbly boom. I could tell by the way the ground shook under my feet that somethin' was wrong. Real wrong. But I was young and stupid... funny how those two always go hand in hand.... and I walked straight into that mine as soon as they gave the all clear... Well, that shaft was sneaky as mines can be. It waited about forty five minutes before it decided to get pissed. Then, that whole mine just sorta belched and shuddered and closed its dark angry mouth on near to fifty-three good men. *(Shakes his head.)* Fifty-three good men... When the rescuers finally burrowed out a hole, I was the only one they pulled out alive.

CORRIGAN.   *(Not knowing what to say.)* Alive is good.

POTTER.   Sometimes it is... Sometimes it ain't. For months, I had to look in the teary faces of all those new widow women. Look in the eyes of all those kids who were suddenly without a daddy. Look in those faces and not be able to tell them why I made it outta that mine, but their husbands and daddies didn't.

CORRIGAN.   Well, I'd sure rather do that then end up under a pile of rocks.

POTTER.   Tell me that again in three months, Corrigan. That's all I could stay in that there town before I moved down here to Lazlo's Mine.

CORRIGAN.   When I get outa here, I'm givin' up minin' for good. I ain't never livin' through this again!

POTTER.   We ain't lived through this one yet, kid.

(They let this sink in. Then, Potter grabs a piece of coal and plays with it. Corrigan paces nervously, searching for a way out.)

CORRIGAN.   How long before they send a rescue crew down here, Sam?

(Potter doesn't look at him, fascinated by the lump of coal.)

POTTER.   Depends on whether they thinks we're alive or dead. If they think we're goners, they'd just might blast a new hole. That could make the rest of these walls collapse. *(Snickers.)* They could rescue us to death. Sorta ironic, don't ya think?

CORRIGAN.   No, I don't think it's ironic! It's damn pitiful if you ask me!

POTTER. Then I better be sure not to ask you. Besides, if the fallin' rock or lack of oxygen don't kill us, the gas surely will.

CORRIGAN. You smell the gas, Sam? Think gas is seepin' in here?! Christ, that's all we need!

POTTER. You never smell the gas, Corrigan. It ain't got no smell. It just makes you drowsy-like, and before you know it, you's sleepin' your way to eternity.

CORRIGAN. I don't wanna die like this, Sam!

POTTER. Seems to me like we ain't got much choice. Old Lazlo's Mine done had its say and arguing ain't gonna amount to nothin'. That's the business, Corrigan. Every miner who walked all blustery proud into Lazlo's mouth knew there was a chance this kinda thing would happen. And every night we walked out at the end of a shift, we knew we beat that cantankerous old mine. If we walk out on our own two legs, we win...Only this time, looks like the mine won...

CORRIGAN. How can you be so damn calm! We're gonna die in here!

POTTER. Maybe... But the more you panic, or the harder you struggle against that rock, the more oxygen you use up. That kills us both. Best be still and wait it out.

CORRIGAN. Not me! I ain't gonna roll over and die like some damn... bug! I'm finding me a way outa this hellhole!

POTTER. Suit yourself. Send me a postcard if you git the time.

CORRIGAN. You're a mean old bastard, Sam Potter. You know that?

POTTER. Never claimed to be any different. Too bad you cain't choose your dyin' companions, ain't it, Corrigan?

(Corrigan glares at the crippled man with pure hatred, then turns and disappears into the darkness.)

CORRIGAN. I'm gonna see if there's an opening in 243. Maybe I can dig us a way out.

(He exits, leaving the stage lit only by Potter's Helmet and flashlight.)

POTTER. You do that, Corrigan. You do that.

(He picks up the coal again. Holds it close to his face, as if trying to unlock some inner mystery.)

POTTER.   It's a damn, pitiful shame. All my life... just rootin underground for this... a piece o' rock-like crap that's stupid enough to burn. *(Chuckles sadly.)* And the durndest thing is that in fifty million years or so, with enough pressure from all this rock, I ain't gonna be nothing more than a lump of coal like you, and some poor bastard futuristic miner is gonna be diggin' me up... *(Tries to move his legs.)* Damn, that hurts! Hell, in fifty million years they probably won't even burn coal no more... Probably just be using some kinda solar energy by then. Then no poor bastard will have to sell his soul to this here darkness, just to feed his family. Yeah... Workin' in the sun's the way it oughta be... The way it oughta be...

(He considers this for a moment, before his body begins to shake uncontrollably. He throws back his head and screams into the darkness.)

POTTER.   I DON'T WANT TO DIE DOWN HERE!! I DON'T WANT TO DIE IN THE DARK LIKE SOME ANIMAL!! *(Weakly.)* I don't want to die...

(Corrigan rushes back on, shining his light in Potter's face. He is abruptly quieted by the older man's fear.)

CORRIGAN.   Sam..?

POTTER.   *(Dragging a sleeve across his eyes.)* What the hell you lookin' at?! Ain't you found a path to China yet?

CORRIGAN.   It's sealed tight as a tomb back there.

POTTER.   *(Still trying to hide his tears.)* Good analogy, Corrigan.

CORRIGAN.   *(Pause, then...)* But I can hear them, Sam. They're comin' for us.

POTTER.   You better not be joshing me, boy.

CORRIGAN.   No, Sam. I can hear them. I think they're close.

(He squats beside Potter, and the two men strain their ears in the darkness.)

POTTER.   I don't hear a durn thing, Corrigan!

CORRIGAN.   They're out there, Sam. They're coming for us.

POTTER.   Ya think?

CORRIGAN.   You lie back and sleep, Sam... I'll do the listenin' for both of us.

POTTER.   *(Like a child)* You can really hear them, Corrigan?

CORRIGAN.   Yeah. Just listen, Sam...

> *(There is no sound but the creaking of the mine and the frightened breathing of the two men. Their flashlights start to DIM, and in the enveloping darkness, we hear Corrigan whisper...)*

CORRIGAN.   Just listen... just listen...

BLACKOUT

CURTAIN

Collaborations

By
Vin Morreale, Jr.

CAST

Hope — A Hollywood literary agent

Tascal — A tough-talking studio executive

SETTING

J.T. Tascal's office at Cypress Studios

Vin's Notes: This piece had an interesting history. One of my first stage plays I turned into a feature film script. It was also one of six plays of mine performed in the first two years of the San Francisco Playwrights Center, which I had the honor to help co-found decades ago. It tells the tale of a mentally unstable ghostwriter who is forced to call in other ghostwriters, when offered a huge opportunity for full credit. But his writing partners aren't all they appear to be, and may not have his best interest at heart. In this scene, his agent negotiates with a tough studio head.

*For royalty information and permission to use this scene in a paid performance, or if you are a Film Producer interested in reading this suspenseful feature screenplay, contact **Academy Arts Entertainment** - vin@academyarts.com.*

Collaborations

AT RISE: A lavish office setting. J.T. TASCAL, 53, the cantankerous head of Cypress Studios, discusses a script under development with HOPE, 33, the writer's literary agent.)

HOPE. So there's no way we can salvage the concept?

TASCAL. The coverage called it interesting, but not worth pursuing.

HOPE. You didn't read it?

TASCAL. My people only give me stuff they're sure I'll like. I rely on their judgment.

HOPE. I really think you should rea...

TASCAL. End of discussion. *Wavering World* is cute and clever and everything I ain't interested in. I need cash, not cute. You tell your boy to start over. And not expect more time either.

HOPE. A complete redo without an extension would be...

TASCAL. A lot of pressure for an unstable writer. I know all about his breakdown, and it don't mean shit to me. I've got media maggots breathing down my neck, and I want to see a first draft on paper in two weeks.

HOPE. I'm not sure that's entirely...

TASCAL. It's entirely the way it is. Look, I'll give your boy everything he needs. A bungalow here on the lot. Catered meals to see he eats right. I'll even throw in an occasional romp with a wannabe starlet on my credit card, if that's what it takes!

HOPE. I don't think Chad's going to need...

TASCAL. Knew you'd say that. I know your history with him, too.

(Hope's face tightens. Tascal knows he's crossed the line.)

HOPE. Then you know I have no problem walking away from this deal and taking Chad to another studio. You want a money-making script? I'm the one that's gonna get it for you. But you don't use him, and you sure as hell don't disrespect me!

(Tascal tries to stare her down. She doesn't flinch.)

TASCAL. *(Pause, then he smiles.)* Look, you're smart, talented, tenacious. A pit bull in a skirt. Why the hell don't you leave the agency game and come work for me? I could use a filly with your fire.

HOPE. 'Cause you're a belligerent old bastard who's used to getting his way all the time.

TASCAL. And that's just my good side. Okay, agent-lady. We still have a deal...provided your boy gets me the story.

HOPE. And you'll read this one yourself?

TASCAL. If I have to.

HOPE. I'll make sure he doesn't use words with more than two syllables.

TASCAL. You're a spitfire, you know that?

HOPE. Try growing up with six brothers.

TASCAL. I have to admit, you carried yourself like a prizefighter during these negotiations. My wallet is still feeling bruised.

HOPE. I'll take that as a compliment.

TASCAL. You should. I like a woman who has the balls to back me into a corner.

HOPE. I majored in 'balls' in agent school.

TASCAL. Most people in this world are cows. You're not.

HOPE. Gosh, I don't know if my little bovine heart can take all this flattery.

TASCAL. So what is it with you and Fisher? This crazy writer still your leading man? Or just a temporary sub-plot?

HOPE. Y.T... You're a smart man, a lot of fun to be with, and probably the biggest sonovabitch in the industry...

TASCAL. That's what it says on my business card.

HOPE. I'd love to work with you to help turn Cypress Studios around. *(Firmly.)* But any feelings I have for Chad Fisher, over and above our agent-client relationship, are none of your damn business.

A PAUSE.

TASCAL. You got an 'A' in that balls course, didn't you?

HOPE. *(Smiling sweetly.)* Damn right. See you in two weeks.

CURTAIN

Her Choice

By
Vin Morreale, Jr.

CAST

Marlene — A woman

Steven — Her boyfriend

SETTING

Marlene's apartment.

Vin's Notes: One of the many scenes written for my **Burning Up The Stage Acting Workshops** that can also be found in my book 150 ACTING SCENES. It's always fun exploring the loving support long-term couples develop to deal with each other's insecurities. Also a useful challenge for actors to make their characters simulataneously frantic and completely comortable with each other.

*For royalty information and permission to use this scene in a paid performance, please contact **Academy Arts Press** - vin@academyarts.com*

Her Choice

AT RISE: STEVEN is trying to calm his frantic wife MARLENE.

STEVEN. You're beautiful.

MARLENE. No, I'm not.

STEVEN. Yes, you are. You're absolutely perfect.

MARLENE. How can you say that?

STEVEN. How can you not see it?

MARLENE. I don't know. I guess because every other time anyone told me how wonderful I am, it doesn't take them long to tell me the opposite.

STEVEN. Then they are crazy.

MARLENE. Or consistent. I'm perfect, until they get to know me. Really know me. Then I'm nothing but a big bundle of flaws, faults, and everything that annoys them.

STEVEN. Sounds like their problem, not yours.

MARLENE. Maybe, but once I fall in love, it becomes my problem.

STEVEN. A problem worth having.

MARLENE. Easy for you to say. I don't think I can go through that again. Watching the respect and admiration in someone else's eyes slowly wither away and die.

STEVEN. Sorry. You can't dissuade or persuade me. I know not every love is real. Not every crush will last. And sometimes promises can bring more pain than happiness...

MARLENE. You know that you're not exactly helping here?

STEVEN. I'm trying to. What I mean is that, just because you've hit a few speed bumps, it doesn't mean you should push love out of your life. Saying you're never going to have these feelings again.

MARLENE. That's exactly what I'm saying.

STEVEN. And what I'm saying is…

MARLENE. Oh, no. Here it comes…

STEVEN. …I love you. No matter what happens. No matter how much pain it may cost me. I love you…and I need to know whether there is even the slightest chance you love me too.

MARLENE. Why are you doing this?

STEVEN. Because every part of my life is better with you in it. And every day I spend without you is killing me a little more.

MARLENE. So, we're talking pity love here?

STEVEN. You can choose to go wall yourself off from everyone and everything… or you can dump your cynicism and self-pity and make my life whole again. Your choice.

MARLENE. Hmmm. That's a tough one…

STEVEN. *(Hurt.)* Really?

MARLENE. Hey, I'm kidding! I'll take door number two. The cuddly couple prize.

STEVEN. Good choice.

MARLENE. But keep this in mind… If you even think about falling out of love with me…I will hurt you. Seriously hurt you. I'm talking intestinal damage, and irreversible groin trauma. You got that?

STEVEN. Absolutely. Clear as a bell.

MARLENE. I mean it!

STEVEN. Irreversible groin trauma. Got it…

MARLENE. You better.

STEVEN. *(Smiles.)* You're so cute when you're trying to be vicious…

CURTAIN

Night Air

By
Vin Morreale, Jr.

CAST

Ethan   A young woman with a cast on her arm

Natalie   A reclusive musician

SETTING

A booth at the local Waffle House

Vin's Notes: In 2018, I launched a 10-WEEK SCREENWRITING INTENSIVE, with the goal of each student finishing the first draft of a screenplay by the end of the course's ten week period. To show them it was possible, I conceived and completed this feature-length screenplay in just seven days. Fleeing from an abusive marriage, a young woman takes a night job as a cashier, drawing on the mysterious voice of a late night radio DJ to give her courage. In this excerpt, a shy customer has just rescued her from the abusive husband who had just tracked her down.

For royalty information and permission to use this scene in a paid performance, or if you are a Film Producer interested in reading the full screenplay, please contact **Academy Arts Entertainment** *- vin@academyarts.com.*

Night Air

AT RISE: A booth at a local Waffle House late at night. NATALIE, 34, with a cast on her shattered arm, sips her coffee with ETHAN, 40, the man who saved her from an attack at the local supermarket.

ETHAN. I'm guessing that was not your typical night at the Hardy Mart.

NATALIE. I've never seen anyone knocked out by a can of stew before.

ETHAN. My weapon of choice. You should be thankful I'm not a Ramen Noodles guy. They wouldn't have dropped him, no matter how hard I threw them.

NATALIE. You probably shouldn't have, but...I do appreciate it.

ETHAN. It's the least I could have done for the Butterfly Lady.

NATALIE. It's funny. You're the second person to call me that.

(She smiles at the memory.)

ETHAN. Your nametag says you like butterflies. That suits you. But what's with the stars on it?

NATALIE. I like astronomy. I'm obsessed with it, really.

(She cradles her coffee with two hands. Calmed by its warmth.)

NATALIE. When I was a kid, my dad had this telescope. He and I used to climb up on top of the garage and aim it at the sky. Just the two of us. Up there on the roof on those clear summer nights... He had a way of making me feel like those stars were twinkling just for me. *(Embarrassed.)* Kinda silly, I know.

ETHAN. It's great to have memories like that. Are you and your dad still close?

(Seeing her face tighten.)

ETHAN. I...I'm sorry. Didn't mean to pry.

NATALIE. It's okay. Dad died a few months before I met Carl. Cancer. Maybe that's why I chose not to see all of Carl's faults. I just needed someone to make me feel the stars were still there in my life.

ETHAN. And Carl made you feel that way?

NATALIE. At first...But then the drinking started. And the bills. Then more drinking. And finally... *(Rubs her arm cast.)* I know I should have left him years ago. But I always kind of blamed myself for setting him off. Like if I just stayed out of his way until he sobered up... But I knew deep inside, that wouldn't have made any difference... *(Blushing.)* Wow. A Waffle House therapy session. Lots more than you bargained for, right?

ETHAN. Waffles with a side of regret. *(Softly.)* Believe me, I do it all the time.

(Their eyes meet in shared anguish.)

CURTAIN

Night Air - 2

By
Vin Morreale, Jr.

CAST

Ethan — A young woman with a cast on her arm

Natalie — A reclusive musician

SETTING

The common room at a Senior Citizen's Center

Vin's Notes: In this second excerpt from my screenplay *NIGHT AIR*, Natalie has inadvertently hurt Ethan after she learns his painful secret. She finally tracks him down at a Senior Citizen's home, where he plays piano for elderly residents. But the once uplifting music he used to sing has grown darker with his hurt feelings.

*For royalty information and permission to use this scene in a paid performance, or if you are a Film Producer interested in reading the full screenplay, please contact **Academy Arts Entertainment** - vin@academyarts.com.*

Night Air - 2

AT RISE: NATALIE, 34, finds ETHAN, 40, after he finishes singing depressing songs at a Senior Center.

NATALIE. That was beautiful. Dark, depressing and totally inappropriate, but beautiful.

ETHAN. Why are you here?

NATALIE. I haven't seen you in the supermarket for a while. I…I was worried.

ETHAN. I'm fine.

NATALIE. I'm not. I hurt you, Ethan. I'm not sure how or why, but I hurt you. And for that, I am sorry. I really am.

ETHAN. Thank you.

NATALIE. That's it? Thank you? You know how much courage it took for me to track you down? To stalk you like some groupie fan fanatic? Do you know I have two whole cases of beef stew in my trunk waiting for you to forgive me?

ETHAN. There's nothing to forgive.

NATALIE. I blew your cover. Isn't that what people on the run say?

ETHAN. I'm not on the run. I'm just tired.

NATALIE. Tired of what? Human contact?

ETHAN. Tired of the gossip. Tired of snap judgements. Tired of betrayal. Tired of the looks.

NATALIE. What looks?

ETHAN. The looks of contempt from people who don't know the whole story. Who don't really want to know, because the only thing more fun than putting someone on a pedestal is watching them fall…

NATALIE. I can't imagine…

ETHAN. No, you can't. I had a life, a career, a following. And suddenly I was just an accident on the highway that people have to slow down and stare at, hoping to get a glimpse of blood on the asphalt. *(Bitterly.)* And who can blame them? Slander is always much more fun than truth. I learned the hard way that it's better to stay invisible...

NATALIE. I've been invisible most of my life. Never making a scene. Never standing up for myself. *(Softly.)* All it ever cost me is everything I ever wanted.

ETHAN. That's not the same.

NATALIE. No, it isn't. I was humiliated in private. You were torn apart in front of everyone. But did I ever judge you? Or give you 'those looks?'

ETHAN. *(Pause, then...)* No.

NATALIE. Do you think I ever will?

ETHAN. I don't know. *(Beat.)* You really have two cases of beef stew in your trunk?

NATALIE. Along with five pieces of Tupperware filled with moldy homemade stew that went bad waiting for you to come see me again. So what do you say we go out to my car and give it the Last Rites, okay?

CURTAIN

VIN MORREALE, JR.

Bewilder Burger

By
Vin Morreale, Jr.

CAST

Hawthorne — A Digestive Facilitator

Customer — A hungry diner

SETTING

The counter at Bewilder Burger Restaurant

Vin's Notes: Here is a zany piece I wrote for a special **Burnng Up The Stage Acting Workshop** that focused specifically on sketch comedy. This scene also appears in my collection, 150 ACTING SCENES. As always, the most effective comedy comes either from putting real characters in ridiculous situations and having them react to the absurdity around them, or dropping ridiculous characters into realistic situations and watching the chaos that results. This comedy sketch does a little of both..

*For royalty information and permission to use this scene in a paid performance, please contact **Academy Arts Press** - vin@academyarts.com.*

Bewilder Burger

AT RISE: HAWTHORNE stands behind a gleaming restaurant counter, as a CUSTOMER walks in.

HAWTHORNE. Welcome to Bewilder Burger! I am Hawthorne, your Digestive Facilitator. How may I serve you today?

CUSTOMER. Uh, I'm not sure. I don't see a menu board.

HAWTHORNE. We at Bewilder Burger are not like the average fast food restaurants. We don't believe in all that corporate marketing overkill.

CUSTOMER. Uh, okay. Do you have a smaller menu I can look at?

HAWTHORNE. No, we don't.

CUSTOMER. You don't have menus?

HAWTHORNE. That is correct.

CUSTOMER. No, menu board? No small menus? No menus at all?

HAWTHORNE. seem to be fixated on this whole 'menu' thing.

CUSTOMER. I mean, um, okay…just give me a Bewilder Burger.

HAWTHORNE. Excellent choice. What kind of faux digestible or inorganic consumable substitution would you prefer?

CUSTOMER. Uh, I don't know. Beef, I guess.

HAWTHORNE. I'm sorry. We do not believe in using beef, or beef byproducts.

CUSTOMER. But you're a burger joint?

HAWTHORNE. A 100% beef-free burger joint.

CUSTOMER. Okay. Do you have chicken?

HAWTHORNE. Sorry.

CUSTOMER. Pork? Lamb? Goat? Venison? Bison?

HAWTHORNE. We at Bewilder Burger do not believe in the slaughter of innocent wildlife just to feed your cruel, self-serving gluttonous hunger pains. But feel free to snatch up any defenseless animal you see wandering the neighborhood and tear it to pieces with your teeth. I hear most domesticated pets are notoriously easy to catch.

CUSTOMER. You realize you are being both insulting and condescending to the only customer in this place?

HAWTHORNE. We at Bewilder Burger do not discriminate based on presence. We believe in being insulting and condescending to ferocious foodians, wherever they may be.

CUSTOMER. All right, wise guy. Just give me a veggie burger. And hold the sarcasm, if you don't mind.

HAWTHORNE. We at Bewilder Burger refuse to be part of your savage desire to take the life of guiltless plants simply to satisfy your contemptuous herba-barbarious needs. Perhaps there is another life form you wish to oppress, murder or masticate?

CUSTOMER. Let me get this straight…You don't serve meat or vegetables? What kind of fast food restaurant is this?

HAWTHORNE. We are not a fast food restaurant. We are a fasting food restaurant. You come here not to eat.

CUSTOMER. Not to eat?

HAWTHORNE. Correct. You come here to fast.

CUSTOMER. A fasting food restaurant?

HAWTHORNE. One of the finest.

CUSTOMER. You don't serve any food at all?

HAWTHORNE. It would be against our Mission Statement and Corporate Philosophy.

CUSTOMER. How do you stay in business?

HAWTHORNE. Tax credits. The Bewilder Burger concept started in California.

CUSTOMER. Well, that explains everything…

Big Plans

By
Vin Morreale, Jr.

CAST

Susan   A newly hired woman

Mike   Her reluctant husband

SETTING

A small, unkempt apartment

Vin's Notes: I always find two-person scenes more interesting when you can juxtapose the two characters' vastly different energy levels, eloquence and emotions. Leaving them to find a way to achieve balance, or surrender to the futility of it all. And as writers, we occasionally base characters on real people and the struggles they have coping with life. This piece also appears in 150 ACTING SCENES.

*For royalty information and permission to use this scene in a paid performance, please contact **Academy Arts Press** - vin@academyarts.com*

Big Plans

AT RISE: *A run-down apartment holding the discards from a dozen yard sales. SUSAN enters, trying to contain her excitement, as her husband MIKE tries to balance their checkbook on a rickety kitchen table.*

SUSAN. I got the job.

MIKE. Uh huh.

SUSAN. I Did you hear me? I got the job!

MIKE. *(Not looking up.)* I heard you.

SUSAN. Well, aren't you going to congratulate me? I mean, this is huge. Huge!

MIKE. *(Flatly.)* Congratulations.

SUSAN. Okay, what is it?

MIKE. What's what?

SUSAN. You. The attitude.

MIKE. Nothing. I'm tired. That's all.

SUSAN. No. It's more than that. There's something else. A hostility or something.

MIKE. I'm tired, Susan. That's all.

SUSAN. What is it? You can't take change? Are you committed to squalor? Afraid of finally having money? Afraid of success? (Slow realization) Or…are you just afraid of my success.

MIKE. Right.

SUSAN. That's it, isn't it? You're jealous! You're jealous that someone finally recognized how good I am. What I have to offer. Admit it! You're jealous because this is about me, and not you, for once!

MIKE. It's always about you! Every stupid dream. Every shattered hope. If I'm jealous, it's because I wish to God that I could be so painfully oblivious to everyone else in my life. So completely unfeeling and uncaring!

SUSAN. Uncaring? Did you hear what I said? I can finally get us out of this hole!

MIKE. And take us where? Another city? Another beautiful house? Another 'perfect life'…which will fall apart in six months, when you decide to quite this latest dream job for whatever ridiculous reason this time.

SUSAN. That's not fair.

MIKE. No, it's not fair. But it's accurate. You won't like the desk they give you. Your bosses will be morons. Your coworkers will have it in for you. Maybe they'll suddenly stop telling you how wonderful you are three times a day.

SUSAN. It's not my fault.

MIKE. It never is. Someone else will get the better parking spot and that'll push you over the edge. Or maybe you'll just get bored, thinking you don't need this. Thinking you can do better.

SUSAN. It won't be like that this time…

MIKE. That's what you say every time. But in six months, you'll find one excuse or another to get pissed off and quit. You'll walk out, cursing the people who gave you this chance. And then it'll start all over again. The drinking. The bitterness. The self-pity. The bill collectors and eviction notices. And then we end up in another pig sty in another town built on your shattered dreams and inflated ego…

SUSAN. It won't be like that. I promise.

MIKE. Sure.

SUSAN. Really. This time it'll be different.

MIKE. Yeah…Congratulations. I'll go pack. *(Exits)*

SUSAN. *(Calling out.)* It'll be different! You'll see! This time, it'll be different!

CURTAIN

House Of The Seven Gables

By
Vin Morreale, Jr.

CAST

Hepzibah — An elderly Victorian matron

Hargrove — A young renter

SETTING

The House of the Seven Gables. Circa 1841

Vin's Notes: When my daughter was in Middle School, she was assigned Nathaniel Hawthorne's 1851 classic HOUSE OF THE SEVEN GABLES. She let me read it after she finished, and my initial reaction was that the book was so stiff and dated, especially in its treatment of women, that it would be impossible to turn into a play for modern audiences. So that is exactly what I did. My stage version of HOUSE OF THE SEVEN GABLES is listed with Dramatic Publishing.

FOR ROYALTY INFORMATION, OR TO REQUEST A COPY OF
HOUSE OF THE SEVEN GABLES, PLEASE CONTACT **DRAMATIC PUBLISHING** -
dramaticpublishing.com/authors/profile/view/url/vin-morreale-jr

House Of The Seven Gables

AT RISE: *The interior of the House of the Seven Gables. In this century, the house is more modestly furnished, as if many items were sold off. Hargrove is seated in a stiff wooden chair by the table, Downstage Left. MISS HEPZIBAH PYNCHEON paces nervously before him. She is far too uncomfortable to sit and speak with the young stranger. Hepzibah is a pale, thin woman, at least sixty years of age. She wears her old-fashioned lace black dress as if she is in a constant state of mourning. Her permanent scowl reinforces the image of someone who has endured unimaginable grief. Once a proud lady, she has gradually been withered by life within this decaying manor. As always, the interior of the House Of The Seven Gables is dimly lit, employing pools of light amidst the gloom and cobwebs to create an eerie visual atmosphere.*

HARGROVE. ...And that is my proposal, Miss Pyncheon.

HEPZIBAH. But why this house, Mr. Hargrove? Surely there are others...

HARGROVE. *(Looking around.)* The House Of The Seven Gables has a certain...charm. An atmosphere I find intriguing.

HEPZIBAH. The charm of a mausoleum. And as for atmosphere... atmosphere is supposed to be breathable. While this house seems to pull the very air from your lungs. *(Shudders.)* Especially at night.

HARGROVE. Nevertheless, Miss Pyncheon. As an artist and photographer, I am drawn to this place. *(His eyes scan the gloomy residence.)* I feel strangely at home here. I wish you would seriously consider my offer.

HEPZIBAH. Mr. Hargrove... I am seriously considering your offer. In fact, this is the longest conversation I have had with an outsider in the last forty years. I...I am not easily drawn to people. Just as people are not easily drawn to me...

HARGROVE. You chastise yourself needlessly, Miss Pyncheon. Why, I...

HEPZIBAH. *(Cuts him off.)* I also am quite experienced in recognizing empty flattery, Mr. Hargrove. Insincerity is another Pyncheon family curse.

HARGROVE. I only meant to say...

HEPZIBAH. Let us speak plainly, sir. People fear me. They fear this house. They fear my face.

HARGROVE. Miss Pyncheon...

HEPZIBAH. I have heard the whispers. The cruel gossip that rises from the street through my window. Hag. Spinster... A face that could make tombstones seem giddy...

HARGROVE. Really, I...

(She silences him with a raised hand.)

HEPZIBAH. It wasn't always so. Once...once I was a lady and was even known to smile on occasion. But this frown is now etched into my soul as deeply as it is etched into my face.

HARGROVE. Perhaps you mistake character for...

HEPZIBAH. I mistake nothing. The house decays, and I decay within it. Such is my fate as one of the last to bear the terrible burden of the Pyncheon name.

HARGROVE. Then let me ease your plight, if only financially. I know you are on hard times. That you have been forced to sell off furniture piece by piece.

HEPZIBAH. This is common knowledge?

HARGROVE. The curse of modern times is that even the ill-informed seem able to know everything that is going on... That is why I am willing to pay upwards of two dollars a month to live here.

HEPZIBAH. *(Stunned.)* Two dollars?

HARGROVE: Every month.

HEPZIBAH. *(Considers.)* There is no denying I need the funds. The Pyncheon family fortune has sidestepped me as surely as the family fate has trampled my bones. All I have left is this house...and the secrets it contains.

HARGROVE. We all have our secrets, Miss Pyncheon. And as for the house, I will be of little distraction to me. I need not even bother you for dinner, as I take my meals at a local tavern. I will keep to my rooms, my politics and my photography. And I will move so silently, you will not even be aware I am in the house.

HEPZIBAH. Another ghost to haunt this place? Just what we need. *(Sighs.)* Well, at least you are a ghost with coinage...and that I can no longer afford to refuse. *(With bruised dignity.)* Very well, Mr. Hargrove. You may move your belongings into the southwest gable, which overlooks the garden. Up that stairway to the end of the hall.

HARGROVE. You will not regret this, Miss Pyncheon!

HEPZIBAH. Then it would be one of the few acts in my life that I shall not.

CURTAIN

House Of The Seven Gables - 2

By
Vin Morreale, Jr.

CAST

Hepzibah — An elderly Victorian matron

Phoebe — Her young niece

SETTING

The House of the Seven Gables. Circa 1841

Vin's Notes: Updating a literary classic from a hundred and fifty years ago requires replicating the author's voice to such an extent that readers cannot tell which lines are from the original, and which are written by the adapting author. With its 1851 chauvanistic attitudes and one-dimensional characters (Hepzibah & Phoebe!), Hawthorne's novel was a real challenge. I ended up creating 80% new dialogue to sound like Hawthorne's voice, which turned out far better than I imagined. I am also working on a musical version of HOUSE OF THE SEVEN GABLES.

For royalty information, or to request a copy of HOUSE OF THE SEVEN GABLES, please contact **Dramatic Publishing** - dramaticpublishing.com/authors/profile/view/url/vin-morreale-jr

House Of The Seven Gables 2

AT RISE: There is an insistent KNOCKING on the door.)

HEPZIBAH.   Be still. All that pounding could wake the dead! *(Glances up at the Old Colonel's painting.)* And some things are better left in slumber.

(She opens the door. Phoebe stands there with a broad smile.)

HEPZIBAH.   I am here!

(Hepzibah abruptly closes the door in her face. More rapping. Hepzibah opens the door a second time.)

PHOEBE.   Please excuse my confusion… This is the House Of The Seven Gables, is it not?

HEPZIBAH.   So it is called.

PHOEBE.   And you are Hepzibah Pyncheon, if I am not mistaken?

HEPZIBAH.   What is it you want, young lady?

PHOEBE.   Why a place to stay for a few weeks.

HEPZIBAH.   Try the blacksmith's shop. They are used to pounding there.

(She closes the door again. More knocking. Even more insistent. With a scowl, Hepzibah opens the door once more. Phoebe takes the opportunity to wedge her foot in the doorway, so the door cannot be slammed in her face again.)

HEPZIBAH.   Forgive me, child. Was the repeated slamming of my door too subtle for you?

PHOEBE.   Cousin Hepzibah…It is I. Your cousin Phoebe. From Virginia.

HEPZIBAH.   I have a cousin Phoebe in Virginia?

PHOEBE.   No. You have a cousin Phoebe on your doorstep. May I come in?

HEPZIBAH. How do I know you are not some well-dressed urchin trying to take advantage of an old spinster?

PHOEBE. You have found me out. In truth, I do this all over town. I am a serial cousin. Now please be kind enough to let me in. I suspect the more curious townsfolk are already believing you have thrown me out before even letting me step across your threshold.

(Hepzibah sees her foot in the doorway, realizes she cannot close it again. She relents and allows the girl to enter.)

HEPZIBAH. Forgive me, child. I do not often let others into my house. I am not what you might call... sociable.

PHOEBE. Oh, I disagree. It was wonderfully social the way you slammed the door in my face repeatedly.

HEPZIBAH. You are being facetious.

PHOEBE. Facetiousness is a city vice. Out in the countryside, we merely see the amusing side of things. (Enters quickly.) But I am forgetting my manners... Forgive me, cousin. It seems my visit has obviously caught you unawares. Didn't you get my letters?

HEPZIBAH. I never read personal correspondence. I find it much too... personal.

(Phoebe drops her bag on the floor and breaks out in a cheerful giggle.)

HEPZIBAH. *(Offended.)* Why are you laughing?

PHOEBE. Oh, I am sorry. I thought you were being witty.

HEPZIBAH. I assure you, child. The next time I am witty, I should be among the first to realize it.

PHOEBE. This is not comfortable for you, is it?

HEPZIBAH. Furniture and bedding are comfortable. I was never designed to be. However...I am also forgetting my manners. You must have traveled a great distance to impose on me. Carolina wasn't it?

PHOEBE. Virginia.

HEPZIBAH. Ah... And you claim we are related in some way?

PHOEBE. *(With a sweet smile.)* Can't you see the resemblance?

> *(The dour old woman examines the beautiful and cheerful face of her cousin. Hepzibah is not amused.)*

HEPZIBAH. That must be the amusing side of things you country folk are so fond of. It seems I must be on my guard with you.

PHOEBE. Oh, no, Ma'am. I was hoping you would open your heart to a forgotten relative as graciously as you would open up your home.

HEPZIBAH. My heart or my home... It is difficult to say which has more cobwebs. *(Sighs again.)* Still, I see you mean well enough, and are merely suffering from the debilitating cheerfulness of youth. You will soon grow out of that. How long do you expect to stay?

PHOEBE. That is entirely up to you, dear cousin.

HEPZIBAH. Is it? Well, then...good day to you, Phoebe. Have a pleasant journey back to Virginia.

> *(Phoebe looks stunned, as Hepzibah crosses to the door and holds it open for her. The young girl lifts her luggage and trudges sadly forward. As she reaches Hepzibah, she detects the flicker of a smile on the old woman's face.)*

PHOEBE. You are having sport with me, aren't you?

HEPZIBAH. *(Wryly.)* I learned it from my Virginia relatives. Now put down that luggage at once and let us get you something to eat. You can cook, I suppose?

PHOEBE. Like the King of England's private chefs!

HEPZIBAH. Hmmmm. This may not be so unpleasant after all. So how did you find your way to the House Of The Seven Gables?

PHOEBE. I was accompanied here by a rather odd gentlemen.

HEPZIBAH. I find most gentlemen odd. And those that aren't odd, I find odder still.

> *(Phoebe laughs again. Catches Hepzibah's stern look and suddenly stops.)*

PHOEBE. Oh... you were not being witty again.

HEPZIBAH. No, I was not. Now tell me... In what way was this escort of yours odd?

PHOEBE. He seemed so grave and somber. Like he carried the weight of generations on his shoulder. And he seemed to know all about me.

HEPZIBAH. I find that neither odd, nor interesting.

PHOEBE. He also knew a lot about you. And this house. How strange... I do not remember this latch being open?

(She bends to inspect the case.)

HEPZIBAH. You will find many strange things in this house. It is sometimes best not to question them.

PHOEBE. As you wish, cousin Hepzibah. I will cause the least disruption in your life as I am able.

(She begins to putter around the house, picking up dishes as she speaks.)

HEPZIBAH. *(Warming to her.)* Disruptions are not always bad things. Be yourself, child...only don't be so very...much of yourself... If you understand my meaning.

PHOEBE. I will happily try to restrain my enthusiasm. And my cheerfulness.

HEPZIBAH. Good. Too much sparkle can hurt the eyes of one accustomed to darkness.

PHOEBE. And too much darkness can blind one to the beauty of the world. Wouldn't you say?

HEPZIBAH. I would not. Seeing only the beauty in things can be a terrible curse. I know from experience.

PHOEBE. Poor Cousin Hepzibah. Has the world treated you so very badly?

(Hepzibah stiffens and searches the younger woman's face. She gradually softens, as she realizes Phoebe's concern is genuine. She sighs.)

HEPZIBAH. God has His favorites, Phoebe. It has always been so. He shows me repeatedly that this branch of the Pyncheon family is not among His chosen... or His blessed.

PHOEBE. I believe this life is meant to be suffered. That is what makes Heaven such a welcomed change.

HEPZIBAH. *(Amused.)* You even say the word 'suffer' as if it were an adventure to be seized. Are all country girls such philosophers?

PHOEBE. Of course. That is what makes churning butter and slopping pigs such an opportunity for enlightenment.

HEPZIBAH. *(Laughing.)* Your good cheer will be the death of me yet, child.

PHOEBE. What a glorious way that would be to end one's days!

(Hepzibah sits and watches Phoebe putter about, cleaning, arranging.)

HEPZIBAH. Not even the cold kiss of the grave frightens you?

PHOEBE. Not when it is followed by the warm embrace of our Father in Heaven. All the evil in this world can surely not match the power of God's grace.

HEPZIBAH. *(Ominously.)* Once you have looked evil directly in the eye, I wonder whether you will remain so strong in your faith.

PHOEBE. I have little doubt.

HEPZIBAH. Then you are one of the fortunate...or the very foolish.

PHOEBE. Perhaps both... Hepzibah is such a stern name. May I call you 'Happy?'

HEPZIBAH. Only if you were the least perceptive person on earth.

(Phoebe and Hepzibah exit together.)

CURTAIN

It's A Mystery

By
Vin Morreale, Jr.

CAST

Constance — A woman in a bar

Woodrow — A guy trying to hit on her

SETTING

An upscale bar on a Friday night.

Vin's Notes: The colorful, tough-talking patter of Film Noir detectives does not have to be limited solely to men. Enfusing female characters with the same hard-boiled attitude gives actresses more opportunity to tackle interesting dialogue. This piece appears in my collection, 150 ACTING SCENES.

*For royalty information and permission to use this scene in a paid performance, please contact **Academy Arts Press** - vin@academyarts.com*

It's A Mystery

AT RISE: CONSTANCE sits alone at a bar, sipping her Bourbon on the rocks. With a wide smile, WOODROW saunters over and takes the stool beside her.

WOODROW. Drinking alone?

CONSTANCE. In a perfect universe.

WOODROW. I'm Walter. Is this seat taken?

CONSTANCE. No. But I am. Feel free to take that chair with you when you leave.

WOODROW. How about if I buy you a drink?

CONSTANCE. Only if you'll do it from across the room.

WOODROW. Cute. Y'know, you look familiar. Have we met before?

CONSTANCE. No. But you do remind me of a fungus I once grew in biology lab.

WOODROW. You're funny.

CONSTANCE. Yeah. My Mom was bitten by a clown when she was pregnant. I must have inherited the gene.

WOODROW. Must have been a really good-looking clown. You're the most beautiful woman in this place.

CONSTANCE. You should have seen me before I got the big red nose fixed. Haven't been able to do anything about the size eighty-eight floppy feet though.

WOODROW. I love a woman with a sense of humor. But don't feel you have to play so hard to get.

CONSTANCE. I'm not playing hard to get. I'm playing impossible to get. And for some reason, you're still not getting it.

WOODROW. One thing you'll learn about me is that I'm tenacious. When I see something I want, I go for it.

CONSTANCE.   So does my dog. And I just had him neutered. Look, Walter, you seem like a nice…well, at least you seem like a guy. So why don't you try your luck with one of those zombie-brained bleach blonde bimbos over there? I hear they're into vintage pick-up lines.

WOODROW.   You're not an easy woman to get to know.

CONSTANCE.   I'm not an easy woman at all. But if you're looking for easy, I will once again refer you to the aforementioned zombie-brained bleach blonde bimbos. Now why don't you be a good boy and go bye-bye before I introduce you to the vet that neutered my dog. (Pause) Oh wait, I did it myself with a salad fork.

WOODROW.   Give me a break, lady. I'm trying my best here.

WOODROW.   Yet somehow, still failing miserably. Okay, Walter. Here's the deal… I'm thirsty and PMS-ing, so this is absolutely not the right time to try to hit on me. I suggest you go back to chest thumping with Bubba and the boys over in the corner, in order to salvage what little is left of your male pride. Otherwise, I may be tempted to let this half empty bottle of Jim Beam get all cutesy with your facial features.

WOODROW.   *(Rising.)* Right. Well, uh…It's been charming.

CONSTANCE.   For you, maybe. Not for me. You ruined a wonderfully intimate moment I was trying to have with this eighteen year-old Scotch, and now you owe me another. So I suggest you leave some cash on the bar. A ten should do it. A twenty would stop me from telling everyone you have herpes and projectile diarrhea.

(He hesitates. Then drops a $20 bill on the bar.)

CONSTANCE.   Good choice. You can say bye-bye now. Come on. Say it!

WOODROW.   Uh, bye-bye.

(He exits quickly.)

CONSTANCE.   *(Sighs.)* I don't get it. Why can't I just meet a nice, normal guy…and somehow resist the temptation to shoot him?

CURTAIN

The Assignment

By
Vin Morreale, Jr.

CAST

Angelica   A high-powered businesswoman

Duncan   Her older, less competent boss

SETTING

Angelica's spacious office

Vin's Notes: This scene was written specifically for the immensely talented Marci Urling of MWU Entertainment, who asked me to write a short film she could both produce and act in. In the end, we actually shot a version of VICTIM, which also appears in this book, and I am extremely proud of the way that short film turned out.

For royalty information and permission to use this scene in a paid performance, please contact **Academy Arts Press** *-* vin@academyarts.com

The Assignment

AT RISE: *A high-rise office setting for a world-famous software firm. ANGELICA, 40, an attractive African-American businesswoman is on her office phone behind a large, well-ordered desk. A warm tone of professionalism in her voice.*

ANGELICA.   *(Into phone.)* I know you're doing your best here, David, but those numbers just don't work for me...

>*(DUNWORTH, 60, appears at her door. His tall, country club casualness is betrayed by his coiffed hair, finely tailored suit and too-easy smile.)*

DUNWORTH.   Got a minute, Angelica?

>*(Angelica nods as she wraps up her phone call.)*

ANGELICA.   *(Into phone.)* Well, take another run at it, and we'll see if we can structure a deal that's a win-win for everyone. I have to go now, so call me this afternoon when you have the new numbers. Thanks, David.

>*(She hangs up. Turns to Dunworth, who has plopped himself down in a chair. Facing the desk.)*

DUNWORTH.   Still working the Teladyne deal?

ANGELICA.   We're close. I think I can finalize next week.

DUNWORTH.   You keep this up and you'll make Executive VP in no time.

ANGELICA.   Thanks, but I'm not at the top of the list, in terms of seniority.

DUNWORTH.   You mean Crenshaw and Williamson? They don't have your fire. Your brains, or your ambition. Besides, it would be good to have a woman at the C-level. Maybe shake things up a little around here. And having a minority face in upper management could be great PR for the company.

>*(She stares him down with icy composure.)*

DUNWORTH.   I, um, meant that as a compliment.

ANGELICA. I'm sure you did. So what can I do for you, Mr. Dunworth?

(He takes a deep breath. Puts on his most engaging smile.)

DUNWORTH. Like I said, you're doing a great job. But not everyone around here is. Take Terrance for example. Showed a lot of promise at first, then failed to live up to our expectations.

ANGELICA. He's had an adjustment period. And a new baby on the way.

DUNWORTH. Procreation doesn't trump productivity in this industry. Too much competition gunning for our clients. That's why we decided to let him go.

ANGELICA. I'm sorry to hear that. But what does that have to do with me?

DUNWORTH. We want you to break the news to him.

ANGELICA. Why? Terrance isn't even in my department. Shouldn't HR be handling this?

DUNWORTH. I'm afraid it's a little more delicate than that.

ANGELICA. Because he's black.

DUNWORTH. No. Because you're more of a people person. You can make even bad news sound like a high school pep rally.

ANGELICA. Cross-departmental firings are not in my job description. I'm not sure I'm comfortable with this.

DUNWORTH. No one ever is. But we need it handled quickly and with discretion. That makes you the best person for the job.

ANGELICA. And by discretion, you mean you want your only African-American woman to fire your one other African-American employee?

DUNWORTH. Now don't go playing the race card with me. You've seen his numbers the past three quarters. You know what a mess Terrance made of the Gavin account. Can you honestly tell me the man is pulling his weight?

ANGELICA. ...No...

DUNWORTH. Then if you want to be a high-powered executive, start acting like one. Sometimes you have to get your hands dirty. That's why God invented manicures. And pedicures for when you really have to kick some butt to get your people in line.

DUNWORTH. I told the board they can count on you for this.

ANGELICA. When would I..?

DUNWORTH. End of day. And we want you to have security escort him out of the building. To make sure no client files or offices supplies go with him.

(Angelica looks distraught. Dunworth, now at her door, is all smiles, having passed off an unpleasant task to an underling.)

DUNWORTH. You know, Angelica, You're going to make a great Executive VP someday. If you can learn to make the right choices.

(He exits. Angela leans back in her plush leather chair, bringing her no comfort.)

CURTAIN

Cruel Wit

By
Vin Morreale, Jr.

CAST

Hadley Oliver III — A sarcastic slacker

Antoinette — A sophisticated lady

SETTING

An elegant ballroom in Washington, D.C.

Vin's Notes: This is the only piece in this book which is actually a work in progress. In 2016, I was commissioned to write a play by a theater in Kentucky. I began writing about an eloquent but self-loathing, slacker named Hadley Oliver III, whose disapproving father was running for President. A few months before the deadline, I wrote a comedic scene, which quickly turned into THE KISS ME CURSE, excerpts of which also appear in this book. I loved that new play so much, I submitted that to the theater instead, and it turned out to be a rousing success. I plan to get back to CRUEL WIT soon, because I have pages of Hadley's self-deprecating quips.

*For royalty information and permission to use this scene in a paid performance, please contact **Academy Arts Press** - vin@academyarts.com*

Cruel Wit

AT RISE: The lights come up on HADLEY OLIVER III, *30, roguishly handsome in a casually indifferent sort of way. He wears a tuxedo and leans against a wall, Stage Right, looking anything but interested. Laughter, and the sound of a waltz wafts through the air.* ANTOINETTE, *45, attractive, in a gown, crosses over to him, carried by the lilting music.*

ANTOINETTE. Isn't it a perfectly lovely evening?

HADLEY. It is only lovely because you are here in that perfectly proportioned dress. Your loveliness must be contagious. I assume that is the only thing about you that might be contagious, isn't it?

ANTOINETTE. You are such a tease.

HADLEY. Am I? Good to know. And speaking of knowing, the answer to my previous question would be..?

ANTOINETTE. Come dance with me.

HADLEY. Sorry to say, I have two left feet.

ANTOINETTE. You are such a liar! I happen to know that you are a wonderful dancer.

HADLEY. Then I must have left the right feet at home. Besides, I'm not sure your husband over there would appreciate my sweeping you off your feet with whatever feet I have on me.

ANTOINETTE. I'm sure he wouldn't even notice. Randall seems to be preoccupied with two senators, three potential donors and his fifth bourbon.

HADLEY. Ah, a true congressional cocktail. At least he has the proportion right. Personally, I find politics so much more palatable when diluted with copious amounts of alcohol. And I find politicians only intelligible when they are lubricated to the point of not being able to speak.

ANTOINETTE. Has anyone ever told you that you talk too much?

HADLEY. Only everyone who has ever met me. Fortunately, they are the last ones I would ever pay attention to. Now back to your husband... And that was a suggestion, by the way. Not a sentence fragment.

ANTOINETTE. Why, Mister Oliver. I get the impression you are trying to get rid of me?

HADLEY. On the contrary. I am merely trying to make sure your husband doesn't get the impression I am paying too much attention to his incredibly attractive wife. And wants to make an impression on my forehead with a blunt object.

ANTOINETTE. You needn't worry. Paying attention is not something my husband ever does. Unless there is money to be made, enemies to be humiliated, or cleavage to be drooled over.

HADLEY. How absolutely male of him. Still, you did make the questionable choice to marry the Congressman. Though I assume your cleavage played an ample part in his decision.

ANTOINETTE. How kind of you to notice.

HADLEY. Not at all. I am merely being up front about your...uh, up front. Besides, I admire a woman who knows what she wants and goes after it.

ANTOINETTE. It's good to know you are not frightened by cougars.

HADLEY. Actually, I enjoy the chase, whether I am the prey or the predator. Besides, I never understood why women who go after younger men are called cougars, while men who go after younger women are called...well, men?

ANTOINETTE. Because you control the vocabulary.

HADLEY. You give us too much credit. If men controlled the vocabulary, there would be only four words in the English language... Sex.... Money...

ANTOINETTE. Power... What's the fourth?

HADLEY. More... That pretty much sums up our entire gender. Though it's not our fault, really. It's that damned Y chromosome. As in 'Y' can't I have More? 'Y' can't I have it all?

ANTOINETTE. And why do we have to endure these fundraising events?

HADLEY. I couldn't agree more. These desperate political events are where we try our best at being our worst.

ANTOINETTE. I see you are wearing your cynical pants tonight.

HADLEY. They were on sale. Fifty percent off-putting. Besides, if I can't laugh at other people, why did God make them so terribly flawed in the first place? And speaking of terribly flawed individuals, have I mentioned your husband lately?

ANTOINETTE. Annoyingly often. And the way you are playing hard to get is starting to become tiresome.

HADLEY. Tiresome is what I do best. I am basically Ambien with a sense of humor. Best taken in small doses, and never while operating heavy machinery. Back in school I was voted 'Most Likely to Cause Seizures.'

ANTOINETTE. Really, Hadley. Are you ever serious?

HADLEY. I seriously doubt it.

ANTOINETTE. Well, if you won't dance with me, I expect you to make up for it next Thursday afternoon. Say around three? Your place?

HADLEY. *(Sighs.)* I'll count the minutes.

ANTOINETTE. Come now. We both know you will do anything but that.

CURTAIN

Plain Speakin'- Political Terms

By
Vin Morreale, Jr.

CAST

Joe Bob Dinkel — A redneck TV Host

Announcer — An Offstage Announcer

SETTING

A simple TV studio

Vin's Notes: Radio comedy is a unique form of entertainment, using distinctive voices, phrasing, pacing and well-planned pauses to sell a joke with maximum impact. Here is another sketch with one of my favorite SENSELESS BICKERING COMEDY THEATRE characters, Joe Bob Dinkel. He was a great tool for adding wry commentary about different social entities, mixed with silly puns.

For royalty information and permission to use this scene in a paid performance, please contact **Academy Arts Press** *- vin@academyarts.com*

Plain Speakin' - Political

AT RISE: An aging country gentlemen, JOE BOB DINKEL, sits in a rocking chair facing the audience. To his left, the ANNOUNCER stands before a podium (or may be played as an offstage voice only.)

JOE BOB. This is Joe Bob Dinkel with another lesson in *Plain Speakin'*. Today we're gonna look at some of them there congressional blabber. You know the high-falutin' words elected officials throw at you so's they can make you think they're earnin' their pay? Let's take a listen at a couple.

ANNOUNCER. House of Representatives.

JOE BOB. The fancy homes your congressmen can buy with the money they get from representin' special interest groups.

ANNOUNCER. Misstatement.

JOE BOB. It's a fancy word for a bald-faced lie. I tried to tell the missus I mis-stated myself when she caught me playing poker instead of workin' late. But she didn't buy it.

ANNOUNCER. Special Legislative Session.

JOE BOB. That's when more than four of 'em are awake.

ANNOUNCER. Bill.

JOE BOB. That's what taxpayers get every time congress decides to pass a law.

ANNOUNCER. Decorum.

JOE BOB. It's what dey do to apples. Dey-core-um

ANNOUNCER. Senate chambers.

JOE BOB. It's what every bimbo and Washington page can get into without having to be elected.

ANNOUNCER. Bi-Partisan effort.

JOE BOB.   That's a get-together when legislators can go either way.

ANNOUNCER.   Congressional Ethics.

JOE BOB.   That's one of them there mutually exclusive terms, like jumbo shrimp, army intelligence or a happy marriage.

ANNOUNCER.   Filibuster.

JOE BOB.   That's a cowboy who breaks in female horses.

ANNOUNCER.   Put it in Committee.

JOE BOB.   That's the Bermuda Triangle of Washington. If you want somethin' to disappear, you put it in committee.

ANNOUNCER.   Franking privileges.

JOE BOB.   That's the $150 million in free postage each congressman spends every single year to tell you how he's figurin' ways to balance the budget.

ANNOUNCER.   Re-election.

JOE BOB.   Don't kid yourself, that's the real job of congress, 'n the only one they really care about. This is Joe Bob Dinkel for Plain Speakin'. I'll be talkin' at ya!

CURTAIN

Fishing

By
Vin Morreale, Jr.

CAST

Stan — A laconic husband

Ethel — His depressed wife

SETTING

Their bedroom

Vin's Notes: I often dealt with specific topics in my **Burnng Up The Stage Acting Workshops**..One class concentrated on portraying believable family bonds: Brother-sister, parent-child, husband-wife. Simple gestures, spatial positioning, and even the length of time an actor holds a look can all contribute to a sense of intimacy and comfort witrh the relationship. Offering these acting tips, supported by in-depth character work can make any scene feel authentic. Like many other pieces in this book, this scene also appears in my collection, 150 ACTING SCENES.

*For royalty information and permission to use this scene in a paid performance, please contact **Academy Arts Press** - vin@academyarts.com*

Fishing

AT RISE: A simple bedroom set.

ETHEL.   I'm fat.

STAN.   No, you're not.

ETHEL.   Look at me! I'm two pounds south of grotesque.

STAN.   Here we go again…

ETHEL.   And I'm old. I'm as wrinkled as a prune left in the washing machine for a week.

STAN.   You look fine to me.

ETHEL.   I don't want to look 'fine!' Wines are fine, and they are purple and aged. When you say people look fine, it means they still have a couple of teeth, a little hair, and their breasts are barely dragging on the floor.

STAN.   At least you wouldn't have to sweep the floor as often. That's a plus.

ETHEL.   I hate you. I hate me. I hate my face. Did I mention that I hate you?

STAN.   Consistently. But I love you anyway.

ETHEL.   What could you possibly love about me? I'm a fat, soggy prune with long, saggy boobs.

STAN.   That's not what I see.

ETHEL.   Oh, and what do you see, Mister Glaucoma?

STAN.   I see a woman in the shape of an angel. Someone so far out of my league, who scowls at herself, but always finds a reason to smile at me. Most of the time, anyway. Whose soft, beautiful eyes only sees faults in herself, never in others. I see a dream I had since I was young, miraculously entering my life. And even more miraculously, choosing to stay with me, when anyone with any sense or taste would probably have dumped my sorry butt long ago.

ETHEL. I meant to. I got busy. And there were all those Gilligan's Island reruns to binge watch…

STAN. I see this warm and weird and wonderful bundle of anxieties making my laugh and smile…and making me feel I'm about as blessed as a man can be. That's what I see every time I look at you.

ETHEL. Really?

STAN. Really.

ETHEL. I kind of like the way you lie.

STAN. I kind of like the way you look. Can't help it. You're much too cute to shoot.

ETHEL. You know, that somehow managed to be both sweet and creepy at the same time.

STAN. Poetry was never my thing. Sorry if I ruined the moment.

ETHEL. That's okay. I'll have it written into the Emergency Protection Order.

STAN. It would take more than that to keep me away from you, gorgeous.

ETHEL. Once again. Sweet and creepy. This would be a good time to shut up and kiss me.

STAN. I can't.

ETHEL. Why not?

STAN. Well, you are kind of fat… *(Yelps with pain.)* Ow! I'm kidding! It was a joke. Owww! Stop hitting me! OWWWWWW!

CURTAIN

We Need To Talk

By
Vin Morreale, Jr.

CAST

Allison   A sincere, hard-working woman

Chuck   Her older brother

SETTING

Allison's Living Room

Vin's Notes: Here is another scene from my **Burnng Up The Stage Acting Workshops** dealing with familiarity and intimacy. In this case, a brother and sister, now fully grown and at cross purposes. There are a number of ways each actor can play this scene with varying intensity and emotion. This scene also appears in my collection, 150 ACTING SCENES, carried by Academy Arts Press.

*For royalty information and permission to use this scene in a paid performance, please contact **Academy Arts Press** - vin@academyarts.com*

We Need To Talk

AT RISE: *A cramped living room dominated by a sofa that has clearly seen better days. CHUCK, 42, is watching TV, sharing the sofa with piles of empty beer cans, pizza boxes, papers and the like. His younger sister, ALLISON enters, looking frazzled and embarrassed.*

ALLISON. We need to talk.

CHUCK. Uh oh. That's never a good sign. Can't it wait until after this commercial? I'm a big fan of dancing farm animals.

ALLISON. I'm serious.

CHUCK. I know. That's why I'm being evasive.

ALLISON. You've been sleeping on my couch for five months now...

CHUCK. It's been that long? Seems like only yesterday.

ALLISON. No, yesterday you threw up on my floor. Last week you told the landlady she looked like she got a face transplant from a baboon. And the week before that you tied the cat to the ceiling fan.

CHUCK. Yeah. Good times.

ALLISON. No. They were not good times. Just the same messes I've had to cover for you ever since we were kids.

CHUCK. No one said you have to cover anything for me. I can take care of myself.

ALLISON. Yeah? Then why are you sleeping on my couch? Why haven't you ever been able to hold even the simplest job for more than three weeks?

CHUCK. I can't help it if the people I worked for were all a bunch of...

ALLISON. It's not the people you worked for. (Cutting him off) Every single one of them knew you had a problem. If not when they hired you, they learned pretty quickly after that. I know you have a problem. The only one who doesn't know you have a problem is you. Or at least you don't admit it.

CHUCK. So...what? You gonna lecture me now? Set me straight? Let me know what a worthless piece of crap brother I am? Because I gotta tell ya, sis. You can't make me feel any more worthless than I do already, I guarantee you that. *(Turns back to the TV)* Man, I love this one! Who comes up with these commercials anyway?

ALLISON. *(Carefully.)* I think it is time for you to go.

CHUCK. What? You're kicking me out?

ALLISON. For your own good.

CHUCK. Ha! That's just what Mom and Dad said. Right before they threw me out on the street. Out on the street, with nothing but thirteen bucks in my pocket.

ALLISON. Thirteen bucks? On top of all the wedding silver and Mom's jewelry you stole! You know what it did to Dad to have to take the bus all the way down to that seedy pawn shop to buy back all of Mom's jewelry?

CHUCK. Hey, you think whatever you want, or use whatever kind of excuse, you think you need to, to let yourself feel better about kicking me to the curb.

ALLISON. I'm not kicking you to the curb. There's a rehab clinic out on Sixth Street. I already booked a room for you. They can help...

CHUCK. I don't need rehab, and I don't need your guilt trip! Got it?! I'm outta here.

(He grabs at his clothes strewn about the room. Shoves them into a large black trash bag.)

CHUCK. See ya around. sis. Sorry about peeing on the couch.

(He storms off. She stands there, broken.)

ALLISON. *(Softly.)* That's what families are for...

CURTAIN

In Mysterious Ways

By
Vin Morreale, Jr.

CAST

Chad — A frustrated office worker

Jacqueline — His coworker

SETTING

Chad's office at the end of the business day

Vin's Notes: A number of years ago, I was hired to write, direct and produce a faith-based film for *Inspiration Ink & Picture Company.* The low-budget Christian feature was entitled IN MYSTERIOUS WAYS, and dealt with themes of forgiveness, loss, guilt and redemption. The independent film would go on to win a few BEST PICTURE awards at film festivals around the country.

For royalty information and permission to use this scene in a paid performance, or if you are a Film Producer interested in reading the award-winning screenplay, please contact **Academy Arts Entertainment** *- vin@academyarts.com.*

In Mysterious Ways

AT RISE: An office setting at end of day. JACQUELINE appears in the doorway, seeing CHAD hard at work.)

JACQUELINE. Hey, workaholic. You forget how to read a clock?

CHAD. What?

JACQUELINE. It's almost six-thirty. And you know how the head office hates to pay overtime.

CHAD. Just a few more things to finish up.

JACQUELINE. So what are your 'big plans' for the weekend?

CHAD. *(Without looking up.)* A little yard work. Watch the game. Fall asleep before I realize how desperately boring my life has become...

JACQUELINE. Quite a weekend.

CHAD. It's not as much fun as it sounds.

JACQUELINE. Why don't you take the wife out for a nice romantic evening?

CHAD. Katy's off on yet another short-term mission trip this week. Florida. Sun, surf and Scriptures...and a hundred teens on spring break.

JACQUELINE. Gospel gone wild, huh?

CHAD. *(With an edge.)* She does good work. *(Closes his laptop.)* There. That should make Wolford happy.

JACQUELINE. Look, Chad. A bunch of us are going out for a bite to eat. It's Debbie's birthday.

(She's a little too close. He looks away.)

CHAD. Be sure to wish her Happy Birthday for me.

JACQUELINE. Afraid to have a little fun?

CHAD. I'm married, Jacqueline. That means I'm not allowed to have fun anymore. *(Catches himself.)* I...uh, didn't mean that to come out as pitiful as it sounded...

JACQUELINE. Exactly how pitiful did you mean it to sound?

CHAD. I'm just tired. It's great. It really is. Marriage, I mean.

JACQUELINE. Except when your wife runs off to play soulmate to everyone else in the world but you.

CHAD. It's not like that.

JACQUELINE. I'm sure it's not. But you're home all alone... And after a while your mind begins to wander a bit. *(Her gaze wanders off.)* And you start thinking about how quiet the house is... and what you could have been doing if you had made different choices... *(Sees Chad's reaction.)* Uh-oh. Touched a nerve.

CHAD. *(Carefully.).* It's time to go, Jacqueline.

(He stands. Gathers his papers. She moves over to him.)

JACQUELINE. You're human, Chad. There's nothing wrong with that.

CHAD. I am not having this discussion with you.

JACQUELINE. We're just talking, that's all. *(Softly.)* But admit it, don't you get that little extra thrill when some stranger smiles at you for no reason at all? When your eyes meet, and they don't look away? How they let you know... with just their eyes... that they find you interesting. Maybe even attractive...

(He hesitates. Grabs his jacket.)

CHAD. See you Monday, Jacqueline.

JACQUELINE. What if Katy feels the same way, Chad? Down there in Florida... hundreds of miles away from her husband?

CHAD. Katy's not like that.

JACQUELINE. Are you sure?

CHAD. *(Firmly.)* She's not.

JACQUELINE. It's perfectly normal, Chad. We all need to feel wanted now and then. *(Her expression turns inward,)* You think you have the perfect relationship, but then you begin to take each other for granted. The excitement slips away and before you know it, you become almost invisible… *(Her eyes moisten.)* …or worse, an annoyance. A constant source of annoyance to someone who swore they'd love you forever…

(An uncomfortable pause.)

CHAD. *(Gently.)* Good night, Jacqueline.

(She is startled by the sound of his voice, lost in a distant memory. She quickly recovers. Tries to cover her embarrassment with a smile.)

CHAD. I said, Good Night…

(She nods. Wipes her eyes with her palm, as she moves to the doorway.)

JACQUELINE.   I'll give Debbie your best.

CHAD. You do that.

(He watches her walk out the door.)

CHAD. *(Softly.)* Yeah. You do that.

(He hesitates, then turns out the light and exits.)

CURTAIN

In Mysterious Ways – 2

By
Vin Morreale, Jr.

CAST

Chad — A bitter widower

Dr. Carelli — His doctor and friend

SETTING

A doctor's examination room

Vin's Notes: IN MYSTERIOUS WAYS tells the story of an increasingly bitter man who distances himself from everyone and everything after losing his wife. Only gradually, do we learn the details of his guilt and isolation. Having a character know important events that the audience has yet to learn can add a wonderfully complex subtlety to an actor's performance.

*For royalty information and permission to use this scene in a paid performance, or if you are a Film Producer interested in reading the award-winning screenplay, please contact **Academy Arts Entertainment** - vin@academyarts.com.*

In Mysterious Ways - 2

AT RISE: DR. CARELLI, 50, with glasses and perfectly groomed white hair. He is extremely professional, but his expression reveals a deep concern and previous friendship with Chad. Dr. Carelli sighs as he jots down a few notes on Chad's chart.

DR. CARELLI. Well, Chad. You don't look too bad, considering.

CHAD. Considering.

DR. CARELLI. And how are you doing otherwise?

(Chad pulls his shirt back on.)

CHAD. So, Mrs. Lincoln, other than that messy business with your husband, how did you like the play?

DR. CARELLI. What I meant to say was…Have you been able to process these feelings about your wife?

(Chad throws him a look of icy hatred.)

CHAD. There's nothing to 'process.' Katy lied. She said she'd love me forever, but forever only lasted…

DR. CARELLI. Katy didn't lie, Chad. *(Gently.)* She died… There's a difference.

(A pause as he struggles with this truth. Then his face hardens.)

CHAD. Not to me.

(The doctor takes a hard look at him, then scribbles a name on a prescription pad.)

DR. CARELLI. Here's the name of someone I want you to see. He may be able to help.

CHAD. Another specialist?

DR. CARELLI. A minister.

CHAD. You know, you can get in a lot of trouble for proselytizing on the job, doc. Separation of church and stethoscope, and all that.

DR. CARELLI. So sue me. That is… AFTER you get better.

CHAD. C'mon, doc…

(Chad gets off the table and leaves the office.)

CHAD. We both know that ain't gonna happen.

DR. CARELLI. *(Gently.)* Have a little faith, Chad.

CHAD. Yeah, like that ever helped anyone…

CURTAIN

In Mysterious Ways - 3

By
Vin Morreale, Jr.

CAST

Chad — A bitter widower

Katy — The ghost of his wife

SETTING

A hospital room

Vin's Notes: In this last excerpt from IN MYSTERIOUS WAYS, Chad is near death, lying in a hospital room, when he is visited by his deceased wfe, who may or may not be a delusion. My lead actors Scott R. Davis and Karen Boles played the scene with touching sensitivity. You can see a trailer for the film here: https://www.youtube.com/watch?v=7F-10b3zMSk

*For royalty information and permission to use this scene in a paid performance, or if you are a Film Producer interested in reading the award-winning screenplay, please contact **Academy Arts Entertainment** - vin@academyarts.com.*

In Mysterious Ways - 3

AT RISE: A hospital room. Chad, near death, opens his eyes to see... KATY, his dead wife, sitting by the side of his bed.

CHAD. Katy?

KATY. I remember those last moments. Those last cold breaths. I was scared. Desperate. But then there you were. Standing over me. Squeezing my hand. And even though I felt everything slipping away, I could sense that you were suffering more than I was. And you were even more scared to be living than I was to be dying. Then suddenly I remembered how much you meant to me. And I...I forgave you.

CHAD. *(Softly.)* You shouldn't have.

KATY. I couldn't say the words, because I was already slipping away. But I forgave you...and it filled me with this incredible peace.

CHAD. I saw it in your face. I saw it in your eyes as you died.

KATY. I know.

CHAD. It would have been easier if you hated me... hated me for what I did to you. How I let you down...

KATY. If you're looking for forgiveness, you will have to look elsewhere, Chad. You already have mine.

CHAD. It's not enough.

KATY. I know.

CHAD. Will...will I feel the same peace when I die?

KATY. That's up to you, Chad. That's up to you...

CURTAIN

Here to Help

By
Vin Morreale, Jr.

CAST

Timothy   A bitter and depressed man

Oldham   A Counselor

SETTING

A cramped Counselling Office

Vin's Notes: Sometimes you just want to thrw out a crazy concept and see if it flies. This was a fun little scene that accomplishes the task of surprising the audience with a little twist. You can find it in my book 150 ACTING SCENES.

*For royalty information and permission to use this scene in a paid performance, please contact **Academy Arts Press** - vin@academyarts.com*

VIN MORREALE, JR.

Here to Help

AT RISE: A small counselling office. OLDHAM sits behind his grey metal desk. A nervous TIMOTHY is perched on a chair facing him.

TIMOTHY.   So how do we do this?

OLDHAM.   That depends on the statement you want to make.

TIMOTHY.   The statement? What statement?

OLDHAM.   Something like this always makes a statement. You want to be remembered. You want to get back at all those who were mean to you. All the people who didn't appreciate you enough.

TIMOTHY.   Well, yeah.

OLDHAM.   You want them to feel guilty. You want the world to realize that you were way too good for it.

TIMOTHY.   Okay. That sounds good. Nobody appreciated me, and I am too good for the world. Way too good.

OLDHAM.   No doubt. And everyone will realize that once this is over.

FIRST ACTOR: Especially my exes. They all better realize that.

OLDHAM.   *(Writing a note.)* Anguish for the Exes. Check.

TIMOTHY.   I mean I want them to really cry. Rend their clothes and gnash their teeth. Real Old Testament-type wailing. Make them feel miserable for years. Decades!

OLDHAM.   Hmmm. Miserable for decades usually requires something dramatic.

TIMOTHY.   What do you mean, dramatic?

OLDHAM.   Something messy. And really, really painful.

TIMOTHY.   Ulp, Is that necessary?

OLDHAM.   If you want decades of unrelenting guilt and sorrow, then yes.

TIMOTHY.   How painful are we talking about?

OLDHAM. Well, we have lots of options. We can throw your body into an industrial woodchipper. Have you fall over a guard rail at the zoo and be devoured by hungry lions or polar bears. Swallow a half-bottle of Drano. Have you dragged under the wheels of a semi-truck for half a mile, or so. You know, the old standards.

TIMOTHY. I'm not sure any of those work for me. I'm not real good with pain.

OLDHAM. Then you may want one of our Premiere Options. Messy, but Instantaneous.

TIMOTHY. How instantaneous?

OLDHAM. You never see it coming. And you're dead before you know it.

TIMOTHY. That doesn't sound too bad. Give me a few examples.

OLDHAM. Falling down an elevator shaft. Accidental clothesline decapitation. Grenade in your underwear drawer.

TIMOTHY. Won't all of those make me look a little…I don't know…stupid?

OLDHAM. Probably. But you'll be splattered into a million pieces. You won't care.

TIMOTHY. Maybe this wasn't such a great idea...

OLDHAM. Hey, you're the one who called the Suicide Hot Line!

TIMOTHY. But I thought you guys were supposed to talk me out of committing suicide.

OLDHAM. That's a common misconception many people have. Now, back to the business at hand. How do you feel about razor blades and poisonous snakes?

TIMOTHY. No way. This all sounds terrible! I would rather live and be miserable than listen to your crazy ideas about killing myself! I'm outta here! (Exits)

OLDHAM. *(Smiling.)* Works every time.

CURTAIN

No Gas

By Vin Morreale, Jr.

CAST

Virginia — An older woman

Bud — Her elderly suitor

SETTING

An empty stage with two chairs

Vin's Notes: With the nearly one thousand original scenes and monologues I have written to date, I have tried to apportion a certain number for actors of every age group. This is especially needed for actors who age out of most lead roles as the years go by. This short scene allows senior actors an opportunity to play age-appropriate romantic interactions. Remember, you are never too old to be cute or loving! You can also find this scene in *BURNING UP THE STAGE: Monologues, Short Scenes & Audition pieces for Actors From Six to Seventy,* which is carried by Dramatic Publishing.

FOR ROYALTY INFORMATION, OR TO REQUEST A COPY OF
BURNING UP THE STAGE, PLEASE CONTACT **DRAMATIC PUBLISHING** -
dramaticpublishing.com/authors/profile/view/url/vin-morreale-jr

No Gas

AT RISE: *Lights come up on a nearly empty set. Downstage Center sits the only piece of furniture – a bench seat from an old sedan. On it sit VIRGINIA and BUD, both in their mid-Sixties, dressed up in nice clothes suggesting a decade past.*

Bud pantomimes driving a car, while Virginia appears to be pressed as far as possible on the opposite side of the bench seat. He steals a few subtle glances at her, then turns the invisible steering wheel, as if pulling off to the side of the road.

VIRGINIA. What's the matter?

BUD. Damn it.

VIRGINIA. What's the matter? Why are we pulling over?

BUD. *(He gestures as if turning off the ignition.)* We're out of gas.

VIRGINIA. Out of gas?

BUD. That's right.

VIRGINIA. Hmm. My dates used to try to pull that trick on me five decades ago... I didn't fall for it then, either.

BUD. I'm telling you the truth.

VIRGINIA. I'm sure.

BUD. What do you want me to do? I don't have any gas!

VIRGINIA. I bet that's a first for you, Bud Filson.

BUD. Give me a break, will ya?

VIRGINIA. *(Looks out her window.)* Why is it men only seem to run out of gas on some dark, deserted road?

BUD. What are you implying?

VIRGINIA. I'm not implying anything. Just making an observation. Women run out of gas on the freeway, or at the shopping center. But men, no, you men always manage to find the most isolated, romantic settings to run out of gas.

BUD. You don't believe me, do you?

VIRGINIA. *(Facetiously.)* Gee, and I thought I was being so subtle.

BUD. Why don't you believe me?

VIRGINIA. Well, for one thing, the gas gauge shows you have more than half a tank.

BUD. It's broken.

VIRGINIA. Broken?

BUD. Uh-huh.

VIRGINIA. Want me to fix it?

BUD. Excuse me?

VIRGINIA. My first boyfriend used to run a service station.

BUD. Really?

VIRGINIA. You bet. I can pop that sucker out and set it right in no time. Got any tools?

BUD. *(Too quickly.)* No! No. uh, I mean...no tools.

VIRGINIA. You're telling me you drive around in this beat up, old death trap, and you don't even carry a screwdriver?

BUD. What kind of screwdriver do you need?

VIRGINIA. A regular flat-head will do.

BUD. Sorry.

VIRGINIA. What if I had said a Phillip's screwdriver?

BUD. Don't have that either.

VIRGINIA. You have no tools at all in this car?

BUD. No tools. No gas. No luck.

VIRGINIA. And I assume you don't have a cell phone?

BUD. Sorry.

VIRGINIA. Well then, I guess we're lucky I always carry my phone and Triple-A card with me. *(Starts to rummage through her purse.)* That's funny... I could've sworn I put it in my purse before we walked out the door...

BUD. Probably left them with my tool kit.

VIRGINIA. Very funny.

(He sighs contentedly, leans back in his seat and stares up through the windshield.)

BUD. Well, looks like we're going to be here until someone drives by this dark, lonely road...

(He smiles, casually mimes the motion of undoing his seat belt.)

VIRGINIA. What did you do that for?

BUD. Do what?

VIRGINIA. Unfasten your seat belt. Why did you unfasten your seat belt just now?

BUD. Well, we're stuck here. I figured...I don't know... we might as well get a little more comfortable.

VIRGINIA. I'm comfortable enough, thank you.

BUD. How could you be? You're plastered to that passenger's side door like one of those suction-cup stuffed toys people stick on their car windows!

VIRGINIA. I'll take that as a compliment. Besides, a man doesn't unfasten his belt in front of a lady.

BUD. Damn it, Virginia! It was just my seat belt. I wasn't trying to moon you! *(Changing tactics.)* Why don't you just relax... slide over here a bit, and let's enjoy this lovely summer's evening.

VIRGINIA. Oh, great. Now it starts...

BUD. What starts?

VIRGINIA. You. The belt. The smooth moves. I bet a dollar you even have a new bottle of Old Spice in your glove compartment.

BUD. I do not!

VIRGINIA. Oh, really?

> *(She reaches for the glove compartment and he stops her. Hesitates. Then fishes a crumpled dollar bill from his jacket pocket. Tosses it to her.)*

BUD. Okay, here!

VIRGINIA. Thank you. (She carefully straightens the crumpled bill, then folds it into her purse.)

BUD. This date isn't working out so well, is it?

VIRGINIA. Gee, and I thought I was being subtle.

BUD. You already used that line.

VIRGINIA. I know. I was so proud of it, I thought I'd use it again.

BUD. C'mon, Virginia... Loosen up. We're both collecting Social Security these days. It's not like a little romance is going to give you a bad reputation...

> *(She hesitates, then slips off her own seat belt. But still sits pressed against her side of the seat.)*

BUD. You look beautiful in the moonlight.

VIRGINIA. Helps hide the wrinkles.

BUD. Cut that out. Why not just you enjoy the stars?

VIRGINIA. Little lights in the sky. I've seen them.

BUD. You're not making this easy on me, are you?

VIRGINIA. 'Easy' is not a word that should apply to a lady on a first date.

> *(Bud grumbles something under his breath.)*

VIRGINIA. What was that?!

BUD. Nothing...

VIRGINIA. No, I definitely heard you say something. What was it?

BUD. *(Grumbling.)* I said I should've asked out the Widow Millford, instead!

VIRGINIA. Constance Millford? You wanted to ask Constance Millford out on a date? That woman could freeze Ben Gay!

BUD. As opposed to the icicles dripping off the dashboard right now?

(She glares at him angrily, then relents.)

VIRGINIA. Oh, all right... you horny old goat. Here's my shoulder. Come get your thrills. But no heart attack! I'm not in the mood for CPR.

(She slides over on the car seat and leans against him. He smiles and throws an affectionate arm around her shoulder, as they both look up at the stars.)

BUD. No heart attack. I promise... You know, it's not just a line. You really do look beautiful in the moonlight.

VIRGINIA. I know. I should have been a vampire.

BUD. Well, if you ever need a victim..?

VIRGINIA. You'd offer me your neck?

BUD. In a heartbeat. Veins and all.

VIRGINIA. That's the single sweetest... and most disgusting thing anyone has ever said to me.

BUD. Thank you.

VIRGINIA. *(Sighing.)* I needed this tonight...

BUD. I know.

(She looks up into his eyes, kisses him tenderly. Then snuggles into his arms.)

BUD. What was that for?

VIRGINIA. This was a really good idea, Bud. You haven't taken me parking since 1952... But you really have to work on that gas gauge story. You nearly blew the whole thing.

BUD. You always were more observant than me, Virginia.

VIRGINIA. Maybe next week we can go skinny dipping down by Old Miller's Pond. You know, like we used to?

BUD. *(Pretending to be shocked.)* Why, Virginia Filson! If I hadn't been married to you for nearly half a century now, I'd swear you were turning into a loose woman.

VIRGINIA. Only with you, sweetheart. Only with you.

(She kisses him again.)

BUD. The kids think we're crazy, you know.

VIRGINIA. The hell with the kids.

BUD. Virginia!

VIRGINIA. Just shut up and enjoy the stars, Bud.

BUD. Anything you say, darlin'.

(They both sit back and snuggle as the lights dim.)

CURTAIN

Captive Christmas

By
Vin Morreale, Jr.

CAST

Bernie   A slightly deranged kidnapper

Five   A department store Santa

SETTING

A dark alley

Vin's Notes: I was encouraged to create a different kind of holiday play for the newly birthed San Francisco Playwrights Center, which I had the honor to help found along with Bill Lees, Harry Hatyer and four other talented writers. So I created this two-act comedy about a disturbed man who kidnaps street corner Santa Clauses on Christmas Eve, in order to recreate a traumatic scene from his childhood. The San Francisco Playwrights Center put on CAPTIVE CHRISTMAS two years in a row, one of the only tites they ever repeated.

For royalty information and permission to use this scene in a paid performance, or to request a full copy of CAPTIVE CHRISTMAS, please contact **Academy Arts Press** *-* vin@academyarts.com

Captive Christmas

AT RISE: The curtain remains closed. The stage is in darkness, as offstage voices are heard.

BERNIE. *(Offstage.)* Come on, move it! Through here. Let's go!

FIVE. *(Offstage.)* Look, buddy, I...

BERNIE. *(Offstage.)* I said move it!

FIVE. *(Offstage.)* You're making a big mistake here...

BERNIE. *(Offstage.)* If you don't stop stalling, you ain't never gonna see New Years, capiche?

FIVE. *(Offstage.)* But I'm not...

BERNIE. *(Offstage.)* Capiche?!

FIVE. *(Offstage.)* Uh... yeah. I capiche...

BERNIE. *(Offstage.)* Then move it!

FIVE. *(Offstage.)* I just want to know something.

BERNIE. *(Offstage.)* What's that?

FIVE. *(Offstage.)* Why me?

BERNIE. *(Offstage.)* Maybe I just like the way you dress...

(The two enter through the audience from the back of the theater. BERNIE is a short, stocky man in his early thirties, with a dark hair and sinister expression. He is dressed in a black muscle shirt and sports an erratic haircut that could only be self-inflicted. He is prodding the other man toward the stage with a large automatic pistol. FIVE, his kidnapping victim, stumbles forward, because of his blind-fold. Five is a mild-mannered man in his early forties, dressed like Santa Claus.)

BERNIE. Watch your feet, man!

FIVE. Whatta you expect with this blindfold on?

BERNIE. Look. Any more whining outa you and it's gonna be Silent Night. You hear me?! *(Softening.)* I don't know why you're complaining anyway. You think I like doing this?

FIVE. Excuse me?

BERNIE. You think I like doing this? You think this brings me any joy?

FIVE. Well, actually...

BERNIE. Well, I don't! I mean, if I got caught, what jury in the world is gonna sympathize with a guy who kidnaps street corner Santas on Christmas Eve, huh? Tell me that, huh?!

FIVE. Then why..?

BERNIE. I mean, it's like you kidnap anybody else and you're a big shot terrorist or a hardened criminal. They show your picture on the Nightly News and Entertainment Tonight. You get like twenty-four hour cable news coverage on CNN and MS-Hey-Look-At-Me. Plus all the buddy letters from head cases all over the world.

FIVE. Look, I'm sorry, but...

BERNIE. Hey, I even heard about this guy who's thing was blowing up Porta-Potties. Don't ask me why. After he splatters his tenth Porta-potty, ISIS 'fiends' him on Facebook. Talk about your fifteen minutes of fame...

FIVE. I don't even like to use Porta-potties. Really, I...

BERNIE. You're missing the big picture here. It's not about kabooming a canned crapper. It's about the notoriety. Psycho street cred. Feeding the media beast. Finding your niche among the nutjobs. You know, standing out. It's not as easy as it sounds, let me tell ya...

FIVE. You have my sympathy. But if you let me...

BERNIE. So Porta-potty boy gets his own fan website...even after that embarrassing premature detonation incident and the thirteen surgeries to remove plastic seat fragments from his face and buttocks... But just try and swipe a Santa and they think there's something wrong with you.

(Shoves him with the gun.)

BERNIE. That's what you think, ain't it? You think something's wrong with me, don't you? Admit it!

FIVE. Hey, I just...

BERNIE. Damned right you do!

FIVE. Really, I know you're upset about something, but I just want to...

BERNIE. Everyone'd think it was 'cause of my childhood or something. That's what they'd all think... Yeah. Like maybe when I was twelve and like my old man mighta put a mousetrap in my Christmas stocking as a joke...

FIVE. A mousetrap?

BERNIE. I'm not saying he did! It's just that, y'know, maybe that's what you might think they'd think. Or maybe they'd say my old man mighta gone hunting on Christmas Eve and brought back a deer he shot... tied it up all tight and bloody on the roof of our old brown station wagon, and y'know, maybe told us kids we was gonna have Donner or Blitzen for Christmas dinner, and us being young and not knowing any better might have believed him...

FIVE. Donner and Blitzen for dinner..?

BERNIE. I'm not saying he done that! I'm just saying that's maybe what they'd think, is all...Or some fancy pants psychologist who ain't never even been to reform school might say that maybe my old man could've gift wrapped a hot watch and then kept his mouth shut when they arrested me for possession of stolen goods and I had to spend my entire Christmas vacation in county lock-up... *(Shudders.)* Sheeesh. You should'a seen the look on Ma's face...

FIVE. Boy, you sure had a rough...

BERNIE. Not that he woulda done any of those things! I mean, my old man, he was okay, y'know?

FIVE. *(Dubiously.)* Uh-huh.

BERNIE. Maybe just a strange sense of humor is all.

FIVE. No kidding.

BERNIE. *(Suddenly cheerful.)* But enough whining. This is Christmas Eve! *(Menacingly.)* Get inside the basement, Santa!

FIVE. Listen, friend. I'm not the real Santa... and I'm not your father...

BERNIE. Don't you say nothin' about my old man!

FIVE. Sure, I just...

BERNIE. You hear what I'm saying?!

FIVE. I only meant...

BERNIE. Just don't say nothin' against my old man, is all.

FIVE. All I meant was... What have you got against me?

BERNIE. *(Reciting.)* Paranoid schizophrenia which manifests itself in the transference or projection of feelings of hostility toward potentially innocent and otherwise uninvolved people.

(Five stares at him in disbelief.)

BERNIE. *(Shrugs.)* I read that in a book somewhere.

FIVE. Remind me to pick up a copy.

BERNIE. Now get in there, elf boy!

CURTAIN

Otherwise Engaged

By
Vin Morreale, Jr.

CAST

Rachel   A very excited woman

Marcus   Her less enthusiastic best friend

SETTING

A blank stage.

Vin's Notes: New materials are invaluable for demo reels, audition pieces, or simply to stretch an actor's abilities by trying on a wider variety of roies than he or she might normally be offered. With limited time to teach, I compiled hundreds of my acting class materials in the books 300 MONOLOGUES and 150 ACTING SCENES. This piece is taken from 150 ACTING SCENES.

*For royalty information and permission to use this scene in a paid performance, please contact **Academy Arts Press** - vin@academyarts.com*

Otherwise Engaged

AT RISE: A sparse set. RACHEL bounces on like she's ready to burst with excitement. She immediately hugs MARCUS, who clearly does not share her enthusiasm.

RACHEL.   Guess what!

MARCUS.   You're getting married.

RACHEL.   What? Who told you?

MARCUS.   Nobody told me. Nobody had to.

RACHEL.   Then how did you know?

MARCUS.   That silly grin on your face. That thrilled-to-death, semi-terrified, what-am-I-getting-myself-into look that says your life is about to change and you're not quite sure if you are ready for it.

RACHEL.   It shows, huh?

MARCUS.   was never your strong suit. Who is it this time?

RACHEL.   What do you mean, 'this time?'

MARCUS.   Do I have to mention 2012? 2015? The two different engagements in 2017. And don't forget that head-over-heels romance last May?

RACHEL.   Okay. Okay! I fall in love easily. Is that my fault?

MARCUS.   Depends on your perspective. What do you say we ask 2012, 2015, the two in 2017, and…?

RACHEL.   I don't know why I tell you anything. Can't you just be happy for me?

MARCUS.   Of course, I'm happy for you. I'm always happy for you. The only one happier than me is the jewelry store that your love life is single handedly keeping in business.

RACHEL.   You think I'm making another mistake?

MARCUS. Don't ask me that. Ask me to throw you a party. Ask me to help you pick out wedding invitations. But please don't ask me if you are making a mistake…

RACHEL. Why?

MARCUS. Because then I'd have to tell you the truth…and we don't want to start all that again.

RACHEL. You don't have to be like that.

MARCUS. I'm trying not to be.

RACHEL. Look. You know how I feel…

MARCUS. I know. It's okay. I was 2012, and that was a long time ago. A very long time ago… So, you go get married and live happily ever after. And I'll just…I don't know…go on living, I guess.

RACHEL. I love you, you know.

MARCUS. I know. *(Smiles sadly)* But I have to go now…

(He turns to exit.)

MARCUS. Congratulations, by the way. *(Exits)*

CURTAIN

Exit Interview

By
Vin Morreale, Jr.

CAST

Natalie — A talented businesswoman

Plotkin — Her boss

SETTING

A business office

Vin's Notes: This piece from my book 150 ACTING SCENES combines some of the my favorite scene devices: strong women, fast resolution and a twist ending. It is also helpful to expand a director's and actor's vision of casting by not limiting these roles to certain age groups, looks or ethnicities.

*For royalty information and permission to use this scene in a paid performance, please contact **Academy Arts Press** - vin@academyarts.com*

Exit Interview

AT RISE: *A modern day office. PLOTKIN organizes files strewn across his large desk, as NATALIE enters.*

NATALIE. You wanted to see me?

PLOTKIN. Yes, Natalie. Please sit down. Tell me, Natalie…are you happy here?

NATALIE. You're kidding, right?

PLOTKIN. Yes Excuse me?

NATALIE. I've been one of the hardest working employees you ever had. I put in overtime almost every week. The quality of my work is the highest in this department.

PLOTKIN. Yes All that has been noted in your annual reviews.

NATALIE. How kind of you. But I bet there's nothing in my file about how I have covered for your mistakes all these years. Or anything about me making you look even close to competent, which is really the hardest part of my job.

PLOTKIN. Yes I'm detecting a bit of hostility here, Natalie.

NATALIE. Really? Too bad you didn't detect it after you passed me over for a raise six years in a row. Or when you promoted your nephew Benjamin over me. Even though he's only been working here four months and has the IQ of a brain-damaged lemur.

PLOTKIN. Yes You'll be happy to know Benjamin was let go this morning. It seems he alienated our biggest client with some…um, inappropriate social media comments and photos.

NATALIE. I know. That's the reason they decided to take their entire account in-house, and then hire me to run the department. It seems they are making me a Vice President at nearly twice the salary I make here. So, you can consider this my exit interview, as well as my two-minute notice. *(Standing)* Have a nice day!

CURTAIN

The Carrie Variations

By
Vin Morreale, Jr.

CAST

Carrie — An impatient middle-aged woman

Danielle — A younger woman applying for a job

SETTING

A cabin away from town

Vin's Notes: One of my favorite concept plays. I wrote a twist-filled mystery one-act called RUTHLESS WHEN NECESSARY with two strong female leads. I then wanted to see if I could use the same setting and premise, same characters and even some of the same lines to create an entirely different plot. It worked so well, I tried it a third time, to see if I could turn these dark stories into a comedy. I put all three together as THE CARRIE VARIATIONS, and it was a huge success in its premier at Kentucky's legendary Alley Theater.

For royalty information and permission to use this scene in a paid performance, or to request a full copy of THE CARRIE VARIATIONS, please contact **Academy Arts Press** *- vin@academyarts.com*

The Carrie Variations

AT RISE: Open on a small, simply dressed den with a stuffy, rustic appeal. Upstage Center is a wooden coffee table bordered on either side by old upholstered furniture angling outward toward Downstage. The furniture consists of a large, well-used recliner on the Stage Right side, and a mismatching, and equally tattered love seat angling out from the Stage Left side. You can almost smell the musty odor rising from these worn and faded pieces. The only other piece of furniture is a rickety and uncomfortable wooden chair sitting Downstage Center, facing the Stage Right recliner. There are no paintings or artwork on the wall, giving little clue to the taste or history of the occupant. The room is dim and empty, the only light coming from the sliver of moonlight through the window, and the soft blue glow of the computer monitor on the Stage Right credenza. Along the Stage Right wall, a heavy curtain obscures a window, leaking only a sliver of moonlight onto the set. The Stage Left wall holds the exterior door, angled so the audience can see whoever is standing in the doorway. At the moment, the door is closed and secured with a chain and two deadbolt locks. The thick silence of the set is shattered by a loud, firm KNOCK on the Stage Left door.

CARRIE. *(From Offstage.)* Hold on a minute!

(CARRIE rushes on through the Stage Right doorway and hits the light switch. The lights flicker on as she spins around the room, making sure everything is in place. Carrie is in her mid-fifties, wearing little make-up, and upscale casual clothes of muted color. Only her expensive, heirloom earrings offer a clue to her personality. She flits around the room, making no attempt to answer the door. Another KNOCK.)

CARRIE. *(Yelling.)* I said Hold on! I'm coming!

(Again, she makes no attempt to answer the door. Instead, she bends to adjust something hidden under the loveseat. After a pause, there's another KNOCK, even more tentative.)

Two Character Chaos

(Carrie angrily stomps to the door and unlatches all the deadbolts and chains. She throws open the door and glares at DANIELLE, 26. A cheap purse draped over her shoulder and a black notebook clutched to her chest.)

CARRIE. What the hell is your problem?!

DANIELLE. I...I'm sorry. I...

CARRIE. Sentences! If you are going to communicate with me, I demand that you speak in full sentences.

DANIELLE. Okay. *(Catching herself.)* I mean, yes. I will. Uh, I will be happy to speak to you in full sentences.

(In contrast to Carrie, Danielle is all sunny colors and optimism. She wears a simple, but attractive sundress. Carrie appraises her with little warmth. Then only reluctantly allows her to enter the room.)

CARRIE. You're late.

DANIELLE. I don't think so.

CARRIE. Then you're late, and you clearly don't think clearly. That's two strikes against you.

DANIELLE. I'm sorry. I mean... I'm not even sure if I'm in the right place?

CARRIE. If you're the right person, then you're in the right place. If you're not the right person, then not only are you late and don't think clearly, but you are also a complete waste of my time. Take a seat.

(Danielle looks around, and then chooses the loveseat as Carrie crosses Stage Right to adjust the angle of the computer monitor again. She turns to see Danielle perched on the end of the loveseat.)

CARRIE. Not there! *(Points to the rickety wooden chair.)* There!

DANIELLE. *(Moving to the less comfortable chair.)* Sorry. Uh, let me introduce myself. My name is...

CARRIE. Ssssh!

DANIELLE. As I was saying, I'm...

CARRIE. Shush!

DANIELLE. What?

CARRIE. Ssssh. Shush. Shut up! Can I make myself any less obtuse?

DANIELLE. I'm just trying to tell you my name.

CARRIE. Listen. I don't need to know you're name. I don't need to know your birthday, your favorite color, or even your favorite sexual position! All I need to know is if you have what it takes.

DANIELLE. *(Nervously)* I do.

CARRIE. You don't sound very confident.

DANIELLE. I do. I have what it takes.

CARRIE. We'll see. Now shut your mouth and let me look at you.

(Carrie stares at Danielle as if she was a bug under a microscope. Circles her chair. Stops. Shakes her head.)

DANIELLE. I uh, brought a resume and a portfolio.

CARRIE. Great. Let me see it.

(Danielle hands her the binder. Carrie tosses it Upstage without even looking at it.)

DANIELLE. Hey! That's mine!

CARRIE. Then why would you give it away so easily? If you don't treat your possessions like they have any value, why should anybody else?

DANIELLE. But I gave it to you to look at. To see what I've done.

CARRIE. Get this straight, sweetheart. What you've done means less than nothing to me. It's what you do from this point on that counts. I don't care about your past mistakes or personal affairs. Your little girl fantasies of growing up to be a ballerina or an astronaut. I care about the here and now, and whether you can perform as required. Now shut up and let me look at you. (Long pause. Shakes her head.) You are not at all what I was expecting.

DANIELLE. Is that good or bad?

CARRIE. It's not good.

(Carrie continues to circle her chair, making a series of disparaging noises under her breath. She pulls a small notepad from her pocket and starts scribbling in it.)

CARRIE. Uh-huh…well, maybe I can work with that…nope.. not at all…

DANIELLE. Can you just tell me if you're the woman who..?

CARRIE. Yes.

DANIELLE. The one who put the…?

CARRIE. That's why you're here, isn't it? (Scribbles a flurry of notes.) Uh-huh…uh-huh…

DANIELLE. What are you writing?

CARRIE. What is this obsession you have with talking?

DANIELLE. Obsession with talking? I'm just trying to figure out what the hell is going on here!

CARRIE. You haven't figured that out yet? Hmmm. Not a good sign. *(Makes a few more notes.)*

DANIELLE. Maybe I should just leave…

CARRIE. Maybe you should.

(A pause. Then Danielle gets up and heads toward the door.)

CARRIE. Sit the fuck down and keep your pretty little mouth shut!

(Danielle is startled, as she scrambles back to the chair. Carrie returns to making notes, as if nothing has happened.)

CARRIE. Okay. Not too tragic…Ummm-hmmm. (Shoves the notepad back into her pocket and smiles.) Well, that about covers it!

DANIELLE. Covers what?

CARRIE. *(Shrugs.)* Still not thinking clearly. Again…not a good sign. (Pulls out the notepad for one more scribble.)

DANIELLE. Okay, I don't know what your game is, but this is getting way too schizo for me. I'm outta here.

(She stands and crosses to the Stage Left door.)

DANIELLE. This has been one complete waste of cab fare. (To Carrie.) Have a nice meltdown.

CARRIE. *(Casually drops into the recliner.)* I am prepared to pay you six hundred and fifty thousand dollars for your services.

DANIELLE. *(Pauses, her hand on the doorknob.)* Did you say six..?

CARRIE. …hundred and fifty thousand. Cash. You can walk out of here with it tonight. But only if you're the right person.

DANIELLE. The ad on Craig's List didn't specify a…

CARRIE. …a salary. That was intentional, as is virtually everything I do. But there it is. Six hundred and fifty thousand. Plus benefits.

DANIELLE. *(Drawn back in.)* What kind of benefits?

CARRIE. Working with me, obviously.

DANIELLE. I'm not sure that counts as a benefit.

CARRIE. *(A sly smile.)* Good. She shows some backbone at last. That's the first positive sign in an otherwise dismal first impression. You can ask your question now.

DANIELLE. What question?

CARRIE. The question that has been rattling around inside your little brain the moment you heard me say six hundred and fifty thousand dollars. Aside from the sparkle of instant greed that also lit you up like a metallic porcupine in a lightning storm. Go ahead. Ask.

(Danielle crosses back to Center. Stands before the loveseat.)

DANIELLE. This job. Is it legal?

CARRIE. Would that matter?

DANIELLE. *(Pause, then…)* Not really. Can I ask if you've seen other people for this job?

CARRIE. Yes.

DANIELLE. Is that a 'yes, you've seen other people?' or 'yes, I can ask if you have?'

CARRIE. Yes.

DANIELLE. Which is it?

(Carrie smiles. Says nothing.)

DANIELLE. You really suck, don't you?

CARRIE. Not often enough to please my husband, apparently. Why don't you grow a pair and ask me the question you really want to ask?

DANIELLE. *(Pause, then...)* Okay...What exactly do I have to do to get this job?

CARRIE. There! That's the question. Cut through all the bullshit and let's get down to business. And it's simple. All you have to do is convince me you are the right person.

DANIELLE. And how do I do that?

CARRIE. It's all there in the ad.

(Danielle pulls out a crumpled piece of paper. Reads aloud.)

DANIELLE. *(Reading.)* " Seeking a desperate and ambitious female. Short-term assignment. Rare opportunity for the right person."

CARRIE. Read the qualifications.

DANIELLE. *(Reading.)* "Great pay for someone who is engaging, intelligent, attractive, resourceful…"

CARRIE. …and?

DANIELLE. *(Reading.)* "…and ruthless, when necessary."

CARRIE. Well?

DANIELLE. I can be ruthless.

CARRIE. I don't believe it.

(Danielle hesitates, then pulls a pistol out of her purse and FIRES.)

(The lamp directly behind Carrie's head SHATTERS.)

CARRIE. Okay. I'm starting to believe it.

DANIELLE. *(Not lowering the gun.)* So when do I start?

CARRIE. It looks like you already have.

DANIELLE. You lost me.

CARRIE. No, I found you. And I've been looking for a very long time, believe me. Uh, you can lower the gun, by the way.

DANIELLE. *(She doesn't.)* You said you'd pay me in cash.

CARRIE. That's right.

DANIELLE. So when do I get paid?

CARRIE. When your assignment is finished. You can put the gun away now.

DANIELLE. How do I know I can trust you?

CARRIE. You don't. That's what's going to make this all so much fun. Uh….the gun?

(The dynamic between them has changed. Danielle is comfortably in charge now with the gun aimed at an increasingly nervous Carrie.)

DANIELLE. Oh, right. The gun. For a second, I almost forget I was pointing it directly at your head. How funny is that?

CARRIE. Hysterical.

DANIELLE. Actually, I'm not pointing it at your head. I'm pointing it at that little crease right between your eyebrows. You know where I mean?

CARRIE. *(Her voice shaky.)* I believe so.

DANIELLE. Why don't you point to it? That little crease right between your eyebrows.

CARRIE. I really don't see why I should…

(Danielle pulls the hammer back again. Aims.)

CARRIE. Because I told you to.

(Carrie hesitates, slowly points to the spot between her eyebrows. Presses her finger there.)

DANIELLE. Exactly. That's the perfect spot. Keep your finger there.

(She sits down on the loveseat. Her gun still aimed at Carrie.)

DANIELLE. Now, can you imagine what would happen if a bullet were to hit you right in that spot? *(No reply.)* Can you?

CARRIE. Yes.

DANIELLE. I mean, think of how much damage it would do! Not only would it splatter your brains out the back of your skull and all over your garage sale mismatched furniture…I bet it would also seriously ugly up that face of yours. Wouldn't you say?

CARRIE. …yes.

DANIELLE. *(A hard edge in her voice.)* Then say it.

CARRIE. *(Softly.)* It would seriously ugly up my face.

DANIELLE. Absolutely. So why don't you go get that six fifty K, and let me help you keep your face intact, okay?

(A tense moment. Then Carrie drops her hand to her lap.)

CARRIE. No.

DANIELLE. No?

CARRIE. No.

DANIELLE. You know this gun is loaded, right?

CARRIE. I have no doubt.

DANIELLE. And you are aware I still have it pointed at your face?

CARRIE. At the crease between my eyebrows. So you've said.

DANIELLE. I can shoot you right now. Shoot you dead.

CARRIE. Then do it.

DANIELLE. You don't think I will?

CARRIE. Actually I do think you will.

DANIELLE. I will shoot you right in the head. Right now. I swear to God I will!

CARRIE. Have you ever considered that maybe I want you to?

CURTAIN

Exploit The Press

By
Vin Morreale, Jr.

CAST

Stephen Shallow — A vapid TV host

Senator Doublespeak — An evasive politician

SETTING

A simple TV studio

Vin's Notes: Another political parody and bit of silliness from my days with the SENSELESS BICKERING COMEDY THEATRE. Politicians, and their ability to ddge direct questions, make such an easy target for comedians.

For royalty information and permission to use this scene in a paid performance, please contact **Academy Arts Press** *- vin@academyarts.com*

Exploit The Press

AT RISE: Two comfortable chairs make up the set for long running news program, EXPLOIT THE PRESS

STEVEN SHALLOW. Welcome to Exploit The Press. I'm Steven Shallow and I'm here with Senator Doublespeak. Senator, how do you justify the 50% pay raise, you and your fellow lawmakers voted yourself while telling the rest of us to tighten our belts to lower the deficit?

SENATOR DOUBLESPEAK. I'm glad you asked that. I felt it was important that the public know how I truly feel on this sensitive issue. That is, as opposed to the media or actual perception of, and perhaps the suggestion that, for all points of view which, in a manner of speaking exist. Perhaps one may construe a contention, of course, and an expectation of something, through which they could imply, with or without, it seems, entirely holding to, from or about, and/or underscoring the image of hard work I perform each day for the common people I represent.

STEVEN SHALLOW. Uh.. yes, but about the raise?

SENATOR DOUBLESPEAK. I believe I have already answered that question.

STEVEN SHALLOW. Okay. Well, moving on. Recently, you used your influence to clear Martin Slimebag, a known drug kingpin convicted of raping an entire parochial school. Since Slimebag's father contributed to your last campaign, you used public funds to travel to another state in order to intimidate the judge on the case. Because of your actions, this convicted criminal got off scot-free. How can you justify this despicable behavior?

SENATOR DOUBLESPEAK. In the matter of, and the issues related to the purported and alleged illegal or immoral activities of Mr. Slimebag, who I might add I have nothing but perhaps, the highest or closest, if indeed these words are appropriate to this situation and/or to any situation in which they might apply.

MORE

SENATOR DOUBLESPEAK. *(Continued.)*. Furthermore, and I cannot emphasize this too strongly, the concept of corruption, much or little, more or less, for all to agree, and enhance, or at least equivocate with a deep sense of responsibility to the common people I represent.

STEVEN SHALLOW. But I still don't see how you can justify getting a dangerous criminal to walk free.

SENATOR DOUBLESPEAK. I don't believe I can make my position any clearer than that which I have already stated and which won the vindication of the common people I represent.

STEVEN SHALLOW. You're claiming an error in judgement?

SENATOR DOUBLESPEAK. Only in the most positive and noble sense of the term.

STEVEN SHALLOW. Senator, aren't you afraid that these "common people you represent" will remember your history of scandal and corruption come election day?

SENATOR DOUBLESPEAK. Hell, the one thing we politicians count on is that voters would rather re-elect an old crook than a new candidate with brains or integrity.

STEVEN SHALLOW. Excuse me, Senator. But that sounded very close to the English language.

SENATOR DOUBLESPEAK. Uh, well, ahem, what I meant to say, in other words and with a deep respect for the common people I represent, that the compassion and proven, or at least continuing continuity of those...

STEVEN SHALLOW. This is Exploit The Press. I'm Steven Shallow. Good Evening.

CURTAIN

Kurt's Apology

By
Vin Morreale, Jr.

CAST

Kurt An abusive husband

Sarah His long-suffering wife

SETTING

A nice suburban home.

Vin's Notes: The essence of a good short scene is the degree to which it can surprise your audience, while offering a variety of emotions for each actor to play. This short piece proved popular in my **Burnng Up The Stage Acting Workshops**, and also appears in my book 150 ACTING SCENES.

For royalty information and permission to use this scene in a paid performance, please contact **Academy Arts Press** *- vin@academyarts.com*

Kurt's Apology

AT RISE: A nice suburban home.

KURT.   I'm sorry. I said I'm sorry.

SARAH.   I heard you.

KURT.   So, we're good, right?

SARAH.   Seriously? You think any of this even closely resembles good?

KURT.   Cut the attitude. You know how I hate that.

SARAH.   Or what? You going to hit me again? Choke me like the last time? Maybe break a finger or something because I finally have the nerve to say enough?

KURT.   You got a mouth on you, you know that?

SARAH.   Yeah. You bloodied it enough over the years.

KURT.   You know I got a temper. You don't like it, don't go pissing me off with that mouth of yours. That's all.

SARAH.   Right. It's my fault. You had me believing that for a long time. But now you gotta smack the kids around. Scare them to death, so they run and hide in their room every time they know Daddy's been out drinking.

KURT.   I work hard. If I want a drink now and then, that's my business.

SARAH.   No. Those kids are your business! You're teaching your seven year-old son that a real man gets flat-out drunk and uses his fist on a woman anytime he feels like it. And you're teaching Emily she can expect more of the same when she grows up.

KURT.   Those kids love me. You can't say they don't!

SARAH.   Of course, they love you! That's the saddest part of all. They love you so much, it makes them swallow your excuses every time you say Mom had it coming, or you promise never to do it again.

KURT.   I won't…

SARAH. It makes them pretend they don't see the bruises and black eyes. Or hear all the screaming and swearing. And it makes them blame the police for arresting you, every time you beat up the neighbors for having the nerve to park their cars anywhere near our house.

KURT. I've got good kids. They stick up for their dad!

SARAH. Yes, they do. Even when he continually beats them down, physically or emotionally. You know, they begged me not to call the police the last time you busted my lip? They were in tears, knowing you were only one more complaint away from doing serious time. My own children would rather I shut up and take your beatings, then let you take responsibility for being a serial abuser. My own children...

KURT. I already said I got a temper! I already said I was sorry! What the hell more do you want me to say?!

SARAH. Say goodbye. To me and the kids. At least until you learn to be a real man. Or at least act like one.

KURT. Goodbye? Oh, so you think you're leavin' me, huh?

SARAH. Just for a while. Until you get your drinking under control.

KURT. I got my drinking under control. But you and your mouth sure as hell don't make it easy.

SARAH. Then let me make it easy for you... Me and the kids are moving in with my mother.

KURT. Yeah? And what makes you think I'm gonna let any of you go?

CURTAIN

Breaking & Entering

By
Vin Morreale, Jr.

CAST

Warren — A charming conman & burglar

Amy — His pre-teen daughter

SETTING

A park bench

Vin's Notes: This romantic comedy with lots of fun twists and turns has been *one* of my most succesful plays worldwide, with productions in Russia, Italy, Kazakhstan, Greece, Great Britain and more. It began as a four character romantic comedy, but a few years ago, I turned it into a feature film as well. This meant adding more characters and locations. In this scene from the movie, a con artist tries to relate to his preteen daughter.

*For royalty information and permission to use this scene in a paid performance, or if you are a Film Producer interested in reading the award-winning screenplay, please contact **Academy Arts Entertainment** - vin@academyarts.com.*

Breaking & Entering

AT RISE: A park bench. Warren sits with his teen daughter.)

AMY.   Look, I really don't want to learn any more about picking pockets, three-card Monty or how to stack a deck.

WARREN.   The deck is always stacked, sweetheart. It's either stacked by you or stacked against you. In this world, you're either a shark or a mark. It's your choice.

AMY.   That's your world. In mine, things aren't so cold-blooded. And Dads do more than just show up every six months for fast talk and felony lessons. In my world, you can trust people.

WARREN.   Then your world is wrong.

AMY.   Maybe. Or maybe it's just a world you know absolutely nothing about. *(Hesitates, then...)* Look, I gotta run. I'm meeting a couple of friends at the mall...

(She sticks out her hand. He hands her a few hundred.)

WARREN.   You know I love you.

AMY.   I know, Dad. *(Sadly.)* But in your screwed up world... does that make me the mark...or you?

(He watches sadly, as she turns away.)

CURTAIN

Breaking & Entering - 2

By
Vin Morreale, Jr.

CAST

Warren — A charming conman & burglar

Jasmine — His current mark

SETTING

An opulent restaurant

Vin's Notes: In this second excerpt from the BREAKING & ENTERING film script, Warren masquerades as European royalty, in order to con a rich woman out of her diamond necklace. It is always fun to watch a deception unfold when the audience is tipped in advance that something shady may be happening. I wrote, produced and directed an Ultra Low Budget production version of BREAKING & ENTERING, which for years held the record for the largest single screening box office premiere of any movie in the Southeast.

For royalty information and permission to use this scene in a paid performance, or if you are a Film Producer interested in reading the award-winning screenplay, please contact **Academy Arts Entertainment** *- vin@academyarts.com.*

Breaking & Entering - 2

AT RISE: An upscale restaurant. Warren is dressed in an elegant suit with a slightly European flair. He sips champagne. JASMINE, rich, gullible and dripping with diamonds, standing over his table..

JASMINE. Thank you for the drawing.

WARREN. *(With a fake accent.)* You are most velcome. I love to capture beauty venever possible. Do...haff a seat.

    (She hesitates, then sits.)

JASMINE. But you got the necklace all wrong. It isn't anything like mine.

WARREN. Forgiffe me. I must haff let my imagination vander. You have zee Tiffany. How silly of me.

JASMINE. *(Impressed.)* You know your diamonds.

WARREN. A hobby of mine. Actually, I drew you vearing zis... by mistake.

    (He pulls the velvet jewelry case and slides it across the table. She opens it. Her eyes widen.)

JASMINE. It's...gorgeous.

WARREN. Eet belonged to Grandmama. Eet holds how you say - sentimental value.

JASMINE. It must be worth a fortune.

WARREN. Can one put a price on sentiment?

JASMINE. Uh... I guess not.

WARREN. Grandmama... passed away last week. I haff carried her necklace vit me since then. *(Starting to tear up.)* Eet is...difficult to let go.

JASMINE. You poor thing.

WARREN. Perhaps I might ask you a kindness? Vould you place the diamonds on for me?

JASMINE.   You want me to wear this?

WARREN.   If eet vould not be so very much to ask.

JASMINE.   No, sure.

WARREN.   Allow me.

(He reaches over and places the diamond necklace around her throat. Staring deeply into her eyes. She is smitten. Behind her neck, he uses a tissue hidden in his sleeve to wipe off any fingerprints. He leans back and smiles.)

WARREN.   You vere born to vear diamonds.

JASMINE.   Ya think?

WARREN.   Certain moi. Yet eet does...overpower your other trinket. If I may..?

(He leans over and unclasps her Tiffany necklace. Drops it in the open jewelry case on the table.)

WARREN.   Ahhh. Far better.

(Jasmine pulls a mirror from her purse and gasps at the reflection.)

JASMINE.   It really is incredible.

WARREN.   You enjoy eet?

JASMINE.   Who wouldn't?

WARREN.   *(Waves it away.)* Zen it is yours.

JASMINE.   You're kidding?

WARREN.   Vat use is eet to me? I vould merely hide eet away vit all my other heirlooms. You bring eet life. Zat is vat Grandmama vould vant.

JASMINE.   I...I don't know what to say.

WARREN.   Say nothing. Just accept.

JASMINE.   But..?

WARREN.   Please. For Grandmama...

JASMINE. Okay... If it'll make Grandmama happy... other than her being dead and all.

WARREN. You are so very kind. Oh...and zere is too a bracelet you must haff.

(He pulls an equally dazzling bracelet from his pocket.)

WARREN. May I?

(She can only nod. He clasps the bracelet around her wrist. At the same time, wiping off his fingerprints. He quickly removes her tennis bracelet and drops it in the open jewelry case with her old necklace.)

WARREN. Eet is lovely on you.

JASMINE. I can't accept this. I don't even know you.

WARREN. *(Leans in seductively.)* Perhaps eet is better zat vay, don't you zink? Haff you never vanted to receive... extravagances...from a stranger?

JASMINE. Sure, but...

WARREN. zen indulge me zis rare moment of romance. Eet vould mean so very much to me.

(He oozes with charm and sincerity. She can only nod.)

WARREN. You are too kind. Now, I must go and tell Grandmama vhat I haff done to keep her spirit alive. *(Grasps her hand gently.)* Eet has been enchanting.

JASMINE. I... I can't thank you enough.

WARREN. Please, do not try. For you haff given me far more zan you realize.

(He casually flips a second white cloth napkin over the case containing her expensive necklace and bracelet.)

JASMINE. Won't you even tell me your name?

WARREN. Vould you spoil zee mystery and romance of zis moment vit such trivialities? *(She shakes her head.)* Zen go. I must be alone vit mine memories of Grandmama.

(As she rises, Warren reaches under the first napkin and grabs the jewelry case he had placed when he first sat down.)

WARREN. Oh, Madame. You forgot your old necklace and bracelet!

JASMINE. I almost forgot. How silly of me.

(He hands her the now empty jewelry case. Sensuously kisses her hand. She strolls dreamily back to her table. Warren reaches under the napkin to the matching case. Slips Jasmine's real necklace and bracelet into his pocket. The switch is successful.)

WARREN. Now go. And go quickly.

(He takes a profound sigh, as she turns and leaves. Then he quickly wipes his fingerprints off the silverware and glass, then quickly exits with her expensive diamonds.)

CURTAIN

Breaking & Entering - 3

By
Vin Morreale, Jr.

CAST

Warren — A charming conman & burglar

Harve — A grizzled old pawn shop owner

SETTING

A seedy pawn shop, late at night

Vin's Notes: This third excerpt from the BREAKING & ENTERING film script, takes place immediately after the previous scene, where Warren tries to fence the diamonds he conned from Jasmine. To add dimension t his character, I built in some backstory between him and Harve, the seedy pawn shop owner. One day, I hope to see this fun and fast-moving screenplay given a remake with a real budget and some name talent.

For royalty information and permission to use this scene in a paid performance, or if you are a Film Producer interested in reading the award-winning screenplay, please contact **Academy Arts Entertainment** *- vin@academyarts.com.*

Breaking & Entering - 3

AT RISE: A pawn shop. A pair of hands opens the case to reveal Jasmine's Cartier necklace and Gucci bracelet. HARVE 60, - a crusty shop owner and part-time jewelry fence, examines the stolen diamonds with a magnifying glass.

WARREN. So how much can you give me for all this?

HARVE. I dunno. Five to ten?

WARREN. Five to ten thousand?

HARVE. Five to ten years. Sooner or later, you're gonna get caught pullin' these high profile cons. Then you'll be playin' butt tag with Bubba and the boys in Cell Block D.

WARREN. Lighten up, Harve. Where's your sense of excitement?

HARVE. You seen my wife? I ain't been excited for years. Look, kid. I know you since you the Three Card Monty days down on Seventh Street.

WARREN. Those were good times.

HARVE. Yeah. The scams. The hustles...

WARREN. The expressions on the marks' faces when they realized they'd been taken...

HARVE. Stayin' one step ahead of the cops, if you was lucky.

WARREN. Luck had nothing to do with it, Harve. It's all about being smart enough to spot a bad situation before it sucks you in... and smooth enough to talk your way out of it, if you get caught.

HARVE. That's what Lucky Larry usedta say.

WARREN. Used to say? What happened to Lucky Larry?

HARVE. Let's just say he'll be needing a new nickname for the next fifteen to twenty. I don't wanna see that happen to you. The flashy con is a kid's game. Maybe it's time you left it to them?

WARREN. It's all I'm good at, Harve. So how much can you give me for all this?

HARVE. Hmmm. Pretty easy to trace. Whatta ya say to a grand apiece?

WARREN. I'd say you're a thief.

HARVE. That's comin' real close to hurting my feelings. Okay, two grand for the necklace, fifteen hundred for the bracelet.

WARREN. Done. Oh, and give me a couple more jewelry boxes and a few of those twelve dollar heirlooms.

(Harve counts out a stack of hundred dollar bills. Then throws three identical fake diamond necklaces on the counter.)

HARVE. Big spender.

WARREN. A man's gotta make a living.

(Warren shoves the cash and fake jewelry into his pocket. Tosses an extra $100 on the counter. Crosses to the door, then turns to his old partner in crime.)

WARREN. I was good in the old days, wasn't I, Harve?

HARVE. You were the best. But sooner or later somethin'...or somebody... comes along to trip you up.

WARREN. That only happens in the movies, Harve.

(He exits. Harve shakes his head sadly.)

HARVE. *(Shakes his head.)* That's the other thing Lucky Larry usedta say...

CURTAIN

Breaking & Entering – 4

By
Vin Morreale, Jr.

CAST

Warren — A charming conman & burglar

Parker — A woman who caught him in her condo

SETTING

Parker's Upscale Apartment

Vin's Notes: This scene is taken directly from the stage version of BREAKING & ENTERING, which is carried by Dramatic Publishing. A charming conman breaks into an apartment he believes to be empty, only to find a beautiful woman dressed only in a towel. The question is, who is conning whom? I did change the female lead's name to Parker in a recent update.

FOR ROYALTY INFORMATION, OR TO REQUEST A COPY OF
BREAKING & ENTERING, PLEASE CONTACT **DRAMATIC PUBLISHING** -
dramaticpublishing.com/authors/profile/view/url/vin-morreale-jr

Breaking & Entering - 4

AT RISE: An upscale residence. The mysterious PARKER, 27, has just caught WARREN, 33, a charming burglar, in her apartment. She tricked him into removing his pants, acting as if she swallowed his story. She now aims a gun at him while he tries to talk his way out of the situation.

WARREN. That's a gun!

PARKER. I find it rather comforting. Nice shorts by the way.

WARREN. What is all this?!

PARKER. My guess would be a Valentine's gift from your mother.

WARREN. Not the underwear! Why are you pointing a gun at me?!

PARKER. So many reasons. For one, this condo does not receive any government subsidies. I know, because my dad owns the building.

WARREN. *(Panicked.)* What about Mister Volgaropoulis?

PARKER. No such guy. I made him up. It has a real Mediterranean flair, don't you think? Besides, your badge was a fake. I used one just like it last Halloween.

WARREN. You tricked me!

PARKER. Don't be so indignant. You're the one breaking and entering here! Then you spout some ridiculous story about government agents and ugly rug violations. Did you honestly expect me to believe that? Do I look like a real blonde?

WARREN. I was under pressure. It was the best I could do.

PARKER. *(Enjoying his panic.)* Improvisation is an art, Warren...A few years in the state pen may help you perfect that art.

WARREN. You seem to be taking this rather casually.

PARKER. Actually, I'm enjoying the diversion. It isn't every day I have a seven break into my apartment.

WARREN. A seven?! Whatta ya mean, 'a seven'?!

PARKER. You know, on a scale of one to ten. Hunkability.

WARREN. Listen, lady, I don't know where you learned the male meat scale, but I ain't never scored under a nine in my life!

PARKER. I'm sure that's true. But I happen to be a little harder to please than most women. *(Points the gun lower.)* And those boxer shorts are good for at least a one point deduction on their own.

He puts on his most soothing voice. Moves slowly toward her.

WARREN. Okay, Parker. You've had your little laugh. Now why don't you just put that thing away? You're far too nice a girl to shoot anybody.

PARKER. That's what the last man who broke in here thought.

WARREN. The last man?

PARKER. Check out the carpet stain in the corner.

WARREN. *(Not really sure.)* That's just a little... red wine?

PARKER. That's what my Dad told the police when they couldn't find the body.

He's baffled by this strange woman and tries to think of a way out. He changes tactics and slowly starts to chuckle.

WARREN. Okay, Parker. You win. The truth is...I'm not really a government agent.

PARKER. Then why are you here?

WARREN. This is difficult for me to admit...

PARKER. I'm sure.

WARREN. I broke in... *(With sincerity.)* ..to see you. There's a note in my jacket pocket telling you exactly how I feel. I didn't have the guts to tell you to your face.

PARKER. Probably because you were so busy staring at my towel.

WARREN. You don't know me, Parker. Or how long I've admired you from afar. Please, go look in my jacket pocket.

(She hesitates, then dashes off to get the jacket. Warren starts to run, but there's no place to go in his underwear. Parker is back in a flash with the jacket. She reaches into the pocket. Pulls out his latex burglary gloves.)

PARKER. I assume you have an explanation for these?

WARREN. *(Shrugs.)* I'm an amateur proctologist. Just read the note.

(She reaches into another pocket and pulls out a note.)

PARKER. *(Reading the note.)* "My dearest one: Of all the love-inspired acts my heart has ever led me to, this is perhaps the most desperate. My passion for you knows no bounds. My soul is forever incomplete without the soft glow of your idyllic face to charm my worthless existence. I love you, though you do not even know I exist. Yet, I will remain true to your perfect inspiration all the days of my life. With undying love... your secret admirer."

WARREN. *(Moving closer.)* So now you know.

PARKER. I...I don't know what to say.

WARREN. Say nothing. Just savor the moment. A love that was hidden in the shadows can now blossom in the pristine light of day.

PARKER. You spelled 'worthless' wrong.

WARREN. What?

PARKER. You talk about your worthless existence. You spelled 'worthless' with two 'l's.

WARREN. Look, lady, this is supposed to be romance, not Grammar 101! If I wanted proof-reading, I would have sent it to my sixth-grade English teacher.

PARKER. I'm sorry. That was very sweet.

WARREN. *(With hurt feelings.)* Damn right...

PARKER. *(Raises the gun again.)* But how do I know this isn't just another lie? It could be a fallback plan in case you're caught. After all, my name isn't even on this note.

WARREN. You still doubt my love? After all I've risked to share this intimacy with you?

PARKER. I'm just a suspicious kind of girl. *(Moves towards her.)* Stay where you are! I'm a suspicious kind of girl with a gun.

WARREN. Parker... Parker... What can I do to prove my devotion?

PARKER. I don't know. I'm still trying to wrap my head around the whole government agent story.

WARREN. What could I do? My heart was on my sleeve. Even my pants were down. I... I panicked. You still don't believe me, do you?

PARKER. There haven't been a lot of men falling in love with me this week.

WARREN. Forget this week. I've loved you for years. If you don't believe me...look in the kitchen.

PARKER. The kitchen?

WARREN. If you don't find something in there to prove my love, then... then you can shoot me dead. *(Sadly.)* It'd be easier on my broken heart if you did.

PARKER. No tricks?

WARREN. You have my word.

PARKER. Why doesn't that bring me a great deal of comfort..?

(She hesitates, then dashes to the table. Parker opens the long box on the table. Opens it to reveal a dozen long-stemmed roses.)

PARKER. Oh, they're beautiful! *(Sniffs.)* Oh... They're fake.

(Warren suddenly sweeps her into his arms.)

WARREN. Not fake. Silk. Each one perfect for today and forever. Symbolizing a love that is timeless and ever vibrant. Ever exciting and alive.

PARKER. Damn, you're good, Warren. These roses are the perfect touch.

WARREN. They're but a pale imitation of your beauty. A face I have loved since the first moment I set eyes upon you.

PARKER. *(Moving away.)* So you've loved me since the first moment you first saw me?

WARREN. That's right.

PARKER. Where exactly was that?

WARREN. *(Too quickly.)* Was what?

PARKER. Where you first saw me.

WARREN. Uh...You don't remember?

PARKER. No.

WARREN. You never saw me around? Following you like some heartbroken puppy?

PARKER. Sorry.

(She raises the gun. He backs away.)

WARREN. Well, at least I should be thankful for that. If you had seen me in those first few days, you might have thought I was some kind of blathering, love-struck idiot. Man, I was pathetic.

PARKER. Now that you mention it, I do remember a few pathetic idiots. Anyway, where was it?

WARREN. Where was what?

PARKER. Where you first saw me? You never told me.

WARREN. Of course I did.

PARKER. No. I'm sure you didn't. You mentioned that you were pathetic and must have gotten sidetracked by your wretchedness.

WARREN. That was probably it. God, I was miserable.

PARKER. Miserable and pathetic. Sounds like most of the guys I know.

WARREN. You don't like men very much, do you, Parker?

PARKER. Only the disposable kind. So where was it?

WARREN. Where..?

PARKER. ...was it? Where you first saw me.

WARREN. Where I first saw you?

PARKER. Do you have to answer every question with a question?

WARREN. Do I do that?

PARKER. Yes. It's miserable and pathetic. So where did you first see me? And if you answer with another question, I'm going to shoot you in the right thigh. Though this gun usually shoots a little higher than what I'm aiming at...

(She aims the gun at his shorts. Warren realizes what she's aiming at. He frantically scans the room. Spots the pennant on the wall.)

WARREN. Uh...um... At the college!

PARKER. The college?

WARREN. *(A confident smile)* Yes. University of Louisville.

PARKER. Interesting. And where on campus did you see me?

WARREN. All over. Strolling the grounds between classes. I remember this one time you dropped your books and I rushed over to help pick them up. But I don't think you gave me a second look.

PARKER. Probably because you were so miserable and pathetic.

WARREN. Thank you so much.

PARKER. Tell me more.

WARREN. Tell you more? *(She aims again.)* All right, I'll tell you more! I mostly remember you...um *(Notices the Greek items on the wall.)*...hanging out with your sorority sisters!

PARKER. Yeah, great bunch of girls, that sorority. Which one?

WARREN. *(With a smile)* You're toying with me.

PARKER. It's what I do best. What sorority?

WARREN. *(Examining the insignia)* Sigma Alpha Epsilon.

PARKER. Good guess.

WARREN. I'm not guessing, Parker. I used to spend hours admiring you from afar. Watching you go to the campus library...

PARKER. Hastings Hall?

WARREN. That's right. Hastings Hall. Sometimes I'd catch a glimpse of you walking with your sorority sisters, and I'd just wish I had the guts to say hello. *(Sighs.)* I remember how the sun during that fall semester would splash gentle golden highlights on your hair...as if it longed to caress you as much as I did.

PARKER. I... I never knew...

WARREN. No. You never saw me in all my love-inspired anguish. There were times I'd hear you laughing - that sweet melodic laugh of yours - and it would make me smile for days. I'd dare to imagine it was me who could bring you such joy. Your gentle laughter was like a symphony to me.

PARKER. Most people tell me I snort when I laugh.

WARREN. They don't hear you the way I do.

PARKER. *(Turning away.)* So you really followed me around campus?

WARREN. Like a puppy. I'm surprised you never notice me.

PARKER. I'm not. After all, I never went to college.

WARREN. What?

PARKER. I thought about it but decided to become a secretary instead. By the way, there is no Hastings Hall at U of L. Or so they tell me.

WARREN. But...but what about the mug... and the pennant?

PARKER. My sister gave them to me.

WARREN. Your sister?

PARKER. Mabel.

WARREN. That's… That's…uh, really funny. I guess you two look so much alike, I got confused.

PARKER. You really think we look that much alike?

WARREN. Doesn't everyone?

PARKER. No. Mainly because she's South Korean.

WARREN. Ulp, South Korean?

PARKER. My Mom adopted her when she was five.

WARREN. Uh… well, she certainly doesn't look South Korean.

PARKER. That's true. A lot of people mistake her for North Korean. So, the question is…do I shoot you now? Or do I call the police?

CURTAIN

Thanks, Mom

By
Vin Morreale, Jr.

CAST

Catelynn A giggling woman

Roger A frustrated man

SETTING

A bedroom

Vin's Notes: Relationships are always rich fodder for comedy, since we are never as pretensious, vulnerable or simply human than when we are in a romantic situation. This scene was an actor's favorite in my **Burning Up The Stage Acting Workshops**. It can also be found in my book 150 ACTING SCENES.

*For royalty information and permission to use this scene in a paid performance, please contact **Academy Arts Press** - vin@academyarts.com*

Thanks, Mom

AT RISE: A bedroom. ROGER pulls off his shirt with a romantic swagger. CATELYNN chokes and covers her mouth.

ROGER. What are you doing?!!

CATELYNN. Uh. Nothing. Sorry.

ROGER. You were laughing at me!

CATELYNN. No, I wasn't.

ROGER. Giggling then.

CATELYNN. Well yeah... I kind of was. But I'm better now. Please continue undressing.

ROGER. Are you crazy?

CATELYNN. Do you really need a copy of my psych evaluation?

ROGER. What? Of course not. I just wanted to know…Wait. You have a psych evaluation?

CATELYNN. Don't change the subject. Just get back to taking off your clothes.

ROGER. (Drops his pants) You're giggling again!

CATELYNN. No, I'm not!

ROGER. Laughing then.

CATELYNN. I can't help it. How old are you anyway?

ROGER. Old enough to do this. Old enough not to like you doing that while I'm doing this!

CATELYNN. I wouldn't be doing this, if you hadn't done that.

ROGER. Done what?

CATELYNN. Wrote your name on every piece of your clothes! Even your underwear. What are you? Eight years old and going on your first sleepover?

ROGER. Huh? My name isn't on my…? *(Checks his underwear.)* Really, Mom?

CATELYNN. *(Giggling again.)* Your Mom wrote your name in your clothes? Sorry. Let me try that again without the falsetto. *(Much lower voice.)* Your Mom wrote your name in your clothes?

ROGER. She called me all upset. A pipe burst in her basement this morning, and I rushed over to fix it.

CATELYNN. And she wrote your name in your clothes as a reward? Man, plumbers have been getting overpaid for years.

ROGER. Very funny. I got filthy, and Mom said she'd throw these in the wash for me. She must have written my name in while doing the laundry.

CATELYNN. That is such a Mom thing to do.

ROGER. Old habits die hard, I guess. You can stop laughing now. Or giggling. Either one.

CATELYNN. Unlikely.

ROGER. Um, I'm guessing this isn't going to happen tonight.

CATELYNN. Even more unlikely. But there is one good thing that came out of this…

ROGER. That would be?

CATELYNN. *(Looking inside his waistband.)* At least I know you used your real name when you married me.

ROGER. Maybe I shouldn't have.

CATELYNN. Oh, my poor baby… You poor widdle man…

ROGER. Well, that just killed the mood…

CURTAIN

A Day At The White House

By
Vin Morreale, Jr.

CAST

Crenshaw Sparx   Groucho Marx as President

Mae Waist   Mae West as a lobbyist

SETTING

The Oval Office of the White House

Vin's Notes: Sir Isaac Newton once said "We stand on the shoulders of giants," when referring to the debt all scientists owed to those who came before them. The same is true of comedy. In this excerpt from my zany musical, A DAY AT THE WHITE HOUSE/THE SPARX BROTHERS GO TO WASHINGTON, a Groucho Marx-type character is elected President, and stacks his cabinet with other famous comedians of the 1930's and 40's. It's a fun filled romp with music by the amazing Erick Siroca.

For royalty information and permission to use this scene in a paid performance, or to request a full copy of A DAY AT THE WHITE HOUSE, please contact **Academy Arts Press** *- vin@academyarts.com*

A Day At The White House

AT RISE: CRENSHAW SPARK, a Groucho Marx lookalike, struts around the Oval Office, after an election snafu makes him the new President of the United States. On his very first day, he is approached by lobbyists, including MAE WAIST, who looks eerily similar to sexpot comedienne Mae West, filled with double entendre and aggressive sensuality.

CRENSHAW.   Hi. I'm Crenshaw Spark, President of the United States. Most powerful man in America. I control the lives of nearly four hundred million people. How's that for an opening line?

MAE WAIST.   You deliver it well.

CRENSHAW.   Oh, you're just trying to butter me up.

MAE WAIST.   Perceptive, too.

CRENSHAW.   So what's a nice girl like you doing, besides making my blood pressure rise? Among other things…

MAE WAIST.   Mister President, you're going to make me blush.

CRENSHAW.   I'll bet my mustache you haven't blushed in years.

MAE WAIST.   Only when it gets me what I want.

CRENSHAW.   Is that so? And what is it you want?

MAE WAIST.   Mr. President… I'm a lobbyist. I get paid to…influence you…

(She pushes him down on the sofa, then sits very close beside him.)

CRENSHAW.   Is that what they call it these days? It's so hard to keep up with the vernacular. *(He puts his head on her lap like a puppy.)* So who do you lobby for? Wall Street?

MAE WAIST.   They couldn't afford me.

CRENSHAW. The NRA?

MAE WAIST. A bunch of big shots. I prefer men of bigger caliber.

CRENSHAW. Small Business Administration?

MAE WAIST. I don't handle anything with the word 'small' in it.

CRENSHAW. Teacher's Union?

MAE WAIST. Not enough class.

CRENSHAW. Dock workers?

MAE WAIST. I do them on my own time.

(She grabs him in a bosomy embrace. He glances at her ample chest.)

CRENSHAW. Milk Producers of America?

MAE WAIST. How'd you know?

CRENSHAW. Lucky guess.... So what exactly can I do to you...uh, I mean, for you, Miss Waist? *(Suddenly worried.)* It is Miss Waist, isn't it? There isn't a Mister Waist running around, is there?

MAE WAIST. There was a Mister Waist...but he died.

CRENSHAW. I'm sorry. How did he die?

MAE WAIST. Happy.

CRENSHAW. *(Gulps, then..)* Did I mention I have close to unlimited power?

MAE WAIST. Then a big, strong President like you won't have any problem pushing one little itty bitty subsidy through Congress for me, now would he?

CRENSHAW. Uh, what itty bitty subsidy?

MAE WAIST. Just some teensy weensy old price supports.

CRENSHAW. Explain price supports to me. Assume I don't know anything.

MAE WAIST. I assumed that from the first moment I saw you.

CRENSHAW. Well then... *(Suddenly getting it.)* Hey!

MAE WAIST. You know how the federal government pays farmers not to grow wheat to keep crop prices from crashing?

CRENSHAW. They really do that sort of thing?

MAE WAIST. Ever since the Great Depression. In good times and bad, taxpayers pay farmers not to grow things. So in keeping with that great government tradition, my people want to be paid a lot more not to milk cows.

CRENSHAW. A little teat for tat, huh?

MAE WAIST. You can say that. Besides, it will keep their poor little hands from chaffing. Can I count on your support?

CRENSHAW. *(Looking at her chest.)* I don't know. There's a lot there to support. *(Jumps up.)* But wait, won't that mean little kids will have to pay more for their milk?

MAE WAIST. Sure. But all those extra pennies could wind up in the pocket of your re-election campaign. Or maybe even your own pocket… *(She drags him back onto the sofa again.)* Besides, aren't some things worth a little…extra attention?

> *(She kisses him passionately. His foot raises off the floor. When she lets him go, he has a dazed and dopey smile on his face, as if his libido just short-circuited.)*

CRENSHAW. Well, when you put it that way… *(Dreamily.)* Where do I sign?

MAE WAIST. You don't have to sign anything. I'll just go tell those boys in Congress that you're going to support my legislation. And if they fight it, they'll have to answer to you.

CRENSHAW. *(Still entranced.)* Yeah. They'll have to answer to me…

> *(She stands up suddenly, spilling him onto the floor.)*

MAE WAIST. Thank you, Mister President. It was a business doing pleasure with you.

CRENSHAW. Hey! When do I get my big pay-off?!

MAE WAIST. If you're lucky, I'll show up in the next act.

(She exits, Stage Right. Crenshaw collapses happily onto the sofa.)
CRENSHAW.   I think I'm in love!

CURTAIN

Being Somebody

By
Vin Morreale, Jr.

CAST

Jeremy — A narcissistic musician

Kendal — His long-suffering girlfriend

SETTING

A small apartment

Vin's Notes: Somewhere along the line, we began defining ourselves by what we do, not who we are. We often consider ourselves failures or successes based on what we have accomplished, rather than the quality of our character or the depths of our relationships. I am as guilty of that as everyone else. Something I tried to explore in this scene from my **Burnng Up The Stage Acting Workshops**. One of my most popular pieces in my collection, 150 ACTING SCENES.

*For royalty information and permission to use this scene in a paid performance, please contact **Academy Arts Press** - vin@academyarts.com*

Being Somebody

AT RISE: A small apartment. JEREMY slowly picks at notes and chords on his guitar. KENDAL enters quietly. Hands him a beer.

KENDAL. Still working on that song?

JEREMY. *(Grabs the beer without looking at her.)* Uh huh.

KENDAL. How's it going?

JEREMY. Fine. I need to concentrate.

KENDAL. You need me to go away?

JEREMY. Not go away. Just…go away for now.

KENDAL. I do that, you know. Every day and half the night. I go away. Tip toe through this apartment like a ghost, so I don't disturb your 'creative process.'

JEREMY. Can we talk about all this later?

KENDAL. No. Because later never comes. Later is always 'after I nail down this verse,' or 'after I fix this messed up chord progression,' or 'after I unblock whatever creative constipation is keeping everyone from recognizing how friggin' brilliant I am!'

JEREMY. Hey, I don't need this right now.

KENDAL. You mean, what you don't need right now is me.

JEREMY. What is it you want from me, huh? I'm working here. Working hard, trying to kickstart this career. Trying to make this more than just some side gig or hobby. Make it something that'll bring in serious money. For you and for me.

KENDAL. Be honest. It's not about the money. It never was.

JEREMY. Okay. Maybe it's not. Maybe it's this obsession I have. Or fear. Or a crazy need to prove something to the world. Prove something to

KENDAL. Prove what?

JEREMY. That I'm not just another loser trying to be something he's not. That I have what it takes to make it. That I can be somebody! I mean, really be somebody. You know what I'm saying?

KENDAL. But you are somebody. Whether you hit it big, or you never do more than play that guitar at our kitchen table every night. Either way, you will always be somebody to me.

JEREMY. Maybe... But that kind of somebody is not enough. I don't know why, but it isn't.

KENDAL. I guess that's the difference between you and me. You want fame. Hunger for it. You need to be loved and admired by millions of screaming fans. You don't want the art, just the acclaim. That's your idea of being somebody.

JEREMY. Every artist feels that way. It's what keeps us going. Keeps us creating. Why the hell is that so bad?

KENDAL. It isn't. It's just that, I want to be somebody, too. What I want...all I ever wanted...was to be somebody to you. But that's not enough, is it? I'm not enough.

JEREMY. Listen...

KENDAL. It's okay. Get back to work. *(Walking away.)* That chord progression sucks, by the way.

CURTAIN

The Kiss Me Curse

By
Vin Morreale, Jr.

CAST

Angie   A slightly zany widow

Dale   A mild-mannered dreamer

SETTING

An airport lounge, late at night.

Vin's Notes: This comedy was commissioned by Kentucky's venerable Little Colonel Playhouse in 2016. I also was given the privelidge of directing its world premier, which turned out to be one of the most successful full length plays in the theater's sixty year history. What began as a simple comedy sketch grew into one of the funniest and most deeply personal works of my career.

*For royalty information and permission to use this scene in a paid performance, or to request a full copy of THE KISS ME CURSE, please contact **Academy Arts Press** - vin@academyarts.com*

The Kiss Me Curse

AT RISE: An airport lounge. DALE, a mild-mannered dreamer, notices ANGIE, attractive but a bit spacey, sitting a few tables away in the otherwise empty lounge. She sees him looking at her and quickly repositions her chair so her back faces him. As she does this, her purse falls to the floor.)

DALE. Excuse me. Excuse me, Miss?

ANGIE. Don't even think it.

DALE. Huh?

ANGIE. I'm not available, okay?

DALE. Available for what?

ANGIE. Available for anything. Whatever you have in mind. So forget it. You don't want to fall in love with me. Trust me.

DALE. Fall in love with you?

ANGIE. Look. You're smitten. I know. It's my eyes. My hair. My smile. The graceful sweep of my neck. The soft, smooth elegance of my recently shaved legs. Best to get all that out of your head.

DALE. Your legs weren't in my head…

ANGIE. A butt man, huh? Well, mine's equally impressive, but since I'm sitting down, you'll have to take my word for it.

DALE. I only wanted to tell you…

ANGIE. Don't give up, do you? But believe me, it won't end well. Just move on. Get over me. Don't make this harder than it already is.

DALE. There's something wrong with you, isn't there?

ANGIE. Wrong with me? I'm not trying to pick up strange women in an airport lounge at midnight! What's the matter? The local meat market lose its appeal? Your subscription to Desperatesingles.com run out?

DALE. I'm not trying to pick you up. I just wanted to tell you that you dropped your purse.

ANGIE. Ha! That is the lamest pick-up line I've ever heard.

DALE. It's not a line. Your purse is on the floor.

(She notices the purse. Bends to pick it up.)

ANGIE. Oh, I'm sorry. I thought you were trying to….

DALE. I wasn't.

(She nods, turns her back to him again.)

DALE. But if I was….

ANGIE. *(Too quickly.)* I'm married.

DALE. Oh. I'm sorry.

ANGIE. My husband will be here any minute.

DALE. Terribly sorry.

ANGIE. Sorry that I'm married? Or sorry about how badly you just crashed and burned?

DALE. Honestly? Both.

ANGIE. Honesty and humility. That's refreshing.

DALE. I'll leave you alone then….

(He turns back to his drink. After a moment, she starts smacking her cheeks, moaning and wailing with obviously artificial sobs.)

DALE. Excuse me… Excuse me…

ANGIE. What now?! My purse is on my lap!

DALE. I just wanted to see if you are all right.

ANGIE. Of course, I'm all right. Don't I look all right?!

DALE. Honestly, no.

ANGIE. What is it with you and honesty, huh?

DALE. Sorry. I'll leave you alone.

ANGIE. You said that before. And we both know how that turned out!

DALE. Are you always this rude to people trying to be nice to you?

ANGIE. Honestly? No...

(Pause. Then she grabs her chair and drags it to his table. Sits.)

ANGIE. It's...it's my husband. I'm supposed to meet him in Baggage Hold.

DALE. I hope you don't mind me asking, but your husband... he's not beating you or anything, is he?

ANGIE. Anything but. He is hopelessly devoted to me.

DALE. Then..?

ANGIE. I'd rather not talk about it.

(She pulls her chair back to her own table. Dale returns to his drink. After a beat, she grabs her chair and again drags it to his table. Sits close beside him.)

ANGIE. It's just that he was always such a good man...

DALE. Was a good man.? And now he's..?

ANGIE. In Baggage Hold.

DALE. I see. *(Beat.)* Not really, but...

ANGIE. I don't know why I'm telling you this. I should know better.

DALE. It's okay. My friends tell me I'm a good listener. They prefer it to hearing me speak. My name is Dale, by the way. Dale Watterson.

ANGIE. Angie. Angie... *(Pauses. Thinks for a moment.)* Uh, Buckner.

DALE. You don't seem very sure.

ANGIE. My life is a mess. You wouldn't believe it.

DALE. Try me. Let's start over. You're married.

ANGIE. Chronically. And usually with bad results.

Two Character Chaos

DALE. So he is not your first husband?

ANGIE. Not even close.

DALE. And he's down in Baggage Claim.

ANGIE. No, Baggage Hold.

DALE. You lost me.

ANGIE. No, I lost him. He's in a box. A coffin, actually. Down in Baggage Hold. We were on an extended honeymoon, when he…he…

DALE. On your honeymoon? That's awful! How did he die?

ANGIE. Smiling.

DALE. Poor thing. You must be devastated.

ANGIE. Not really. I'm used to it.

DALE. You are used to your husband dying?

ANGIE. Not this one, obviously. It was his first time.

CURTAIN

The Kiss Me Curse - 2

By
Vin Morreale, Jr.

CAST

Angie — A slightly zany widow

Father Lawrence — A blind priest

SETTING

The priest's office

Vin's Notes: Poor Angie has a problem; every man she meets wants to marry her. But after their lips meet, her future husbands only have three months to live. And thanks to an old curse, the ghosts of her fourteen spouses continue to be lovestruck, even after death. This zany romantic comedy blends hilarity with touching insights on love, loss and forgiveness.

For royalty information and permission to use this scene in a paid performance, or to request a full copy of THE KISS ME CURSE, please contact **Academy Arts Press** *- vin@academyarts.com*

The Kiss Me Curse - 2

AT RISE: ANGIE mutters nervously to herself, FATHER LAWRENCE 67, enters. Even with his dark sunglasses, he looks uncomfortably like Angie's dead gangster husband, SLIGO, only with a black clerical shirt and priest's collar.)

FATHER LAWRENCE. Hello?

ANGIE. Oh, hi, Father.

FATHER LAWRENCE. Who are you speaking to, my child?

ANGIE. I was just, um, talking to myself.

FATHER LAWRENCE. I see. My name is Father Lawrence Berg. Berg as in German, not Jewish.

ANGIE. I got that from the collar.

FATHER LAWRENCE. Of course.

(The priest feels for the table, then backs himself into the chair without removing his sunglasses.)

ANGIE. You're blind.

FATHER LAWRENCE. Ah, that explains why I don't get much from these books! *(Smiles.)* That's a joke. Blind priests are allowed a modicum of humor. Please. Have a seat.

ANGIE. I'd rather pace, if you don't mind.

FATHER LAWRENCE. How can I help you, child?

ANGIE. I need an exorcism! Or an un-haunting or de-spiriting. Whatever you guys do here.

FATHER LAWRENCE. I am afraid you have seen too many movies. The church does not do that kind of thing on a regular basis.

ANGIE. Who does?

FATHER LAWRENCE. Do you feel you are possessed?

ANGIE. No. I just see my husband way too much.

FATHER LAWRENCE. Well, marriage counseling is something we do a great deal of. Where is your husband these days?

ANGIE. Here. In this room. In your chair.

FATHER LAWRENCE. Sorry?

ANGIE. When I look at you, I see Sligo.

FATHER LAWRENCE. *(Confused.)* Is this Sligo a man of the cloth?

ANGIE. No. Although he did have a lot to do with funerals.

FATHER LAWRENCE. And he looks like me?

ANGIE. It's hard to tell. I don't know what you look like.

FATHER LAWRENCE. I'm afraid you have other issues that may require more help than I can offer…

ANGIE. No, it's just that I can't see your real face. To me, you look like my husband.

FATHER LAWRENCE. Sligo?

ANGIE. My ex.

FATHER LAWRENCE. You are divorced then?

ANGIE. I wish. No, Sligo is dead.

FATHER LAWRENCE. You are a widow.

ANGIE. Repeatedly.

FATHER LAWRENCE. *(Takes a drink of water.)* You've been married and widowed before?

ANGIE. A few times.

FATHER LAWRENCE. How many is a few?

ANGIE. Eighteen.

FATHER LAWRENCE. *(Spits his water.)* Did you say eighteen?!

ANGIE. Sorry, I meant seventeen. A few looked so much alike, it's easy to lose track.

FATHER LAWRENCE. I see.

ANGIE. You do?

FATHER LAWRENCE. Actually I can't see. I was speaking metaphorically. Please continue.

ANGIE. The only ones who don't look like my dead husbands are the ones who are about to be my next husbands. Who will then become my next ex-husbands within three months…

FATHER LAWRENCE. When they die.

ANGIE. It's not very considerate of them. Leaving me alone like that.

FATHER LAWRENCE. You mean, until the next future dead husband comes along?

ANGIE. You do see!

FATHER LAWRENCE. In truth, I am somewhat glad I don't. Perhaps we should start at the beginning?

ANGIE. Okay…When I was back in high school, there was this girl, Saggy Maggie we called her, because her face always seemed to drag down.

FATHER LAWRENCE. *(Nodding.)* Saggy Maggie. Go on.

ANGIE. She never had a boyfriend until this one guy asked her out. They went steady for five months, then he asked her to the prom.

FATHER LAWRENCE. So Saggy Maggie was happy?

ANGIE. Until she caught me kissing him. I didn't mean to. Actually I did, but that's why she put a curse on me.

FATHER LAWRENCE. The church does not believe in curses.

ANGIE. Neither did I. At least until husband number six. Then I started to detect a pattern.

FATHER LAWRENCE. A quick learner, I see.

ANGIE. Maggie told me that since I kissed her boyfriend, I could have him. But that everyone I kissed I would have for only a short time. Now whenever a guy sees me, he has an overwhelming urge to kiss me. We get married, and within three months, he dies.

FATHER LAWRENCE. And how do your multitude of ex-husbands die?

ANGIE. The usual ways. Sneeze and crack their skulls on a urinal. Brush their teeth with Ben Gay. Wear a Halloween costume into a bank and get shot by a security guard.

FATHER LAWRENCE. I'm not sure those are the usual ways.

ANGIE. I guess not. But within three months they're dead. Fortunately, I've learned how much of a blessing life insurance can be.

FATHER LAWRENCE. You take out policies on each husband?

ANGIE. Wouldn't you? We usually do about ten million. More than that raises suspicion.

FATHER LAWRENCE. So you are both deadly and wealthy.

ANGIE. Somewhere in the neighborhood of two hundred and sixty million.

FATHER LAWRENCE. Nice neighborhood.

ANGIE. Anyway, after I married Maggie…

FATHER LAWRENCE. Saggy Maggie?

ANGIE. Yes.

FATHER LAWRENCE. Saggy Maggie who cursed you?

ANGIE. Messed up, I know. That's why I need your help.

FATHER LAWRENCE. Because you married the woman who cursed you back in high school?

ANGIE. It's okay. She's dead now. Not that that's okay, but it's why they decided I needed an exorcism.

FATHER LAWRENCE. Who decided?

ANGIE. My ex-husbands. And Maggie.

FATHER LAWRENCE. I thought they were all dead?

ANGIE. They are. But that doesn't mean they stop telling me what to do. You know how men are. And Maggie. Why are you smiling?

FATHER LAWRENCE. I suddenly thought of a subject for my next article in Abnormal Psychology Today.

ANGIE. I'm not crazy. I'm cursed. Doomed to be kissed and married, over and over.

FATHER LAWRENCE. Have you ever thought of simply saying no?

ANGIE. I tried. But they become obsessed. We both do. Besides, it's hard to resist someone who finds you irresistible. You know?

FATHER LAWRENCE. Not really. Celibate and all that.

ANGIE. I'm sorry.

FATHER LAWRENCE. So am I, it seems.

ANGIE. Can you help me, Father?

FATHER LAWRENCE. Tell me, child. Are you a serial killer?

ANGIE. That's what the police thought. Especially this one detective. He tracked me for years, convinced I was offing my exes. But it's hard to say I was responsible when someone spills hundred proof whiskey on their shorts, and they catch fire when they stand too close to the barbecue grill. Usually the cause of death is so silly, they can't charge me. But this one detective refused to give up.

FATHER LAWRENCE. What happened to him?

ANGIE. Snyder? Husband number thirteen. He was the one in Baggage Hold when I met Dale. It's always within three months. Then I start waiting for the axe to fall. Like with Luther.

FATHER LAWRENCE. What happened to Luther?

ANGIE. The axe fell. He worked in the garden department of Home Depot. There was a cleanup in aisle eleven that day. Believe me.

CURTAIN

Big Bug

By
Vin Morreale, Jr.

CAST

Katy — A terrified woman

Willis — A distracted husband

SETTING

Their home

Vin's Notes: Some actors have a natural flair for comedy, while others slip more easily into dramatic roles. A major focus of my **Burnng Up The Stage Acting Workshops** is to give actors the ability to move comfortably between both worlds. And that is accomplished by experience working with all manner of scripts. This is just a fun, light-hearted piece that appears in my collection, 150 ACTING SCENES.

For royalty information and permission to use this scene in a paid performance, please contact **Academy Arts Press** *- vin@academyarts.com*

Big Bug

AT RISE: A simple apartment.

KATY. BigBugBigBugBigBugBigBugBigBug!

WILLIS. What is it? A spider?

KATY. Too big to be a spider. More like a raccoon. Or a coyote. A big black coyote. With eight legs.

WILLIS. You're exaggerating.

KATY. I'm not exaggerating! It's like something out of those cheap 1950's horror flicks. Where insects grow ginormous from a megadose of nuclear waste.

WILLIS. That must be it. They must have installed a leaky nuclear reactor down the street while we were sleeping. (Sighs) I'll get the fly swatter.

KATY. You'll need something bigger than a fly swatter. Like a baseball bat. Or a bazooka. A bazooka would be good.

WILLIS. Aren't you a bit old to be so afraid of one tiny little... (Sees it) SweetJellyMattress! What is that thing?!

KATY. Told ya. Nuclear experiment gone wrong.

WILLIS. Or someone's been feeding it vitamin-enhanced steroids. I don't usually think of insects as tall, but that thing could play for the NBA. And it's got an Ick Factor of ten-point-infinity!

KATY. It's looking at you. With those dark googly eyes. It's looking right at you!

WILLIS. Don't show it any fear.

KATY. Too late. What do we do now?

WILLIS. Well, we can act like adults, and you can go right over there and step on it.

KATY. Me? Why not you? You've got the bigger feet. And the uglier shoes. Besides, stepping on a spider that big might only make it angry.

WILLIS. Then that leaves us with two choices. We can either move to a different city…or run over it with the car.

KATY. I'll get the keys. I hear Seattle's lovely this time of year.

CURTAIN

NASHVILLE

By
Vin Morreale, Jr.

CAST

L.G.   A Nashville music mogul

Bobby Ray   An up-and-coming country singer

SETTING

The lavish offices of a major music label.

Vin's Notes: I chose to close this book with one of my favorite short plays. This was another entry excerpted from my love letter to the South, called SOUTHERN DISCOMFORT, where each scene celebrates the lyrical accents and rich flavor of Southern lifestyles. NASHVILLE won a play contest at the Bunbury Theater and has proven to be an highly effective piece for strong actors.

FOR ROYALTY INFORMATION, OR TO REQUEST A COPY OF
SOUTHERN DISCOMFORT, PLEASE CONTACT **DRAMATIC PUBLISHING** -
dramaticpublishing.com/authors/profile/view/url/vin-morreale-jr

Nashville

AT RISE: A luxuriously furnished office in downtown Nashville. Gold and platinum albums line the walls, alongside frame photos of L.G. MUNROE standing with country music's biggest stars. An expansive desk juts out from the STAGE RIGHT wall. A well-stocked wet bar occupies the UPSTAGE area. A large leather sofa leans against the wall STAGE LEFT. CENTER STAGE is a simple backed wooden chair facing the desk, which looks out of place in such an elegant office.

L.G. MUNROE & BOBBY RAY BURTON enter through the office door, STAGE LEFT. L.G. is in his early 50's, dressed in an expensive designer suit and moves rapidly about the office with confident familiarity. Bobby Ray is younger, handsome, and solidly built. He wears his best jeans and nervously fingers the brim of his baby blue cowboy hat. He looks around the office with undisguised wonder.

L.G. So that's the bum's rush tour, Bobby Ray. Twenty-two floors of state-of-the-art, star-making machinery. Impressed?

BOBBY RAY. Well, I...

(L.G. slaps Bobby Ray on the back.)

L.G. Of course you're impressed. This is country music heaven, boy! And I just gave you a back stage pass through the Pearly Gates!

BOBBY RAY. I'm just a little... overwhelmed...

L.G. That's why we do it like this. We could probably get the same amount of work done on a floor and a half... but who would be overwhelmed with that? Image is everything in this business. Remember that.

BOBBY RAY. I see what you mean.

L.G. Not that you're any stranger to image... are you, Bobby Ray?

BOBBY RAY. What are you saying, Mr. Munroe?

L.G. L.G.... My friends and enemies call me L.G.. Only my accountant calls me Mr. Munroe.

BOBBY RAY. Okay, L.G.

L.G. Now, where were we? Oh, yes... Images. Specifically your image, Bobby Ray.

BOBBY RAY. Hey, I'm just a poor old country boy looking to sing my songs to anyone who'll take the time to listen.

L.G. Well, see? That's your image! And everything about you supports that. The pre-faded jeans and cowboy boots. The old guitar... even the trademark baby blue cowboy hat!

BOBBY RAY. I make no apologies for what I am, Mr. Munroe.

L.G. L.G.

BOBBY RAY. L.G... I'm not one of those vinyl and tin foil cowboys playing country music because they couldn't make it in rock and roll.

(L.G. gestures to the wooden chair. BOBBY RAY sits, looking comfortable at last. L.G. sits on his desk and leans in with the same enthusiasm.)

L.G. You're country through and through.

BOBBY RAY. That's right.

L.G. A good old boy with good old American values.

BOBBY RAY. They're what makes this country great.

L.G. You probably drive an old Ford pick-up, right?

(Now it's BOBBY RAY's turn to flash a wicked smile.)

BOBBY RAY. It's parked out back.... right next to your Jaguar. *(Leans back in his chair)* Look, Mr. Munroe. I know you're the head of this here record company and a very important man in the music business... But I'm not looking to change who I am for nobody. I'm Bobby Ray Burton and that's all I want to be.

L.G. A man of integrity. How refreshing.

BOBBY RAY. If that means I don't become as big a name as Garth Brooks... I guess that's how it's gotta be then.

L.G. A man who knows himself and is true to his inner core.

BOBBY RAY. *(Deadly serious.)* I'm not gonna change, Mr. Munroe.

> *(L.G. crosses behind his desk. He picks up a manila folder containing information about Bobby Ray.)*

L.G. And who'd want you to? I've been following your career for months. *(Scans through the folder.)* You're beginning to develop a small, but loyal following... You just put out a CD on a tiny independent label. You have four songs you wrote yourself...

BOBBY RAY. Five. I'm almost finished with my fifth. It's a love song about this woman I've been seeing.

L.G. Sad one, I hope.

BOBBY RAY. Beg pardon?

L.G. Come on now, Bobby Ray! This is country music! Love songs dipped in tears sell the best. (Back to the folder) Anyway, you've been playing small clubs and bars around town hoping for your big break.

BOBBY RAY. You do your homework.

L.G. It's my job. You also told a music reporter in a small Kentucky newspaper that Bobby Ray Burton would rather: "be the kind of man my momma would be proud of, than some plastic-haired, no-talent, country music sell-out."

BOBBY RAY. *(Shrugs.)* That's who I am. Take it or leave it.

> *(L.G. crosses UPSTAGE to the wet bar and begins to pour a drink for himself and one for Bobby Ray.)*

L.G. *(With gleeful malevolence.)* Oh, we'll take it. Bobby Ray. We'll take it all the way to the bank. And you're gonna love the ride, believe me!

BOBBY RAY. So you're gonna sign me?

L.G. We can start small. Major album release, with option for three more. Half million in promotion. Two music videos with the stereotypical blondes in halter tops. And a year-long national tour, fronting for some big name band. Sound good so far?

BOBBY RAY. Sounds great!

L.G. We'll put press releases in all the trade papers. Book appearances on all the major talk shows. And maybe we can get you in as a presenter on the next Country Music Awards. Create a lot of buzz about you. Still happy?

BOBBY RAY. You bet!

L.G. *(Hands Bobby Ray the drink.)* Don't feel like you're compromising your identity with all this success, do you?

BOBBY RAY. Just because I'm country, don't mean I don't know a good deal when I see one... As long as you take me just like I am, then I'm yours all the way.

(L.G. pulls a contract off his desk and hands it to Bobby Ray.)

L.G. Oh, and we throw in the standard $25,000 signing bonus.

BOBBY RAY. *(With a wink.)* You're not taking advantage of me, are you?

L.G. *(Smiling in return.)* I am. Make it $50,000.

BOBBY RAY. Where do I sign?

L.G. The bottom of page four, seven and nine. Initial the other pages at the top.

BOBBY RAY. You got a pen?

L.G. Ain't it funny how real cowboys never carry pens? *(Tosses him a pen.)* Anyway, I suggest you get your lawyers to read it first. I'll guarantee ours did.

BOBBY RAY. *(Starting to sign.)* No need. You look like an honest man. I trust you.

L.G. *(Turns his back to Bobby Ray.)* I'm glad. However, I suggest you read Page six, Sub-paragraph seven. It's not a standard clause in these things.

(As L.G. stands and drinks by the wet bar, his back stiffly facing the other man, Bobby Ray reads the paragraph in question. His face

drops.)

BOBBY RAY. What the hell..?

L.G. Read it carefully.

BOBBY RAY. Is this some kind of joke?

L.G. No, Bobby Ray. It's an iron-clad, got-you-by-the-balls contract that will make your career if you sign it... Or leave you singing to a bunch of drunks for $25 a night if you don't. The choice is yours.

BOBBY RAY. *(Leaping up.)* This is bullshit!

L.G. Sub-paragraph seven? No. It's a standard business agreement. I make you a star... *(Turns to face him.)*... and you agree, in writing, to stay the hell away from my wife.

(Bobby Ray leans menacingly over the older man.)

BOBBY RAY. I oughta kick your ass!

L.G. Or I oughta kick yours.

(He steps out from under Bobby Ray's hulking frame.)

L.G. However, this contract will accomplish pretty much the same thing. I want you to keep your hands and your... other things... off my wife. Because I love Crystal, I'm willing to take some no-talent country gigolo and make him a star, if he breaks off his cheap little affair before she gets hurt.

BOBBY RAY. She won't get hurt.

L.G. I'm here to see that she doesn't. According to the clause in question; you call her up... Tell her you found some other bimbo. And then never contact her again. If you do, you agree to give every dime of royalties you earn on your next four albums back to me. *(Sarcastically.)* Of course, if you really do love her, losing all that fame and fortune won't matter so much to you.

(Bobby Ray grabs L.G. and slams him against the STAGE RIGHT wall, his forearm pressed tightly against the other man's

throat.)

BOBBY RAY. Now I know why Crystal hates you so much... You're a manipulating little sonofabitch!

L.G. Unlike you. You love her for her mind... not her husband's position with the biggest country music label in the world.

BOBBY RAY. I'm gonna break your neck.

L.G. That's your choice. But if you do, I assure you, no one else in this company... or this city...has any intention of signing that contract. They know how much talent you really possess.

(Bobby Ray backs off, crosses to STAGE LEFT, though his anger doesn't diminish.)

BOBBY RAY. This is blackmail.

L.G. No. This is a man with a star-struck wife doing what he has to do to survive! A man who can't compete anymore with your kind... all you wannabe country stars who don't mind using some poor, middle-aged woman who can't help falling for any young guy with a guitar and tight jeans.

BOBBY RAY. It's not like that with me and Crystal.

L.G. Then prove me wrong. Tear up the contract.

(The two men glare at each other for a long, tense moment. Bobby Ray is the first to break.)

BOBBY RAY. Give me a couple of days to think about it...

L.G. You've got an hour.

(Bobby Ray grabs the contract and starts walking toward the office door. As he grabs the handle, L.G. begins reading from Bobby Ray's file. Bobby Ray listens but doesn't move.)

L.G. Bobby Ray Burton... Real name -- Martin Harold Borelski. Born and raised in Cambridge, Massachusetts. Father was an economics professor at MIT. Young Martin holds a Masters in Theater from Boston College. The closest he ever got to a farm was on a fifth grade field trip.

> *(Bobby Ray turns to face L.G.. He crosses to the desk, with hatred in his eyes.)*

L.G. The man who has to be true to who he is. Your fans are going to love this.

> *(Bobby Ray leans over to sign the contract.)*

BOBBY RAY. You'll say good-bye to Crystal for me?

L.G. The contract permits you to say good-bye yourself.

> *(He finishes signing and tosses the contract and the pen on the desk. he turns to leave.)*

BOBBY RAY. What's the point?

L.G. Welcome to Nashville, Bobby Ray.

> *(Bobby Ray exits without another word. After he's gone, L.G. takes a long, slow drink, then presses his telephone intercom button.)*

L.G. *(Into Intercom.)* Marie? I've got another contract to go in my... special file. Bobby Ray Burton... You know the process. Call promotions. Notify our best songwriters... and God Almighty, let's get someone to teach this kid to sing!

CURTAIN

About The Author

Vin Morreale, Jr. is an award-winning screenwriter, acting teacher, casting director and internationally produced playwright.

Vin was a founding member of the San Francisco Playwrights Center and the Senseless Bickering Comedy Theatre. He has directed hundreds of works for stage, screen and radio across the country.

As president of *Vin Morreale Casting,* along with his nationally known *Burning Up The Stage* acting workshops, he has helped nearly 30,000 actors find work in movies, TV, stage and video.

Vin was awarded the prestigious *Al Smith Writing Fellowship*, and his scripts, stage plays, documentaries, museum exhibits and radio comedy have received hundreds of productions around the world, as well as being translated into Chinese, Italian, Russian and Spanish.

Vin has sold material to network and cable television networks, had screenplays optioned and produced, and his work has been seen in more than 15 countries. He was named a top screenwriter by both The International Screenwriters Association and TheBlacklist.org.

You can find more of his books at *academyartspress.com.*

And be sure to check out the exciting opportunities at *300monologues.com.*

Also by Vin Morreale, Jr.

DRAMATIC PUBLISHING
dramaticpublishing.com/authors/profile/view/url/vin-morreale-jr

Breaking & Entering
Uncool
Nicky's Secret
Burning Up The Stage
The Happy Holidays Collection
Slight Indulgences
Southern Discomfort
House of The Seven Gables

ACADEMY ARTS PRESS
academyartspress.com/titles

300 Monologues
150 Acting Scenes
Monologues & Scenes For Young Actors
The Kiss Me Curse
Knowing When To Leave
Dark Wilderness & Other Stories
Mabel The Maple
Too Many Rules

ELDRIDGE PUBLISHING
histage.com/search?q=Morreale

The Fairyland Detective Agency
Sonoma White & The Seven Dolts
Fairies, Fantasies & Just Plain Fun

OFF THE WALL PUBLISHING
offthewallplays.com

Exquisite Anxieties
Temp Work
The Ladies Guild Pre-Christmas Planning Session

www.ingramcontent.com/pod-product-compliance
Lightning Source LLC
Chambersburg PA
CBHW070530010526
44118CB00012B/1089